Assessing Learners' Competence in L2 Chinese 二语汉语能力测试

Assessing Learners' Competence in L2 Chinese is the first book intended to answer the question on whether existing standardised and classroom-based assessments can reflect learners' competence in L2 Chinese.

The Chinese language has enjoyed increasing global popularity amongst second/foreign language learners and has become one of the major modern languages for school and university curricula. However, to many teachers and researchers, it has been difficult to answer with confidence whether the existing standardised and classroom tests can reflect learners' competence in L2 Chinese. This book defines and redefines the constructs for assessing L2 Chinese competence that have been overlooked or misplaced because of the unique features of the Chinese language.

The book provides theoretical backgrounds and practical methodologies for assessing competence in L2 Chinese trainees and experienced teachers of Chinese as a second language. It will provide invaluable guidelines and ready-made workshop materials for postgraduate teacher training programmes. Researchers and academics will find innovative frameworks on the subject for further studies and debates.

Yang Lu is a retired lecturer of the Chinese language who taught at the University of Nottingham, UK. Her research interests have covered the assessment of L2 Chinese and spoken competence in ESL, teaching methodology for L2 Chinese grammar, and comparative studies of Western and Chinese literature. Yang has published an edited collection, *Teaching and Learning Chinese in Higher Education*, and research articles on standardising L2 Chinese competence with the Common European Framework of Reference, the criterion-referenced validity of the New HSK Intermediate tests, explicit instruction of L2 Chinese grammar, Chinese EFL test-takers' spoken discourse competence and the impacts of examiners' conversation styles on learners' performance.

Routledge Chinese Language Pedagogy
Series Editor: Yongcan Liu

The Routledge Advanced Language Training Course for K-16 Non-native Chinese Teachers
Hong Gang Jin, Lian Xue, Yusheng Yang and Lan Zhao Zhou

Teaching and Learning Chinese in Higher Education:
Theoretical and Practical Issues
Yang Lu

Manual for Teaching and Learning Chinese as a Foreign Language
Bo Hu

Technology-Assisted Instruction in Teaching Chinese as a Foreign Language
Amber Navarre

Interculturality in Learning Mandarin Chinese in British Universities
Tinghe Jin

Identity of Chinese Heritage Language Learners in a Global Era
Zhen Li

Assessing Learners' Competence in L2 Chinese 二语汉语能力测试
Yang Lu

For more information about this series, please visit: www.routledge.com/Routledge-Chinese-Language-Pedagogy/book-series/RCLP

Assessing Learners' Competence in L2 Chinese
二语汉语能力测试

Yang Lu

LONDON AND NEW YORK

Designed cover image: Routledge

First published 2023
by Routledge
4 Park Square, Milton Park, Abingdon, Oxon OX14 4RN

and by Routledge
605 Third Avenue, New York, NY 10158

Routledge is an imprint of the Taylor & Francis Group, an informa business

© 2023 Yang Lu

The right of Yang Lu to be identified as author of this work has been asserted in accordance with sections 77 and 78 of the Copyright, Designs and Patents Act 1988.

All rights reserved. No part of this book may be reprinted or reproduced or utilised in any form or by any electronic, mechanical, or other means, now known or hereafter invented, including photocopying and recording, or in any information storage or retrieval system, without permission in writing from the publishers.

Trademark notice: Product or corporate names may be trademarks or registered trademarks, and are used only for identification and explanation without intent to infringe.

British Library Cataloguing-in-Publication Data
A catalogue record for this book is available from the British Library

Library of Congress Cataloging-in-Publication Data
Names: Lu, Yang (Lecturer of Chinese language) author.
Title: Assessing learners' competence in L2 Chinese = Er yu Han yu neng li ce shi / Yang Lu.
Other titles: Er yu Han yu neng li ce shi
Description: Abingdon, Oxon ; New York, NY : Routledge, 2023. | Series: Routledge Chinese language pedagogy | Includes bibliographical references and index.
Identifiers: LCCN 2022030425 (print) | LCCN 2022030426 (ebook) | ISBN 9781138052192 (hardback) | ISBN 9781138052222 (paperback) | ISBN 9781315167923 (ebook)
Subjects: LCSH: Chinese language—Study and teaching—Foreign speakers. | Chinese language—Ability testing.
Classification: LCC PL1065 .L88 2023 (print) | LCC PL1065 (ebook) | DDC 495.180071—dc23/eng/20221012
LC record available at https://lccn.loc.gov/2022030425
LC ebook record available at https://lccn.loc.gov/2022030426

ISBN: 978-1-138-05219-2 (hbk)
ISBN: 978-1-138-05222-2 (pbk)
ISBN: 978-1-315-16792-3 (ebk)

DOI: 10.4324/9781315167923

Typeset in Times New Roman
by Apex CoVantage, LLC

Contents

Acknowledgements   vii

Introduction   1

1 Construct for L2 assessment: concept and approaches   7

    1.1 *Construct for language assessment: concept, theoretical background and techniques 7*
    1.2 *Approaches for defining the construct for assessing L2 competence 17*
    Further readings 24
    Reader activities 24

2 Framework-based assessment of L2 Chinese and a CFL model   25

    2.1 *CEFR-based assessment of learners' L2 competence 26*
    2.2 *EBCL-based assessment of learners' competence in L2 Chinese 29*
    2.3 *ACTFL-based assessment of learners' competence in L2 Chinese 35*
    2.4 *ICCLE-based assessment of learners' competence in L2 Chinese 39*
    2.5 *A CFL model of construct definition for assessing learners' L2 competence in Chinese 46*
    Further readings 52
    Reader activities 52

3 The CFL classroom-based summative assessment: process, validity and reliability   54

    3.1 *Classroom-based assessment 54*
    3.2 *The context, purpose and consequences of the CFL classroom-based assessment 56*
    3.3 *The process of developing CFL CBA for summative purposes 63*

vi *Contents*

    3.4 The validity of assessing L2 competence in Chinese 73
    3.5 The reliability of assessing L2 competence in Chinese 77
    Further readings 82
    Reader activities 82

4 The CFL formative assessment and teachers' knowledge and competence for assessment   84

    4.1 Introducing formative assessment 84
    4.2 Teacher strategies for effective formative assessment 89
    4.3 CFL teachers' knowledge and competence for assessing competence in L2 Chinese 102
    Further readings 106
    Reader activities 106

5 Assessing vocabulary, grammatical knowledge and competence in L2 Chinese   108

    5.1 Assessing vocabulary knowledge and competence in L2 Chinese 108
    5.2 Assessing grammatical knowledge and competence in L2 Chinese 118
    Further readings 129
    Reader activities 130

6 Assessing Pinyin and spoken language competence in L2 Chinese   131

    6.1 Assessing Pinyin competence (PC) 131
    6.2 Assessing listening competence in L2 Chinese (LCC) 138
    6.3 Assessing speaking competence in L2 Chinese (SCC) 147
    Further readings 163
    Reader activities 163

7 Assessing written language and orthographic competence in L2 Chinese   165

    7.1 Assessing orthographic competence in L2 Chinese 165
    7.2 Assessing reading comprehension in L2 Chinese 174
    7.3 Assessing productive written language in L2 Chinese 185
    Further readings 203
    Reader activities 204

References   205
Index   222

Acknowledgements

I am grateful that Routledge, UK, has given me the opportunity to put my knowledge and twenty-two years of experience as a CFL teacher in this book. I must thank Andrea Hartill and Yongcan Liu for their unreserved support and understanding during the journey for this project. Their invaluable comments and suggestions will always be appreciated. In addition, I also feel grateful to the UK universities that have had me as an external examiner and the colleagues in China, Germany and America who have provided me with much- needed information. Without their experiences and information, I would not have been confident to present the original ideas in this book.

Finally, my daughter has been a constant support and never complained when I skipped holidays and festivals to write this book.

Yang Lu
Nottingham, UK

Introduction

This book is the first attempt to solve issues and concerns in the field of assessing L2 competence in Chinese with a wide range of up-to-date literature research and abundant illustrative examples. The existing principles and practices, rather disorganised and conceived inconsistently, for assessing abilities in a very different language, Chinese, are examined, re-defined and structured around the fundamental concepts of language assessment (e.g. the construct definition of assessment, validity and reliability). Such an attempt has been long called for as it has been challenging to apply the established theoretical system and techniques for assessing English or other languages in the Indo-European family. This effort needs a comprehensive understanding of L2 language assessment and the characteristics of the Chinese language that have been perceived as unique so that, the validity and reliability of L2 Chinese tests are not at a risk. Most importantly, this book will greatly help the in-service and pre-service teachers of Chinese as a foreign/second language (CFL) to measure their learners' achievements more accurately and motivate them for further learning.

Educating teachers to assess learning at primary, secondary and tertiary levels and for lifelong studies should be a top priority for postgraduate courses or teacher-training programmes to ensure the validity, reliability, fairness and usefulness of assessments. The reality, however, is that CFL teachers have been in the same predicament as teachers of other languages, learning the 'trade' of assessment on the job through trial and error from their mentors or by following the established institutional practice. Most of the postgraduate or pre- and in-service training programmes have not provided adequate input about theoretical backgrounds and techniques for teachers to develop and manage assessment. The recent unprecedented attention to classroom-based assessment (CBA) for learning rather than of learning has challenged CFL teachers and programmes, which are facing overwhelming responsibilities and expectations from their learners, parents, educational authorities and potential employers. The challenge is intensified not only because of the rapidly increasing number of CFL learners worldwide in the past two decades but also because of the issues and dilemmas for assessing the unique features of the Chinese language (e.g. the script is made up of characters written in strokes, radicals and components constructed in different structures which do not have a clear grapheme-phoneme relationship with the written words; the

DOI: 10.4324/9781315167923-1

tonal phonology is represented by a Romanised phonetic system which does not bear much resemblance to the logographic script; the topic-prominence discourse is built with some unusual syntactic structures, etc.). In addition, CFL learners' backgrounds are much more diverse. For instance, there are those who are from character or non-character backgrounds and heritage learners born overseas who speak Chinese dialects or Putonghua with little competence for writing.

Furthermore, the CFL professionals have been uncertain about the relevance and consistency of the influential language frameworks, such as the Common European Framework of References for Language (CEFR); the American Council on the Teaching of Foreign Languages (ACTFL); the European Benchmarks for the Chinese Language (EBCL); or the International Curriculum for Chinese Language Education (ICCLE). Firstly, they question if the language competence descriptions based on the linguistic features of the English language or other Indo-European languages could be applied to the Chinese language, which is a Sino-Tibetan language. Secondly, it seems to them that the benchmarks and guidelines developed specifically for teaching and assessing L2 Chinese either overseas or in China are not well aligned with the CEFR or ACTFL standards, although they are more closely drawn towards the features of the Chinese language. Thirdly, the high-profile standardised L2 Chinese proficiency tests (CPTs) may have overly influenced the learning objectives and assessment criteria for summative, diagnostic and placement purposes by CBA. In some cases, there have been serious problems with the CPTs' washback on learning. As a result, many CFL practitioners are often at loss to deal with the business of assessment on the courses they teach with mentors who are neither provided with adequate training on assessment. They are presented with specific issues every day. For example, they need to be well informed on how to develop effective placement tests for heritage learners or those from Hong Kong who speak Chinese dialects and can read or write much more and better than they can speak Putonghua. What should they do to achieve fairness when writing summative tests to assess the competence of learners from both character and non-character backgrounds in receptive and productive written language? What can they do to persuade the students who see the script as impossible to handwrite and resort to Pinyin instead in exams? And the number of issues could be a long list depending on the learning contexts.

Understandably, the language frameworks or benchmarks mentioned earlier are not intended for answering those specific questions as general guidelines. The CFL classroom teachers should learn and become knowledgeable and competent on language assessment to resolve issues and problems and assure the validity and reliability of their developed assessments. Moreover, we must realise the importance of the assessment occurring in the classroom and during the interaction between teachers and learners and amongst peers. CFL classroom teachers must have the competence to guide their students in exploring the learning journey and succeeding in the process. Thus, this book is for teachers and those who manage CFL programmes, those taking postgraduate courses to study CFL and organising teacher-training programmes. It also provides CFL academics and L2 Chinese test developers with insights and useful information about CBA for summative and formative purposes and about the impact of CPTs on learning and teaching. This book will help teachers to resolve difficulties during the cycle of teaching, learning and assessment through the good practice of developing assessment, rating test-takers' learner performance and organising formative assessment to facilitate learning.

This book starts with and focuses on the concept of *construct* to help teachers understand what constitutes L2 competence in Chinese and how they are organised and interact with each other. The book develops around the construct definition for assessing CFL learners' abilities for spoken and written language in receptive and productive modes, introducing measures and techniques to improve validity and reliability. Exclusively, the book provides a comprehensive exploration of strategies and practices for formative assessment to help teachers reflect on their performance in the classroom. The interface between language assessment and the L2 acquisition of Chinese is the foundation for examining the issues for testing L2 Chinese, which is well informed of the latest research on L2 Chinese relevant to the assessment. Specifically, the book endeavours to answer the following questions:

1 Construct related:
   What changes should we make to the existing principles and practices for defining the constructs for assessing L2 competence in Chinese?
2 Standardisation related:
   How should we apply the existing language frameworks and language-specific benchmarks to accommodate the unique features of the Chinese language so that the validity of L2 Chinese tests is improved for different purposes?
3 CBA related:
   How should we operate the cycle of summative assessment by CBA to ensure the quality of tests? What should teachers do to support learning in the classroom through formative assessment with much-desired knowledge and competence?
4 Reliability related:
   What are traditional and new techniques that we can employ to effectively assess CFL learners' competencies in Pinyin, vocabulary, grammar, listening, reading, speaking and writing? What can the examiners and raters do to guarantee the reliability of assessments?

This book has seven chapters. At the end of each chapter, there is a list of *further readings* and *reader activities* for teachers, researchers and academics to further explore the theoretical backgrounds and practical work related to the discussion in the chapter. The chapters structured as such are also for the teacher-training programmes or postgraduate courses to select materials and topics for teaching or training. The contents of the chapters are briefly introduced as follows.

Chapter 1 introduces the essential concept of *construct* for language assessment and explains how a construct is operated in a test with different techniques either as a discrete-point knowledge or integrated communicative ability. The theories about languages and language competence that influence different construct definitions are introduced along with specific approaches applied to implement them. Examples of test items/tasks in Chinese are provided to illustrate the connection between the approaches and the constructs so that readers can relate to the tests that they need and develop in their teaching, learning and research contexts. The examples are also very helpful as the readers will understand the crucial roles played by a task's context and domain and goal, along with the interaction between them that affects the operationalisation of the construct defined for a specific assessment and the test-takers' performance. Chapter 2 continues with the theme on construct definition for assessing L2 Chinese by tackling complicated issues for defining construct in assessing L2 Chinese in line with influential language frameworks, guidelines and benchmarks. The CFL programmes in different parts of the world have either attempted or been required to standardise their courses with the competence descriptors proposed by frameworks such as CEFR, ACTFL or ICCLE. Some of them do not account for the unique features of the Chinese language, whereas the others are language-specific benchmarks with curriculum recommendations for L2 Chinese language programmes. The Can-Do Statements or proficiency descriptions of the frameworks have been considered lacking relevance to the unique features of the Chinese language, and the language-specific benchmarks, unfortunately, have shown inconsistencies in terms of construct definition for assessment. The issues and concerns of practitioners will be discussed in the chapter to resolve those irrelevance and inconsistencies. In addition, the *Model of Construct Definition for Assessing Learners' Competence in L2 Chinese*, based on up-to-date empirical research on L2 Chinese acquisition, will be proposed and introduced to rectify the existing principles and practices, and improve the appropriateness and consistency of the influential frameworks and benchmarks.

Chapter 3 and Chapter 4 focus on the practice of CBA for formative and summative purposes and its validity and reliability for assessing L2 competence in Chinese. Chapter 3 first introduces the development of CAB, its advantages and the differences between assessment of learning and assessment for learning. Then, the chapter introduces the contexts, purposes and consequences of CFL CBA before the process for developing summative CBA is described and presented. The principles of the different stages in the process are identified, and the different types of validity and reliability are introduced about L2 Chinese tests to help the readers understand how high-quality assessments can be produced and administered for CBA with high-stakes or moderately high-stakes consequences. Chapter 4 focuses on the theoretical background for formative assessment and the strategies for classroom practice during the interaction between teachers and learners and amongst peers. The originality and practicality of the strategies are exemplified with not only the specific measures usually taken by teachers but also the learning activities that they often organise. The introduction to the strategies for formative assessment is followed by a section that discusses the knowledge and competence for assessing L2 competence that CFL professionals should have, which identifies the different components of the competence and levels expected from the CFL teachers.

Following the *Model of Construct Definition for Assessing Learners' Competence in L2 Chinese*, Chapters 5, 6 and 7 aim to define the constructs for assessing CFL learners' linguistic knowledge and their competence for receptive and productive spoken and written language. The specific features of the language and related recent research on L2 acquisition of Chinese are critical to identifying and ascertaining individual constructs for the assessment of different language abilities. Chapter 5 tackles the assessment of vocabulary or character knowledge and grammatical knowledge in L2 Chinese. The proposed construct definition for assessing vocabulary knowledge on breadth and depth in terms of form, meaning and use takes account of the graded lists of characters and lexical items for different levels of proficiency. The unclear boundary between words and the derivational- and inflectional-like processes of the Chinese lexicon are instrumental not only to construct definition for assessing vocabulary competence but also to assessing grammatical competence for applying the basic and unique syntactic structures of Chinese. Both conventional and innovative techniques for assessing vocabulary and grammatical knowledge and competence are presented and demonstrated with both items and tasks for the assessment of different purposes.

Chapter 6 and Chapter 7 concentrate on the assessment of CFL learners' competencies in spoken and written language in the receptive and productive mode. Pinyin and orthographic competence are defined as parts of the components for spoken and written language competence, respectively. Both chapters follow the structure of Chapter 5, defining constructs based on the unique features of the Chinese language and supported by research on L2 acquisition. In addition, the cognitive processes involved with the performance of tasks are discussed where necessary, and the measures for improving the validity and reliability of listening, reading, speaking and writing tests are recommended. Chapter 6 describes the constructs for assessing Pinyin competence, listening and speaking abilities and identifies the distinct subcomponents of those constructs (e.g. Pinyin competence consists of the articulation of combined initials and finals, and the different tones and changes of tones). Cognitive activities and loads are especially important to CFL learners' listening comprehension due to the features of spoken Chinese. Concerns have been expressed about the frequent use of indirect measures for assessing speaking. Chapter 6 discusses those issues and proposes resolutions and various techniques to elicit task performances for assessing competencies in spoken Chinese.

On the other hand, Chapter 7 describes the constructs for assessing written Chinese, including orthographic control, which has been neglected by some CFL teachers, programmes and learners. The chapter debates that orthographic competence for the logographic script and handwriting ability significantly impacts learners' reading and writing competencies. Innovative and practical techniques are recommended for assessing both orthographic knowledge and competence. Although word segmentation processing is unique to reading in Chinese and the CFL learners' understanding of the written language, the construct definition for reading comprehension ability is based on the fact that bottom-up and top-down processing in reading and the interaction between them are critical factors for assessment. The approach for defining the construct for assessing writing also emphasises the importance of cognitive activities. As a result, the assessment techniques are adapted according to the characteristics of the written language. Moreover, the two chapters reveal that design items and tasks are critical to the construct validity when assessing competence in the receptive mode, and examiner/rater reliability can ensure the accurate interpretation of the test-takers' performance when their competencies are assessed in the productive mode.

The assessment of L2 Chinese competence is still a very young academic field. Compared to the fully developed theoretical and practical systems for assessing English as a second/foreign language, it calls for substantial research and study of L2 Chinese proficiency tests and CBA for summative and formative purposes. The present situation must change, in which the CFL professionals either apply the well-established principles and techniques for assessing Indo-European languages or develop tests without knowledge and competence for assessment. The practice of neglecting the importance of assessing the written language must also change. Furthermore, it is time that the CBA of the CFL programmes develop assessments with construct validity and reliability improved by representing construct definition, appropriate item/tasks and accurate marking and rating. This book is the first step towards those goals. The framework and construct definitions proposed for assessment are drawn from an extensive review of literature on L2 Chinese acquisition and the established theoretical background for language assessment. It is hoped that the chapters in this book will help readers to understand the nature of L2 Chinese competence and the principles for assessing the CFL learners' abilities.

1 Construct for L2 assessment
Concept and approaches

The first question that a CFL programme, teacher or testing professional will ask is which knowledge and competence are to be assessed before they write the test specification, design the test items/tasks, and decide on the marking criteria. Testing professionals ask the question because they need to identify language knowledge and competence for assessing a specific proficiency level. The CFL classroom teachers ask the question because they need to know if the expected learning outcomes have been achieved so that they can record and report the students' progress and achievement to the authorities or parents or other stakeholders. They may also ask this question when a 'diagnosis' of a CFL learner's competence in certain aspects needs to be conducted for placement or diagnostic purposes so that they can know whether the students have learnt, for example, the differences between 的 and 得 to adjust the teaching plan. To achieve the goal, the CFL teachers and test professionals must have the knowledge and competence to identify, describe and decide the constructs for assessments for specific purposes. It is known that there have been long-debated issues on the construct for assessing L2 Chinese which are intertwined with many facets of validity issues. Hence, this chapter introduces the concept of the *construct* for language assessment, admittedly a complex concept by nature (Davies et al., 1999), because theories on second language learning and acquisition have significantly influenced how it is understood and how the identified constructs should be operated in language assessments. Therefore, it is especially important that before we discuss other issues related to assessing competence in L2 Chinese, we need to understand the concept of construct, the different approaches for defining constructs and the techniques for implementing the construct identified.

1.1 Construct for language assessment: concept, theoretical background and techniques

Jones and Saville (2016) suggest that agreement on construct definition is critically important to curriculum designers, classroom teachers and testing professionals. The agreement involves not only the understanding of the nature of language proficiency but also the usefulness of language competencies to society at large. To the CFL professionals, the agreement that should be reached as soon as possible

DOI: 10.4324/9781315167923-2

is mainly related to whether the learners' competence in the written language, especially in the productive mode, should be assessed at all levels and with the same standards as those for the spoken language (Ling, 2007). The confusion has been due to the unique features of the Chinese script and the difficulties to define the constructs for assessment. Specifically, the characters, morphemes or words are logograms and different from the scripts of languages with a grapheme-phoneme relationship such as English or German. *Hanyu Pinyin* (Pinyin hereafter), the Romanised phonetic system, on the other hand, has a weak or sometimes no association with the meanings of the logograms, which has made reading and writing the script even more difficult for CFL learners. As a result, Pinyin and characters have been considered by some as the 'concurrent coexistence scripts' (DeFrancis, 2006: 1), and some classroom assessments and proficiency tests have tested reading and writing much less or with much lower standards (Guder, 2014). Furthermore, as the characters are modified and adjusted 'symbols (technically, graphs or glyphs)' (Myers, 2019: 2), writing the script does not involve alphabets but strokes, radicals or different components of a character in specific constructions. This means that reading, writing and especially handwriting the *logographic script* (a term used not exclusively in this book as characters can also be used as a syllabary for loan words) entail much more complex cognitive processes than developing literacy in languages with a grapheme-phoneme relationship (Perfetti et al., 2005; Seymour, 2006; Shen, 2019; Li et al., 2014).

Consequently, a rather unique situation has existed for some CFL programmes and high-profile standardised Chinese proficiency tests (CPTs), where the Chinese written language is not only taught less but also assessed less and more easily (Guder, 2014; Lu, 2017). Some have even proposed a computer-assisted 'penless' approach for teaching and assessing L2 Chinese (Xu and Jen, 2005). To seek a resolution, CFL professionals and academics have heatedly debated the pros and cons of such practices, and whether orthographic control is indispensable to L2 acquisition in Chinese. However, research has not provided substantial evidence to conclude the debates, leaving the CFL professionals yet to reach an agreement based on their thorough understanding of the basic concept of language assessment—the construct of language competence. It is time for a framework of construct definition be established for L2 Chinese assessment to ensure the validity and reliability of formative and summative CBA and CPTs.

To put it simply, a *construct* for language assessment is the attribute(s) that contributes to language ability. However, defining a construct theoretically and implementing it in a specific test successfully is not as straightforward. Davies et al. (1999: 31) state:

> The **trait** or traits that a test is intended to measure. A construct can be defined as an **ability** or set of abilities that will be reflected in test **performance**, and about which inferences can be made based on test **scores**. A construct is generally defined in terms of a theory; in the case of language, a theory of language.
>
> (ibid.: 31; bold in original)

There are three elements in the definition which are critical for our understanding of what *construct* means for language assessment. Firstly, a construct is a trait or an attribute or several attributes that construct a language *competence*. Secondly, the *performance* or the behavioural and observable characteristic(s) produced on a test should demonstrate the defined construct of competence which is judged against a set of criteria and presented by a score or grade. Thirdly, the construct for an assessment is not randomly chosen but defined according to a specific theory of language which denotes the nature of language learning and language acquisition. In other words, testing a language competence demands an explicitly defined profile of the constructs to describe the specific knowledge and competence intended for assessment. The expected outcome elicited by test items or tasks should be observed by the examiner and interpreted through a measurable scale. Theoretical backgrounds about the nature of a language, how it is learnt and what constructs the competence in the language will direct and support such an endeavour.

For example, a teacher for a beginner class is required to write a test to measure if the learners have achieved one of the learning objectives, introducing people. She/he may do this with two different tests. One is a test that requires the learners to read aloud sentences in Pinyin, e.g. *zhè shì wǒde péngyǒu, tā jiào Lǐ Qiáng, shì yīngyǔ lǎoshī.* (This is my friend. His name is Qiang Li. He is an English teacher.) The other one is a test in which three learners are asked to do a role play of introducing people. The Pinyin test reflects the view that though reading aloud is an indirect technique to test speaking, the performance can indicate whether the learner has achieved the ability for making introductions. Furthermore, the design of the test reflects the theory that a language learner must grasp the separate elements of a language to acquire it (Lado, 1961). As a result, the set of traits or constructs defined for the test is as follows.

- Accurate pronunciation of the initials, finals and tones
- Accurate changes of the third tone for wǒ, Lǐ and lǎo
- Fluency with natural pauses

The role play, on the other hand, involves more sets of traits as the construct implemented by a task for assessing interactive competence. The criteria for judging the learners' performance expect a conversation amongst the three test-takers as follows (see Example 1.1). The example shows that besides the traits listed previously, the constructs also include the following:

- Production of the vocabulary for utterances called for in the language functions
- Grammatical accuracy (e.g. using 是 and 叫 as the predicates with corresponding objects and native-like speech with a zero-subject sentence in 是英语老师)
- The ability for turn-taking in the context to realise the communicative goal (e.g. initiating a topic or responding to questions and given information)
- Sociolinguistic knowledge about greeting and introducing people to each other, etc.

Example 1.1:

Student A: 你好，玛丽 (Hello, Mary.)
Student B: 你好，杰克。这是我的中国朋友，王燕。 (Hello, Jack. This is my Chinese friend, Yan Wang.)
Student A: 你好，认识你很高兴。 (How do you do? Glad to meet you.)
Student C: 你好,认识你很高兴。 (How do you do? Glad to meet you, too.)?
Student A: 你也在北京大学学汉语吗? (Do you also study Chinese at Beijing University?)
Student C: 是的，你也是北大的学生吗? (Yes. Are you also a student at this university?)
Student A: 是，我学外国文学。 (Yes. I study foreign literature)

Noticeably, the theoretical background for a construct definition to assess the learning objective of introducing people is very different from that of the Pinyin task. It is a communicative approach that views language ability as the communicative competence in a real-life situation and tasks as the most effective instrument to measure learning and competence (Hymes, 1972; Canal and Swain, 1980). In addition, the examiner's interpretation of the performance will involve many more factors than that of the pronunciation of utterances in Pinyin.

As the examples have shown, the theoretical backgrounds about languages and language competence play a vital role when we define and describe the construct(s) for assessments and work to implement the construct of competence in a test (Chapelle, 2012). According to Green (2014: 174), there have been six theoretical trends for defining constructs for language assessment: *pre-scientific/traditional, psychometric structuralist, psycholinguistic sociolinguistic, communicative, mastery learning* and *formative*. Each trend views language learning and competence differently, and they adopt different techniques for assessment.

In the pre-scientific/traditional era, the *grammar-translation* trend dominated language assessment, and the favoured techniques were translation exercises, grammar questions and essay tasks. The construct of language competence was viewed as the ability to understand and render literature texts into one's first language and vice versa (Richards and Rodgers, 2001). The *psychometric-structuralist* trend assumes that language ability is mastering the separate elements of the linguistic features of a language—e.g. elements of phonology, vocabulary or grammar (Lado, 1961). The assessments, therefore, were usually designed with discrete-point measures that contribute to reading, writing, listening and speaking skills. The *psycholinguistic-sociolinguistic* tendency perceives language learning as 'developmental' rather than 'correct or incorrect' (Corder, 1981; Selinker, 1992), focusing on the constructs of a unitary or integrative competence assessed by test items that combine various language skills (Oller, 1979). The favoured techniques are cloze tests, dictation, oral interviews, translation and essay writing.

When language ability was interpreted as *communicative competence* in a real-life situation, how a language learner uses the target language became the primary concern of assessment. The tasks reflecting authentic situations were employed as the most effective instruments to assess learning and competence. In Green's view (2014), after the communicative approach became the mainstream for L2 assessment, validity issues have been the priority for test developers, whereas reliability was the main concern for the previous trends. In other words, defining constructs of competencies for assessment is critical to the validity and reliability of a language test. Green (ibid.) refers to the next trend as the *mastery learning movement*, which concentrates on the formative role of language assessment and considers the construct of language competence as behavioural objectives later adopted by the Can-Do Statements by language frameworks such as CEFR or ACTFL. The sixth trend is drawn from the increasingly prominent principles of *formative assessment*, which view assessment as shaping learning and contributing to learning. This trend derives from the constructivist and sociocultural perspectives on learning. The preferred techniques are supported assessment, self- and peer assessment or teacher consultation.

The research on L2 Chinese tests, especially the influential standardised tests, such as Hanyu Shuipin Kaoshi (HSK, CPTs), Test of Chinese as a Foreign Language (TOCFL) and the Chinese tests in the USA, have been mostly published in Chinese (Teng, 2017; Chang, 2017; Liu, 2017). Recently, nonetheless, publications in English have emerged on the validity and reliability of the L2 Chinese tests (Lu, 2017; Teng, 2017; Liu, 2017; Chang, 2017; Zhang, 2017) and formative assessment on CFL programmes (Ke, 2006; Wang, 2017). Although it is still early to describe the theoretical trends followed by the construct definition for assessing L2 Chinese, a brief review of the techniques having been employed by the existing CPTs, and classroom-based assessment (CBA) reveals that the trends of grammar translation, psychometric structuralism, psycholinguistic sociolinguistics and communicative competence have all significantly influenced assessing L2 Chinese.

The grammar-translation theory is still popular amongst CFL classroom teachers and programmes with the view that translation tasks can assess several abilities 'single-handedly', including vocabulary, grammar, script writing and reading comprehension, when the learners mediating between their first languages and Chinese. The psychometric structuralist trend has also been applied to test L2 Chinese through discrete-point elements of linguistic knowledge or separate skills/components. The influence can be observed in both CPTs and CBA by CFL programmes through techniques such as multiple choice, true/false question, filling blanks with grammatical, phonetic or vocabulary elements—for instance, a multiple-choice question on Pinyin to see if beginner learners have mastered the three retroflex initials/consonants, *ch*, *sh* and *zh* (see Example 1.2). Example 1.3 illustrates a more complex application of the psychometric-structuralist approach to examine if learners at lower-intermediate levels (approximately at CEFR B1 level) have mastered the grammatical use of the three particles 的, 得 and 地 through the gap-filling items, which also demand reading comprehension. The advantage of the technique by the psychometric-structuralist trend is that the interpretation of the performance rarely involves subjective marking, producing satisfactory reliability. This advantage has been appealing to the existing CPTs and CBA, as multiple choices with visual aids and filling blanks have been widely used, particularly when assessing low- or lower-level learners (see Example 1.4 and Example 1.5). Those techniques have been applied when developing assessment for learners with higher proficiency levels to test listening and reading comprehension (see Examples 1.6 and 7).

Example 1.2: Which of the following is the initial for 水 (water) ?

    A ch   B sh   C zh   D s

Example 1.3: Fill in the blanks in the following sentences with 的, 得 or 地.

1   她说中文说 ____ 太快。(She speaks Chinese too fast.)
2   我们高兴 ____ 唱了两个小时的歌。(We happily sang for two hours.)
3   三位上海 ____ 学生还没来。(Three students from Shanghai have not arrived)

Example 1.4: Listen to the times heard and tick the corresponding clocks.

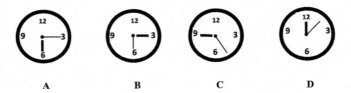

Figure 1.1 Telling the Correct Time

Example 1.5: Match the sentence you hear with the picture.

    The test-takers hear 他很喜欢踢足球。

Figure 1.2 Favourite Sport

Example 1.6: Read the passage and choose the correct answer.

人们曾经把西红柿当做有毒的果子，直到 18 世纪，人们才知道它的食用价值。现在它是人们餐桌上的美味，生食、煮食都可以。它是世界上种植非常普遍的蔬菜，中国作为主要生产国之一也在不断扩大它的种植面积。

A 西红柿吃法多样　　　　　　B 过去西红柿是有毒的
C 西红柿的种植范围在缩减　　D 18 世纪前人们就开始食用西红柿

(Level 5 HSK Past Paper, 2018)

Example 1.7: Listen and select the answer.

The candidates hear 中国人经常说：早饭要吃好，午饭要吃饱，晚饭要吃少。

Question: 根据这句话，可以知道_____：

A 早饭要少吃　　B 午饭要多吃　　C 不要吃晚饭

(HSK Level 3 Sample Paper, 2018)

The third trend that has significantly influenced the construct definition in L2 Chinese tests is the psycholinguistic-sociolinguistic perception or the integrative view of language assessment, which assumes that language ability is a *unitary* competence, 'a unified set of interacting abilities which cannot be separated apart and tested' (Oller, 1979: 37). It argues that language competence is decided by a global factor rather than discrete points of linguistic features. In other words, language users communicate with integrated linguistic knowledge and skills involving abilities in phonology, orthography, morphology, syntax and discourse. The techniques applied are mainly cloze test and dictation as they consist of 'a language panacea' that could solve all the difficulties for assessing overall language ability (Hughes, 2003: 189). The test items require the test takers to rely on both linguistic knowledge and world or experiential knowledge of the subject matter or topics. Example 1.8, a mock reading paper in the traditional character version for TOCFL Band C, can illustrate such a view. To make the right choices for the two questions, the learners need to know the exact meanings of the four four-character idiomatic expressions presented for question 13 and the four words all ending with 然 in 14. Reading comprehension is undoubtedly essential, and experiences or world knowledge about having a pet cat is vital, too, so that the test-takers can infer the nickname '小女生' is for a cat. This type of test item (cloze tests provided with answers in multiple choices) has been favoured by CPTs and CBA in that the test-takers do not have to write the characters, which is a challenging task.

Example 1.8: Choose the answers for the gaps.

整個冬天，小女生用她前所未有的沉重鼾聲提醒我，她老了。小女生是我養的一隻貓，以人的年齡換算，她早該是老太太 _____ 13 的年紀。我詫異地發現，老貓打鼾的節奏和鼻息，乍聽來 ＿＿＿ 14 是人熟睡時的呼吸聲。

13　A 裝瘋賣傻　B 牙牙學語　C 含飴弄孫　D 少年老成
14　A 固然　　　B 儼然　　　C 縱然　　　D 斷然

(TOCFL Mock Test, Reading Paper for Band C)

Dictation is another technique often applied by the integrative test for testing L2 Chinese, though it has been mainly used as a formative assessment by CFL teachers as a weekly classroom exercise or as a continuous assessment during an instruction period. The teachers dictate not only words and sentences but also a paragraph or passage to help learners to memorise newly learnt characters. Such exercises have been considered necessary because the task of writing characters in specific constructions with radicals or different components can consolidate vocabulary knowledge and the skills for writing the script. The format also has the advantage of integrating listening, lexical, textual and orthographic competencies.

The paradigm of communicative competence has profoundly influenced assessing competence in L2 Chinese. From the early 1980s, the CPTs and CFL CBA have started to develop tests based on the construct definition for communicative language ability (CLA) to assess both the linguistic knowledge and competence in using the L2 in real-life contexts. Speaking tests, for example, have used techniques such as oral-proficiency interviews and interactive and presentational tasks to assess learners' competence in the spoken language through face-to-face, computer-delivered, online or automated tests. To assess CLA in the Chinese written language, CPTs and CBA have provided prompts online or through paper-and-pencil exams to elicit the performance of real-life tasks such as writing formal or informal correspondences (see Example 1.9).

Example 1.9: Read this email from a friend and write a response.

发件人：林平
邮件主题：课外活动
真没想到，学校的舞蹈队和网球队都录取了我。从时间上看没什么问题，一个是周三活动另一个是周二周四活动。但是我担心要是同时参加两项活动，哪项都做不好。你觉得我应该参加哪个队比较好？你参加过哪些课外活动？请谈谈你的经验或者看法，非常感谢。

(AP Released Paper, 2007)

As Chapelle (2012) states, the development of theories for languages and language learning has affected the views and trends for defining the constructs for language competence, following which comprehensive profiles and descriptions of L2 language ability have evolved and been established for assessment (e.g. CEFR, ACTFL). Nevertheless, the theoretical paradigm for construct definition to assess L2 Chinese has been underdeveloped and hindered by specific issues. Firstly, as mentioned earlier, there has been a dilemma whether the Romanised phonological system Pinyin should be included in the constructs for the assessment of written language. Some CPTs have provided Pinyin with Chinese characters in reading comprehension tests developed for the beginner or lower-intermediate proficiency levels (CEFR A1 and A2 levels, see Example 1.10). Some CFL programmes have accepted Pinyin amongst answers to listening, reading and writing tasks. Some language frameworks for L2 Chinese have attributed the ability for writing words or sentences in Pinyin as one of the competencies for productive written language (e.g. EBCL).

Example 1.10: Match the sentences in A with those in B.

A	B
Jīntiān de tiānqì hǎo ma? 今天的天气好吗？	*Tā shì Běijīng yī gè dàxué de lǎoshī。* 她是北京一个大学的老师。
Nǐ jiějie zài nǎr gōngzuò? 你姐姐在哪儿工作？	*Xiàyǔ ne。* 下雨呢。

The second issue is whether the ability for written language in both receptive and productive modes should be assessed using the same standard for listening and speaking at the same proficiency level. It has been noticed that some high-profile CPTs with large annual candidatures have overlooked the importance of competence for writing and assess it with tasks at much lower ability levels than claimed or do not assess writing (Lu, 2017; Teng, 2017). For example, the writing papers of HSK represent such a construct definition (see Table 1.1). Evidently, except for the writing paper for Level 6, the writing tasks are either not provided or much easier than the proficiency levels though claimed as aligned

Table 1.1 Test Items in the Writing Papers by HSK (Chinesetest.cn, 2019)

HSK Levels (Equivalent to CEFR)	Part I	Part II
1 (A1)	Not provided	Not provided
2 (A2)	Not provided	Not provided
3 (B1)	Construct five sentences with the words provided	Fill in the blanks with the characters provided with Pinyin in five sentences
4 (B2)	Construct ten sentences with the words provided	Write five sentences based on pictures and with the words provided
5 (C1)	Construct eight sentences with the words provided	a. Write a passage of about 80 characters with the words provided. b. Write a passage of about 80 characters based on a picture provided
6 (C2)	Read a narrative article of about 1,000 characters within 10 minutes. Then the article will be taken away. Rewrite it into a shorter article of about 400 characters within 35 minutes	

16 *Construct for L2 assessment*

with the CEFR competence description (refer to Test Introduction at chinesetest. cn). Examples 1.11, 1.12 and 1.13 are such items, designed to assess writing abilities equivalent to those of CEFR B1, B2 and C1; however, according to the CEFR standards (CoE, 2001a: 27), CFL learners at those levels should be able to write, for example, simple and connected text on familiar topics (B1), write clear and detailed texts on a wide range of subjects (B2), and write well-structured opinions at some length (C1). A related issue is how orthographic competence should be tested if an assessment is not administered in paper and pencil because typing Chinese on computers and digital devices is much easier than handwriting characters (Liu, 2017; Chang, 2017).

Example 1.11 (CEFR B1): Fill in the blank with the character according to the Pinyin.

认识你很高 _____ (xìng)

Example 1.12 (CEFR B2): Construct a sentence with the words provided and write on the line.

越来越高　变　得　他　这两年　了

Example 1.13 (CEFR C1): 请结合这张图片写一篇 80 字左右的短文。(Please write a passage of about 80 characters based on the picture.)

Figure 1.3 Picture of a City

The third concern is about the intense interest by some standardised and high-profile CPTs in assessing competence in speaking with indirect tasks (e.g. repeating sentences, reading aloud, recognising tones of words and retelling what the test-takers have read). Although their validation studies have supported the constructs defined and the techniques employed based on a psycholinguistic tradition (see details in Chapter 6.3), there have been doubts about construct validity and communicative value (Lu, 2014). Finally, there has been little attention given to formative assessment and assessment for learning (AfL) in L2 Chinese classrooms. According to Zhang and Lin (2017: xii), this is due to a widespread 'knowledge gap' amongst CFL professionals about the significance of and strategies for formative assessment. The lack of knowledge, skills and competence for language assessment has severely affected the quality of CBA developed by classroom teachers. Thus, CFL professionals should equip themselves with the much-desired expertise on different approaches to defining the constructs for assessing competencies in L2 Chinese and improve the quality of assessments.

1.2 Approaches for defining the construct for assessing L2 competence

The last part has discussed that it is critical to understand the concept of 'construct' for language assessment, the theoretical backgrounds for different construct definitions and the techniques applied. This part introduces the different approaches for defining constructs for the assessment of L2 competence, which will help us to understand the other dimensions of construct definition. According to Purpura (2016: 193), 'approaches' means, in this context, the different ways 'not only for meaningful interpretation of performance consistencies, but also for assessment design and operationalisation, interpretation, and use'. Some of the approaches have inspired the creation of language frameworks standardising teaching, learning and assessment. Some have contributed to comprehensive descriptions of the different components of constructs and the interaction between them. Others have served as guidelines on elicitation methods that are different from traditional test items and tasks. Four main approaches are introduced here as they have been 'broadening the construct of L2 proficiency' (Purpura, ibid.): *trait-based, task-centred, interactionist* and *socio-interactional* approaches.

The trait-based approaches

The *trait-based approaches* to construct definition perceive test-takers' performance as a reflection of their language knowledge, skills and competence as hypothesised by the different theoretical models of language learning (Purpura, 2016). Designed test items or tasks are the prompts to stimulate the performance of those traits in unspecified or specified contexts, based on which the examiner or rater interprets and judges the test-takers' language competence. The demonstrated trait(s) is considered generalisable across contexts. This approach has significantly influenced L2 assessment and dominated the trends for construct definition with three well-known models: the *discrete-point, unitary* and *communicative competence* models.

The discrete-point model, as mentioned earlier, considers language proficiency as the accumulation of the acquisition of individual units of knowledge or skills that should be assessed separately. Although tests based on this model are applauded for reliability resulting from the techniques used (e.g. multiple choices and filling blanks), they have been challenged for neglecting the contexts for language use and breaking down language competence into discrete points rather than observable behaviours (Brown, 2004). In contrast, the unitary model considers language competence as a unified set of interacting abilities that cannot be tested separately for the strong positive correlation between the test-takers' performance on listening comprehension, oral interviews and grammar (Oller, 1979). This model, therefore, proposes that language tests can only measure a *global construct* of language ability. The test techniques applied by this model are cloze tests or dictation, known for their practicality and low cost. The criticism has been that the model fails to distinguish the global construct from the specific constructs that build the overall L2 competence demonstrated by performance assessment (Bachman and Palmer, 1982). As discussed in the last part, these two models have influenced the assessment of L2 Chinese with the often-employed techniques such as multiple choices, gap filling, dictation exercises, etc. Nonetheless, it is the *communicative competence model* that has undoubtedly impacted L2 Chinese tests most in theory and principles for assessment.

The theoretical backgrounds for communicative language teaching have revolutionised L2 assessment, defining the constructs of communicative language competence as consisting of grammatical, sociolinguistic and strategic competence (Hymes, 1972; Canal and Swain, 1980). The contributions of Bachman (1990) and Bachman and Palmer (1996, 2010) have been widely acknowledged for a comprehensive profile of the constructs of communicative language ability (CLA, see Table 1.2). Such a construct definition for language assessment has clarified some confusion for operationalising the traits of CLA in test items/tasks with appropriate and practical authenticity in communicative contexts.

Firstly, to ensure the usefulness, validity, reliability and practicality of a test, Bachman and Palmer (Bachman and Palmer, 1996) proposed 'to define the construct componentially' so that more sub-scores as pieces of information can be collected to reach a 'composite' score to report confidently about the test-takers' CLA

Table 1.2 Components of CLA (Bachman and Palmer, 1996, 2010)

Communicative Language Ability		
Language Knowledge		*Strategic Competence*
Organisational knowledge *Grammatical*: vocabulary, syntax and phonology/graphology *Textual*: cohesion, rhetorical or conversation organisation	Pragmatic knowledge *Functional:* ideational, manipulative, heuristic and imaginative functions *Sociolinguistic:* dialects/ varieties, registers, natural or idiomatic expressions, cultural references and figures of speech	*Goal setting*: deciding what one is going to do *Assessment*: assessing what is needed, what one should do with and how well one has done *Planning*: deciding how to use what one has

(ibid.: 117). Secondly, they distinguished the construct based on syllabus from that on theory, because the assessments of the competencies based on the two types of constructs are not the same. The former is to measure learning achievement over an instruction period to improve and diagnose learning on a specific language programme. The latter is to assess proficiency levels at any time regardless of the test-takers' learning backgrounds. The tests developed with syllabus-based constructs are the CBA for summative or formative purposes, whereas the theory-based constructs are usually norm-referenced standardised proficiency tests. Thirdly, Bachman (1990) differentiated real-life task-driven methodology from an interactional-authenticity approach to communicative language testing, claiming that construct definition for assessment should select not only the traits of language use in real-life contexts but also the underlying traits of communicative competence with the same or similar cognitive processing. As a result, an oral-proficiency interview, though not the same as a job interview, is a valid task for assessing an L2 learner's competence in the target language. Fourthly, Bachman and Palmer (1996: 74 and 119) redefined strategic competence as a set of metacognitive components always 'implied in our construct definitions of language ability and can always be assumed to be part of the construct'. Such a notion distinguishes the constructs for language competence from strategic competence and clarifies that strategic competence consisting of the metacognitive components of CLA interacts and supports language competence to achieve successful communication in an L2.

The communicative-competence trait model for construct definition has profoundly influenced ESL tests, providing theoretical background for revisions or the regeneration of high-stakes and high-profile standardised English tests (Green, 2013). It has also been the theoretical foundation for the CEFR standards (CoE, 2001a, 2001b; Harding, 2014). Though CFL practitioners and test developers are fully convinced that this model is a much more meaningful and appealing paradigm for learning and testing L2 Chinese, it has been challenging for them to apply a mostly cognitive model that pays insufficient attention to the social and interactive dimensions of language use in real life (Weir, 2005a; Harding, 2014). In the CFL context and with the complexity due to the long-debated issues, though the communicative-competence trait model is plausible and convincing, the difficulties in working with a largely cognitive approach have resulted in the existing situation described earlier: a combination of the techniques derived from the discrete-point, unitary and communicative models has been applied by CPTs and CFL CBA.

The task-centred approach

The task-centred approach, also known as the task-based or performance-based approach, has gained a considerable profile because of the popularity of task-based language teaching and learning developed from the principles of communicative language teaching. This approach regards a task as the 'fundamental unit of analysis motivating item selection, test instrument construction, and the rating of task performance' (Long and Norris, 2000: 60). The construct definition for assessment is—though influenced by the communicative approach—focused on the language skills necessary for accomplishing selected tasks within specific settings, communicative goals and outcomes (Purpura, 2016). Furthermore, the approach emphasises the importance of authenticity and the ability to perform tasks that replicate as much as possible the setting and operation of the real-life situations. However, practicality is another essential quality of a language test because assessing what people do in life is not always feasible and realistic for test administration. To resolve the issue, McNamara (1996) distinguishes the strong version of authenticity for task performance from the weak version. The strong version of task-performance authenticity reflects what exactly the learners can do in real-life situations in the countries the target language is spoken. The weak version of task-performance authenticity, on the other hand, can be interpreted as predicting the competence or demonstrating the underlying ability in real-life settings. For instance, Example 1.9 (see P. 14) is a task of the strong version of authenticity which people often do in their daily life. Example 1.6 (see P. 13), in contrast, is a weak version of authenticity since doing a multiple-choice test when reading is not what people always do. For practicality, the latter may have been applied more often, because test-taker performance at present is still mostly provided in classroom, online settings or mediated through a computer. Tasks on the continuum of authenticity will provide testers with useful information about test-taker competence if the construct is defined distinctively and the tasks, whether direct or indirect, can facilitate the observable behaviour in an L2 as expected.

The task-centred approach has been appreciated and applied by the language frameworks (e.g. CEFR) expressed through Can-Do Statements for construct definition of assessment (Purpura, 2016). EBCL as a language-specific benchmark following the CEFR standards has also adopted a task-centred approach for construct definition to assess L2 Chinese competence (EBCL, 2012a). For example, CFL learners studying to achieve CEFR A2 may often perform an interactive task, 给一个中国朋友买生日礼物 (buying a birthday gift for a Chinese friend), which represents the required competence in interactive spoken discourse. The constructs of the competence for this task are found amongst the EBCL Can-Do Statements for Interaction Spoken Competence at A2 (EBCL, 2012a: 19–27), for example:

- Can ask and answer questions and exchange ideas and information on familiar topics
- Can understand enough to manage simple, routine exchanges without undue effort
- Can make and respond to suggestions
- Can agree and disagree with others

The task-based approach has also gained considerable recognition for using L2 production features; complexity, accuracy and fluency, to measure speaking performance through automated tests and for validation studies (Purpura, 2016). It has also been noted that the approach attends to only performance and task outcomes rather than to capacity for use that reflects learners' knowledge and competence (Skehan, 1998). Moreover, it seems that the approach has overlooked the fact that the completion of interactive tasks is contributed by all participants, and their backgrounds, affective and cognitive characteristics and communicative strategies which impact their participation and performance. Therefore, the two approaches introduced in the following part are concerned with the issues overlooked by the task-centred approach to defining constructs for L2 assessment.

The interactionist and socio-interactional approaches

The *interactionist* approach argues that the constructs for language competence as defined by the trait-based approaches are not context independent because performance in an L2 test depends on test-takers' language ability, the contextual factors of the test task and the interaction of the two assisted by cognitive strategies (Chapelle, 1998). The approach assumes that when language learners are asked to perform a task with a specific context and agenda, their language knowledge and cognitive strategies are activated to meet the demands. For example, the seemingly alike discussion tasks, 给一个中国朋友买生日礼物 (buying a birthday gift for a Chinese friend) and 给中国女朋友的父母买见面礼 (buying a gift for a Chinese girlfriend's parents for the first meeting), provide the test-takers with rather different contexts for communication, though the domain and themes are similar. Since the gift receivers are different and the relationships between them and the gift givers are different, the demanded vocabulary for the gifts (e.g. the vocabulary for gifts for young and older people) will vary, and the sociocultural knowledge demanded is also different (e.g. gifts that a young Chinese would like and those that the older and would-be in-laws would appreciate, the social etiquette for gift giving in Chinese culture and the cost of the gifts, etc.). Consequently, although the goals of the tasks may be similar, the contents of the discussions and the language knowledge and strategies involved in the tasks' contexts will differ, which decides the construct definition for the assessment. The interactionist approach, therefore, proposes an 'ability-in-individual-in-context' construct that emphasises the importance of the interaction between language use, contexts and strategies for construct definition (Chalhoub-Deville, 2003).

The other issue that the interactionist approach attempts to resolve is the construct definition for assessing language ability for specific purposes. It views the learners' background knowledge involved in the contexts of tasks as vital to the language learners' performance on an assessment, proposing that the interaction between the test-takers' subject knowledge and language ability be mediated by their metacognitive strategies and integrated into the development of assessment based on a specific-purpose language-ability construct (Douglas, 2000). Such a recommendation has been widely applied to tests developed for young learners, businesspeople, immigrants, nurses, pilots, etc. Those tests integrate the specific background knowledge accessible for or required of test-takers with their language competence and communication strategies. As a result, the interactionist approach has significantly broadened the construct of L2 proficiency and addressed and resolved the role that topic, theme, and content (topical or disciplinary) play in L2 performance elicited from contextually rich tasks (Purpura, 2016).

The *socio-interactional* approach, on the other hand, argues that L2 learners' performance on a task for a speaking test that provides a specific context and domain involves a locally social activity constructed by all the participants' interaction (McNamara, 1997). The interaction involves two or more people who are subject to how each participant does at the time based on their social relationship. This is not difficult to understand if we examine the dynamics in a speaking test, no matter the communication is through face-to-face, a computer screen or a voice over the headphones or telephone, and with an examiner or the test-takers' peers. Therefore, the spoken discourse is co-constructed when the participants work toward the communication goal designed by the interactive task. The outcome of the co-construction is that the constructs defined before the interaction may not all be demonstrated by the performance due to the different choices of language use and strategies by the participants. The resulted variations endangering the validity and reliability of a speaking test are sometimes caused by the examiners interacting with test-takers and sometimes by peer examinees of different ages, genders, personalities, cultural and educational backgrounds and experiences of learning the target language (McNamara, 1996; He and Young, 1998). As a result, during local and social activities, indigenous assessment activities would occur and lead to indigenous assessment criteria for evaluating test-takers' performance on unexpected discourse structures and individually selected L2 use (Purpura, 2016).

According to research, indigenous activities and criteria significantly impact learners' performance and the examiner's judgement of their performance. For example, the oral examiners with either a 'teacherly' or 'casual' conversation style affect test-takers' performance (Brown, 2003). With the 'teacherly' examiner, the test-takers become more effective communicators, whereas with a more 'casual' examiner, they tend to be less cooperative and effective in communication. Native and non-native interviewers (NSI and NNSI), on the other hand, may also behave differently in oral tests (Lu, 2005). The NSIs are more engaged in interaction, eliciting more extended speech from the examinees. The NNSIs are likely to provide information, ask more questions, and tend to cut short the learners' speech. In other cases, the examiner interlocutor variables would be insisted upon even when they are provided with a strict script (O'Sullivan and Lu, 2006).

The interlocutor effect produced by test-takers could also cause indigenous activities, and the examiners must adapt the marking criteria to assess their performance. Learners' cultural and educational backgrounds influence their discourse styles, and their social status, age, gender, etc. also cause different behaviours in conversations (Young and Halleck, 1998). Their choices of language use could be personal preferences too. Thus, the interaction intended to mimic social activities can turn out differently from what the construct definition has prescribed with individually preferred lexis, syntactic structures, speech acts or different strategies for managing turn-taking and opening and closing topics in conversation (He and Young, 1998). For instance, when assessing learners with the task, 给一个中

国朋友买生日礼物 (buying a birthday gift for a Chinese friend), the construct definition is based on a reciprocal, collaborative and goal-oriented conversation. However, the following could occur:

1 Candidate A recommended various gifts without responding to Candidate B's disagreement.
2 Candidate B disagreed with all A's suggestions for different reasons without suggesting alternatives.
3 No agreement on the gift was reached.

He and Young (1998) conclude that as performance consistencies during interactive communication are co-constructed, interactional competence (IC) should be defined as a practice-specific rather than general and a practice-independent competence. Through such a proposition, the socio-interactional approach has broadened the L2 competence construct and the dynamics of the co-construction and intersubjectivity is identified for assessing interactive spoken competence. The approach has also helped to explain the construct definition for dynamic assessment (DA) often developed for CBA, which utilises mediation in the forms of intervention by the teacher, a more capable peer or the widely operated e-learning system. Through interacting with different forms of mediation, learners can narrow down the gaps between the existing learning status and learning objectives, assessing themselves and setting goals for future learning.

To conclude, this chapter has introduced the concept of construct for L2 assessment, theoretical background and different techniques for implementing the construct definitions to assess L2 knowledge and competencies. Although L2 Chinese tests have attempted to follow the construct definitions based on different theories about language and language competence in their specific methodologies, it has been challenging for CFL professionals and academics to reach an agreement or consensus on construct definition for competencies in the written language due to the unique features of the Chinese language. The chapter has introduced disagreements and issues and identified inconsistencies in the existing practice for assessing L2 competence in Chinese. Furthermore, this chapter has introduced approaches for defining constructs, their theoretical background and perceptions of L2 competence. The trait-based approaches have been substantially applied in L2 CPTs and CBA, and multiple choices, gap filling, dictation, etc. have been widely employed by teachers and test developers, though standardisation aligned with influential language frameworks has been problematic, especially for competencies in written language. The task-centred, interactionist and socio-interactional approaches for construct definition have dealt with issues related to the importance of task contexts and domains, the co-constructed nature of interaction in spoken language, and their impacts on test-takers' performance. Those approaches will assist CFL classroom teachers and academics to understand the complexities involved in defining constructs for assessing L2 Chinese competence and to improve the validity and reliability of their assessments.

Further readings

1 Chapters 1 and 4 in Lado (1961) provide theoretical background for discrete-point construct definition and strategies for testing.
2 Chapter 3 in Oller (1979) discusses pragmatic tests and integrative testing techniques.
3 Chapters 3 and 4 in Bachman and Palmer (2010). This is an updated version of Bachman and Palmer (1996) with a framework for testing development based on the Assessment Use Argument approach. Chapter 3 describes language competence and its different components. Chapter 4 discusses the concerns of the task-based and interactionist approaches to construct definition for assessment.

Reader activities

1 Find a written exam paper that you or your CFL programme have used for beginner learners and a mock or past HSK paper at the same proficiency level (available at www.chinesetest.cn). Compare the two papers and answer the following questions.

   a) In general, which paper defines the constructs for assessment based on the trait-based approaches? Which model (discrete-point, integrative or communicative competence) is applied more than the others?
   b) What are the techniques used?
   c) Is there a section for assessing Pinyin competence? If yes, what are the abilities being assessed?
   d) Is there a section for assessing writing Chinese characters? If yes, what are the abilities being tested?
   e) Has the paper been developed by you or your Chinese programme include syllabus-based constructs to assess learners' learning achievement?
   f) Offer two suggestions for each paper to be improved.

2 Find a speaking test for advanced learners and examine the tasks on the following:

   a) What do you think about the authenticity of the task(s)? Are they tasks for a strong or weak version of authenticity? If they are tasks for the weak version, what are the constructs of competence that can be used to predicate the learners' ability for real-life settings?
   b) Select one of the interactive tasks and, firstly, examine the constructs for the language abilities assessed. Make a list. Secondly, discuss with a colleague, peer trainee or student in your post-graduate course about the potential diversions from the construct defined which might happen during the interaction. Make a list of the diversions that the examiners or learners could make. Offer some suggestions to reduce the negative impact on learners' performance.

2 Framework-based assessment of L2 Chinese and a CFL model

Fulcher and Davdison (2007: 36) distinguish three levels of increasing details regarding construct definition: theoretical models, assessment frameworks and test specifications. They argue that a framework 'mediates between a model, which is a high-level abstract document, and test specifications, which are generative blueprints or plans for a specific test'. In other words, language frameworks that standardise learning and assessment, though less abstract than theoretical models for defining construct for assessment, are not test specifications, which are adjusted to a specific learning objectives and contexts. The competence descriptions by language frameworks present the generally expected language abilities rather than the exact learning achievements required by a language course. This chapter reviews the frameworks that have influenced and shaped the practice for assessing L2 competence in Chinese. Amongst those frameworks are the Common European Framework of Reference for Languages (CEFR); the American Council on the Teaching Foreign Language (ACTFL); the European Benchmarking the Chinese Language (EBCL); and the International Curriculum for Chinese Language Education (ICCLE). The CEFR and ACTFL have been influential general guidelines followed by L2 programmes in many parts of the world.

In contrast, the EBCL and ICCLE are the language-specific benchmarks that have been applied as the standards for CFL curriculum development, teaching, learning and assessment mainly in Europe and China. Although not all CFL practitioners are completely convinced by the frameworks, it has been a common practice that CFL programmes standardise their courses at different proficiency levels with the relevant language frameworks. It is also a widespread practice that CPTs and CBA develop tests by following the competence descriptors or Can-Do Statements (hereafter CDSs) established by the frameworks. This chapter, therefore, reviews the frameworks and explores their usefulness, suitability and practicality for the CFL contexts. In the last part, a CFL model for defining the construct for assessing competence in L2 Chinese is proposed based on recent studies on the nature and different components of communicative language competence. It is hoped that the model can provide solutions for assessing L2 competence in a language with unique features.

DOI: 10.4324/9781315167923-3

2.1 CEFR-based assessment of learners' L2 competence

As mentioned in Chapter 1, the CEFR has been an influential language framework for standardising L2 teaching, learning, and curriculum development and assessment in Europe and beyond. It has served not only as a 'framework of reference' to energetically promote the learning of modern languages but also 'a linguistic policy choice at a crucial point in the history of Europe' (Council of Europe hereafter CoE, 2001a: 134). It aims to help language learners 'integrate with peoples from the member countries with the linguistic competence and their own cultural identities in the diversified experience of otherness'. The 2001 CEFR document has been translated into 40 languages, and the Self-Assessment Grid, specifically designed for language learners, has been in 32 languages. Apart from the languages of the EU countries, standards for teaching, learning and assessing languages such as Chinese, Japanese, Korean and Russian have also been aligned with the CEFR guidelines.

In 2015, to ensure complete coherence and continuity with the existing CEFR scales, the Education Policy Division of the Council of Europe commissioned a project to review the existing competence descriptors and develop the new and necessary additions. The result of the project is the *Common European Framework of Reference for Languages: Learning, Teaching, Assessment, Companion Volume with New Descriptors* (the Volume hereafter CoE, 2018), which owes much to the contributions of about 130 experts and professionals of language teaching and assessment across Europe and in other parts of the world. The Volume is an extension and complement to the CEFR published in 2001, with changes and additions to the CEFR illustrative descriptors and scales. For example, the new descriptors for mediation and plurilingual/pluricultural competence, online interaction, understanding and responding to creative texts and literature were created beside the new scales for the plus level (e.g. B1+), pre-A1 level and phonological control. The Volume also updated descriptors such as those for the C2 level and A1 to C1 levels. Furthermore, it creates seven scales for signing competence and descriptors for young learners aged 7–10 and 11–15.

The following is the *Structure of the CEFR, a Descriptive Scheme* of overall language proficiency, with details incorporated as much as possible (CoE, 2018: 30) for the three bands of *Global Scales* of language competence (Basic User, Independent User and Proficient User), subdivided into six levels: A1, A2, B1, B2, C1 and C2 (See Figure 2.1).

As the figure shows, the CEFR adopts a task-centred or 'action-oriented approach' for defining the construct of language ability, regarding language learners as 'language users and social agents' and a language as a 'vehicle for communication rather than as a subject to study' (CoE, 2018: 27). Thus, language education aims to enable learners to act in real-life situations and complete tasks of different contexts in the target language under various conditions and constraints in specific domains. Furthermore, the traditional perception that language ability is constructed by listening, speaking, reading and writing skills, to such an approach, is inadequate to explain the complex reality of communication. On the other hand,

Framework-based assessment of L2 Chinese and a CFL model 27

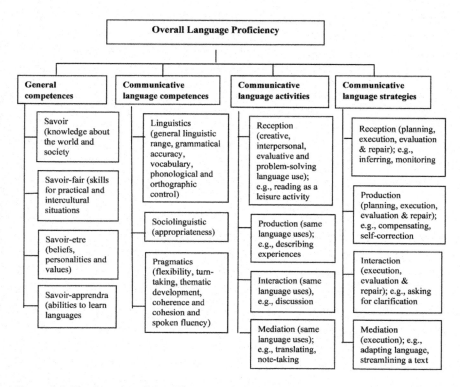

Figure 2.1 The Structure of the CEFR Descriptive Scheme

language proficiency is constructed with the learners' general language competencies and the strategies they apply when performing the communicative activities of various contexts, domains, goals and constraints.

As the Volume claims (CoE, 2018: 29–30), the CEFR descriptive scheme of overall language proficiency is highly compatible with the task-based and ecological approaches to second language learning and drawn from the sociocultural and socio-constructivist theories. The influences of those theoretical approaches are presented by the illustrative descriptor scales and the CDSs for a continuum of L2 proficiency levels, which have been amongst the most widely explored and employed aspects of the CEFR by the curriculum development, learning and teaching of foreign languages. The descriptors are seen by many as transparent, practical and closely related to the language learners' progression and achievement and are taken as reference tools and sources for standardisation by large-scale proficiency tests and local or institutional assessments. The main reason for such a wide reception of the descriptors is that they not only consist of independent scales referring to the aspects, elements, contexts and processes of language use but also describe language competencies in quantity, or the communicative activities, and quality, or the effectiveness and efficiency of language use (CoE, 2001b).

The CEFR descriptor scales and CDSs have been perceived by many as the constructs of L2 competence or the criteria for assessing learning outcomes (Little, 2014). In particular, the descriptor scales are supplemented by the *Self-Assessment Grid* that has influenced many language learners in Europe and other parts of the world as the learning objectives or building blocks of their language proficiency. For example, chatting with a friend about likes and dislikes is often an oral exam task for CFL learners working towards the CEFR A1 level. In this case, the teachers can find the specific CDSs in the CEFR illustrative descriptors and apply them as the assessment criteria when necessary. The following are some of them.

> *A1: Spoken Interaction: informal discussion (with friends)*
> Can exchange likes and dislikes for sports, food, etc. using a limited repertoire of expressions when addressed clearly, slowly and directly.
> *A1: General Linguistic Range*
> Has a very basic range of simple expressions about personal details and needs of the concrete type. Can use some basic structures in one-clause sentences with some omission or reduction of elements.
> *A1: Overall Phonological Control*
> Pronunciation of a very limited repertoire of learnt words and phrases can be understood with some effort by interlocutors used to deal with speakers of the language group concerned. Can correctly reproduce a limited range of sounds and stress on simple, familiar words and phrases.
> (CoE, 2018: 86, 131 and 136)

As Green (2014) observes, the CEFR is one of the best-known content standards and frameworks that can improve the coherence of the national and international language education systems. Doubts, however, have been expressed about whether the CEFR scales and levels can be employed as clear and unambiguous constructs of test content for language proficiency tests (Hulstijn, 2007; Weir, 2005a; Harsch, 2014). It has also been noticed that inconsistency exists between the constructs included in L2 tests and the CEFR descriptors (e.g. Wu and Wu, 2010; Harsch and Hartig, 2015). Difficulties have also been reported in aligning local or institutional tests with the CEFR competence descriptors (e.g. Harsch et al., 2010).

For the L2 Chinese tests, there have been challenges and concerns to align with the CEFR standards and competence descriptors. For example, the New HSK developed since 2010 has encountered complications as the CEFR is a general guideline and not intended for the unique features of the Chinese language (Teng, 2017). The early version of TOCFL, Test of Chinese (TOP), also found it problematic to map levels with the CEFR due to the overlapped domains by the CEFR CDSs (Chang, 2017). Understandably, the CEFR is not a language-specific framework or a test specification to standardise the assessment of L2 Chinese and expected to provide the construct definition. The next part will introduce a project founded by the Council of Europe that applies the CEFR standards for Chinese as a foreign language.

2.2 EBCL-based assessment of learners' competence in L2 Chinese

The European Benchmarking Chinese Language project (EBCL) is the only language-specific benchmark for L2 Chinese outside China. The project's mission is 'to create a benchmark framework for Chinese, based upon CEFR, for Europeans learning the Chinese language in universities and schools, privately, or for professionals to use as a common framework of standards' (EBCL, 2013: 6). The mission was put forward because, at the time, Chinese Mandarin had become a widely taught foreign language in European schools and universities, which prompted an urgent need to standardise learning objectives and describe language competence for assessment and broader educational purposes. The project was launched in 2010, and the team members were from four universities in Europe; each of them also had a school collaborator. There were four highly respected European scholars of Chinese language studies in the advisory board. The project was completed at the end of 2012 (for further details on the project, see EBCL, 2013).

At the outset, the team members were fully aware of the challenges of applying the CEFR for benchmarking L2 Chinese. Therefore, the questions they aimed to answer were as follows:

> *Can Chinese, which is vastly different from European languages both in linguistic terms and in terms of its sociocultural context, be incorporated within the CEFR? If so, how can this be achieved? What specific characteristics does the Chinese language possess, and how should these be dealt with?*
>
> (EBCL, 2013: 3)

The answers were that the CEFR 'is largely applicable to the Chinese language with some amendments. The writing of Chinese, a non-phonetic script, needs special attention when taught and assessed' (EBCL, 2013: 4). The amendments made are mainly those for the graphemic control of the script and the ability for the phonetic system. In general, the following are the products of the project:

1. A proposed Conceptual View of EBCL Language Proficiency Levels: A1.1, A1, A1+, A2, A2+, B1, B1+, B2, B2+, C1, C1+, C2
2. 120 CDSs for A1 and A2 with examples for spoken and written language in receptive, productive and interactive modes, including those for *graphemic/ orthographic control* (GOC hereafter) and communicative strategies on targeted themes/topics and domains (see Table 2.1 for the descriptor scales in comparison with the corresponding CEFR CDSs)
3. Supporting documents including proposed Lists of Themes/Topics, Language Functions, lists of A1 and A2 Characters, A1 and A2 Lexical Items for Written Production, and A1 and A2 Lexical Items for Oral Production

Table 2.1 The EBCL CDSs for Interaction Spoken: Understanding a Native Speaker Interlocutor (EBCL, 2012a: 22)

Level	CEFR CDS	Level	EBCL			
			Coded CDS	Topics/ Themes	Functions	Lexical Examples
A2.2	C-IS2-A2.2–1 Can understand enough to manage simple, routine exchanges.	A2	E-IS2-A2–3 Can understand enough to manage simple, routine exchanges with some effort and asking for repetition.	N/A	F6.4 重复	1 请你再说一遍。你能不能再说一遍？ 2 请你说慢一点儿。 3 对不起，我没听懂。/我不懂。

One of the main challenges the EBCL project encountered was the application of the CEFR descriptors to define the competence for writing the Chinese script because the CEFR descriptors for orthographic control are about the accuracy of spelling and the intelligibility of a blend of spelling, punctuation and layout. They are not related to knowledge of the script and the ability for remembering, retrieving and writing Chinese characters in prescribed constructions and with, components, radicals and strokes. The EBCL project decided to expand and modify the CEFR descriptors for orthographic control and created the notion of GOC that deals with the specific features of the Chinese script. GOC is further divided into two subcomponents: *Sinographemic Competence* (SC) and *Pinyin Reading and Writing Competence* (PRWC). SC consists of 'knowledge about stroke order, significance and phonetic character components at A1 and A2; and the awareness of four different construction principles in which iconicity, semanticity and phoneticity all play a role to varying extents' (Guder, 2014: 20). PRWC, on the other hand, is created to fully acknowledge the instrumental functions of Pinyin for European CFL learners who often read and write Pinyin to carry out communication activities in the written language. The General Notes (EBCL, 2012a: 34) about GOC explains the difference between orthographic control in Chinese and other languages, especially at lower proficiency levels.

> Unlike European language writing systems, the Chinese writing system does not consist of fewer than 50–100 graphemes. It is a morpho-syllabic writing system that uses several thousand graphemic units, 汉字 (Hànzì Chinese characters). The consequence is that the CFL learners do not achieve full graphemic competence at A1 or A2 level, which is regarded as a prerequisite even for the A1 level in all phonographic written languages. Because of this uniqueness of the Chinese writing system, the CEFR descriptors of Orthographic Control had to be modified.

In the *EBCL A1-A2+ Can-doD Statements* (EBCL, 2012a), the EBCL SC scales provide detailed descriptions of the competence at A1.1, A1, A1+ and A2. Those for A1.1 Level are:

1   Can tell whether a given text is written in Modern Chinese or Japanese
2   Can understand the functions of the Chinese punctuation marks
3   Can handwrite any character, lexical item or short phrase by following the stroke-by-stroke visual demonstration

The suggested knowledge for the beginner learners is the basic principles of stroke order and stroke direction, the division of characters into smaller components, the main rules of composition of complex characters and the differences between words, characters and components, and single (独体字) and complex (合体字) characters. They should also know that the di- or polysyllabic words have a morphemic function.

The SC CDSs for A1 require the following from learners:

1   Can copy familiar words and characters as well as unfamiliar characters of simple signages or names
2   Can write characters with Pinyin as input
3   Can handwrite personal details

The SC CDSs for A1+ require the following from learners:

1   Know how to use dictionaries or electronic devices to know the meanings of unknown lexical items
2   Can tell the meanings of 15 semantic components in unknown characters (e.g. 亻/人, 女, 氵/水, 口, 艹)
3   Can distinguish Chinese traditional characters from simplified
4   Can identify the differences between semantic and phonetic components in a Chinese character

The SC CDSs for A2 are as follows:

1   Can copy characters confidently with reasonable graphemic accuracy, which can be recognised by readers and optical recognition devices
2   Can copy short phrases on everyday subjects by hand without hesitation

Furthermore, they should also know the functions of Chinese punctuations and the strategies for learning the main categories of characters (pictographic/indicating characters, semantic compound, phonetic loan and semantic-phonetic compound).

The other GOC, PRWC, is the competence for the Romanised phonetic system, which the EBCL explains as:

> by far the most widely used transcription system for the Chinese language and . . . necessary for the visualisation of pronunciation, for the usage of most

dictionaries and digital input of Chinese characters in text processing and other applications.

(EBCL, 2012a: 36)

In specific, the PRWC CDSs require the following from learners at A1.1:

1   Can understand familiar words and sentences written in Pinyin
2   Can write the Pinyin for words or short sentences with most tones correct
3   Know the functions of letters and tone marks of the Pinyin alphabet as a transcription system for the script
4   Can associate Pinyin with the corresponding Chinese characters

At A1, the CDSs require the learners:

1   Can write syllables in Pinyin with tone marks mostly accurate
2   Can type characters and sentences using Pinyin as the input
3   Can read aloud correctly any Pinyin syllable

At A2, the following is required from learners:

1   Can read, write and understand short sentences in Pinyin on everyday subjects
2   Can write example sentences in Pinyin for grammar study
3   Can write the Pinyin of any Chinese word with correct tone marks in listening exercises

The EBCL project's notion about GOC with the SC subcomponent has significantly contributed to resolving the long-debated issues of defining the constructs for assessing the CFL learners' orthographical competence. The competence descriptions for SC have assured that writing the script is an essential part of the learning objectives for beginner learners and critical to literacy in the language which constitutes the learners' L2 development in Chinese and their communicative language competence. Furthermore, the SC competence descriptors have communicated with the teachers and learners in Europe the importance of learning the script of the Chinese language without ambiguity. The standards and criteria have been regarded as 'closure' to the debate on whether CFL learners can progress to proficiency in the language without learning the script (Lu and Song, 2017).

Another significant contribution of the EBCL project are the graded lists of characters and lexical items for the proficiency levels of A1 and A2 as the numbers of characters mastered by the CFL learners have been considered the indicators for their overall language competence and proficiency levels. The lists have informed the teachers and learners in EU countries of the standards for teaching, learning, assessment of the CFL learners' vocabulary competence because the graded lists were established in consideration of the distinctive features of the

Chinese vocabulary and modes of language activities. Firstly, words in Chinese are either monosyllabic characters or compounds—for example, 水 (water) as a monosyllabic word can form other words such as 水果 (fruit), 河水 (river water), 泪水 (tears), 水仙 (water lily), etc. Therefore, the number of characters learned is always smaller than the number of lexical items. Secondly, since understanding and producing the spoken language is considered much easier than reading and writing Chinese characters, separate lists of the A1 and A2 lexical items for written production and oral production are established as necessary measures to support learning and assessment. This approach has followed the practice of the CPTs (e.g. HSK, TOCFL) and the benchmarks for CFL courses—e.g. the *Chinese Language Proficiency Scales for Speakers of Other Languages* (Hanban, 2007), and the *International Curriculum for Chinese Language Education* (ICCLE hereafter Hanban, 2008; 2014). Furthermore, the lists were accumulated when practical examples were selected to evaluate the feasibility of the competence descriptors, and they were also based on extensive research conducted during the project (EBCL, 2013).

More importantly, the project's achievements have shown, contrary to the opinion that the CEFR can hardly apply to the Chinese language, that with certain modifications, the CEFR is a relevant and applicable guideline to standardise the learning and assessment of L2 Chinese. The EBCL descriptors have successfully presented the traits of competence in receptive, productive and interactive modes on graded themes/topics and domains. Nonetheless, as reported by the EBCL team (EBCL, 2013), work was not completed on drawing up the descriptors of grammatical and intercultural competence, and it was hoped that future projects can establish the CDSs for the rest of the CEFR levels. Thus, with the descriptors for only A1 and A2 levels, it has been difficult for teachers and CFL programmes to define the learning objectives and constructs for assessment with continuity based on the EBCL standards.

Furthermore, the notion of EBCL's creation and descriptions of the PRWC needs scrutiny and discussion. As introduced in the last part, the CEFR descriptors for phonological control are related to intelligibility, control of sounds and control of prosodic features (CoE, 2018). Those are the essential and universal phonological features that L2 learners should achieve in a target language. Thus, the CEFR CDSs for phonological control have established the standards and criteria for assessment. The EBCL's definition of PRWC have departed from the CEFR notion to accommodate the unique features of the Romanised phonetic system. However, most of the CDSs of PRWC presented earlier are related to reading (not reading aloud) and writing Pinyin. Therefore, Lu and Song have commented (2017: 25):

> Those Can-do Statements have reflected what is proposed by DeFrancis (2006) that the Chinese language is distinctive for this one writing system, two scripts, 双文制 (shuāng-wén-zhì), defined as digraphia, a term which refers to the concurrent coexistence of two scripts—characters and Pinyin.

Reportedly, the EBCL team was fully aware of the disputes and controversy that their concept for PRWC raised through the feedback collected from the attendees at the symposiums organised and the CFL professionals in schools and universities in Europe (EBCL, 2013). The team decided to keep the PRWC descriptors nonetheless, claiming that they were still not sure that the ability to read in Pinyin is not part of a Chinese learner's reading competence. On the other hand, the project insisted that the PRWC descriptors can promote learning the standard Chinese pronunciation and have the practical value for typing texts on computers and digital devices. Such a position is confusing to CFL practitioners and can be misleading to learners who find the script difficult to learn.

Another concern with the EBCL project is, in addition to the absence of grammatical and intercultural competence, that it did not benchmark vocabulary competence (VC) for applying the forms, meanings and use of the Chinese lexis with the lists of graded characters and lexical items. They were provided as supplementary documents which cannot be considered as competence descriptors for vocabulary competence. This has also been observed as inconsistent with the CEFR concept for vocabulary competence, which focuses on 'the breadth and variety of words and expressions used' and the 'ability to choose an appropriate expression from their repertoire' (CoE, 2018: 132 and 134). As VC provides the 'basic blocks of language' (Read, 2000: 1) and interacts with other language competencies in their specific meanings, forms and uses, the usefulness and transparency of the EBCL standards have been affected negatively because of the absence of a lexical component amongst the other essential language competencies.

Finally, the EBCL project considered the situation whereby native speakers of Chinese nowadays usually communicate with electronic devices or keyboards and proposed that SC of A1 and A2 be in two modes: by hand and by electronic devices or computers. The issue is that writing on computers and electronic devices, or converted writing (Xu, 2020), is a process that involves typing the Pinyin of a character without the tone, reading the characters with the same combination of initials and finals, and choosing the character intended. This process does not require the CFL learners' orthographical control but a Pinyin competence disregarding the tones that decide the meaning of a character. Moreover, the EBCL competence descriptors for SC overlooked that writing characters on the screens of computers and digital devices demands orthographic control as writing on paper. As a result, the EBCL benchmark for SC is still an unsettled case and needs to be redefined so that the CDSs can be consulted to define the construct for assessing orthographic competence in L2 Chinese.

To summarise, as a pioneering language-specific benchmark for standardising learning, teaching and assessing competence in L2 Chinese outside China, the EBCL project has transferred the essence of the CEFR principles to standardising L2 competence in Chinese at A1 and A2 proficiency levels. It has also successfully addressed the long-debated issues about the construct definitions of orthographic and phonological competence. The proposed notion for SC has, for the most part, reflected the essential knowledge and competence that CFL learners must obtain for interlanguage development. However, the other GOC component, PRWC, has deviated from the CEFR standards and raised questions for further debate. The graded lists of characters and lexical items have been tailored for the characteristics of the Chinese lexis and the capacity that learners can use in oral and written production, though no vocabulary competence was defined which consists of learners' knowledge and competence in the lexical form, meaning and usage. As funding for further project has not materialised to complete the unfinished work (e.g. benchmarks for the higher CEFR levels—B1, B2, C1 and C2—and grammatical and intercultural competence), we need to consult other influential general language frameworks or language-specific guidelines to define the constructs for assessing L2 competence in Chinese.

2.3 ACTFL-based assessment of learners' competence in L2 Chinese

Since the 1960s, the American Council on the Teaching of Foreign Languages (ACTFL) has been an influential organisation for foreign language education in the USA with its established language framework and guidelines for classroom teaching and assessment based on studies of second language acquisition (Liu, 2017). At present, the most well-known ACTFL documents include the *ACTFL Proficiency Guidelines 2012* (ACTFL, 2012a); the *ACTFL Performance Descriptors for Language Learners* (ACTFL, 2012b); and the *ACTFL and NCSSFL (National Council of State Supervisors for Languages) Can-Do Statements* (ACTFL and NCSSFL, 2017). These documents represent the ACTFL standards for teaching and learning and the construct definition for assessing language performance and proficiency.

The difference between the CEFR and ACTFL guidelines is that the former is the standardisation for teaching and learning English as a second/foreign language (EFL) and alignment with it is highly recommended for other language programmes. The latter, in contrast, is committed to the improvement and quality of the teaching and learning of all languages at all levels of proficiency, providing performance and proficiency standards for language programmes and assessment. In addition, ACTFL administers tests for other languages besides English (e.g. Arabic, Chinese, Russian, Indonesian). However, the ACTFL proficiency and performance descriptions for the different levels in speaking, listening, reading and writing are not modified for the specific features of the languages. It is the test samples and *Rationale for Rating* that are language-specific and assist in the application and adjustment for teaching and assessment. The following is the rationale for rating a written sample (filling a visa application form) by a CFL learner at the Novice level. As can be seen, the rationale explains how the rating is reached based on the ACTFL standards for written production and how the rating takes into account the performance of writing the logographic script. Further, the rating does not accept Pinyin in the test-taker's response instead of Chinese characters.

> This Novice-Level sample shows the ability of the writer to reproduce a modest number of words and phrases on basic biographic information, such as name (blocked for privacy purposes), nationality and gender. There is an instance when the writing is in phonetic form instead of a character form

(*fǎ*国人). The writing could be difficult to understand for readers who are not accustomed to the pinyin system.

(ACTFL, 2020)

The *ACTFL Performance Descriptors for Language Learners* (hereafter, the Descriptors; ACTFL, 2012b) consists of competence descriptors for language learners' performance at Novice, Intermediate and Advanced Range. As defined by the ACTFL, performance is 'language performance that is the result of explicit instruction in an instructional setting'. The Descriptors constitute 'a roadmap for teaching and learning that help teachers create performance tasks targeted to the appropriate performance range while challenging learners to use strategies from the next higher range' (ACTFL, 2012b: 3). They also help classroom teachers set realistic expectations and create assessments for summative purposes such as achievement, placement or diagnostic tests. There are two dimensions for describing the performance by the Descriptors. Horizontally, the Descriptors present the over-time progression of the instructed learning that gradually takes on the characteristics of the next higher level's performance in the *interpersonal, interpretive and presentational* modes of communicative activities. Vertically, there are *Domains*, namely *functions, contexts and contents, text type, language control, vocabulary, communication strategies* and *cultural awareness*. The first three are the parameters for the language learner's performance. The following five are the areas in which learners' performance is distinguished in terms of the quality of the tasks in different modes. For example, text types prescribe the texts that learners can understand, control, manage and produce in the target language (e.g. levels of words, phrases, sentences, paragraphs). Cultural awareness describes the cultural perspectives or practices that language learners express and apply to communicate more effectively. Table 2.2 shows the performance descriptions of the language learners' ability with text type in interpersonal activities (ACTFL, 2012b: 14).

The *ACTFL Proficiency Guidelines* (the Guidelines hereafter ACTFL, 2012a), on the other hand, describe what an L2 learner can do in speaking, writing, listening and reading 'in real-world situations in spontaneous and non-rehearsed context' (ACTFL, 2012a: 3). The competence descriptions are for five proficiency levels: Novice, Intermediate, Advanced, Superior and Distinguished. The Advanced, Intermediate and Novice levels are further divided into high, middle and low, creating in total nine sublevels— e.g. Advanced High (AH), Intermediate Low (IL) and Novice Middle (NM). According to the Guidelines, the proficiency descriptions have been the resources for selecting the constructs to assess language ability in academic and workplace settings. The following is the overall description of Novice level learners' ability in writing.

Writers at the Novice level are characterised by the ability to produce lists and notes, primarily by writing words and phrases. They can provide limited formulaic information on simple forms and documents. These writers can reproduce practised material to convey the most simple messages. In addition, they can transcribe familiar words or phrases, copy letters of the alphabet or syllables of a syllabary, or reproduce basic characters with some accuracy.

(ACTFL, 2012a: 14)

Table 2.2 ACTFL Performance Descriptors for Test Type in Interpersonal Activities

Domains	Novice Range	Intermediate Range	Advanced Range
Functions	....	....	......
Context/Content	....	......	......
Text Type	Understands and produces highly practised words and phrases and an occasional sentence. Able to ask formulaic or memorised questions.	Able to understand and produce discrete sentences, strings of sentences and some connected sentences. Able to ask questions to initiate and sustain conversations.	Able to understand and produce discourse in full oral paragraphs that are organised, cohesive and detailed. Able to ask questions to probe beyond basic details.
Language Control	....	....	....
Vocabulary	....	....	....
Communication Strategies	....	....	....
Cultural Awareness	....	....	....

As mentioned earlier, the ACTFL provides proficiency tests in speaking, listening, reading and writing based on the proficiency competence descriptions. The Chinese tests, for instance, cover all the language skills for the overall five levels—for example, the ACTFL Chinese Writing Proficiency Test and the Chinese Oral Proficiency Interview. Besides, the ACTFL also develops online tests for pupils in the US. The most known are the tests for K–12 to K–16: Assessment of Performance Toward Proficiency in Languages (APPL). The tests are performance based and standardised with the Descriptors and the World-Readiness Standards (National Standards Collaborative Board, 2015). The tests are offered in 13 languages assessing abilities in *Interpersonal Listening/Speaking*, *Presentational Writing*, and *Interpretive Reading and Listening*. The typical tasks for a Presentational Writing test would require the test-takers to type texts in response to different contexts and communication goals—e.g. writing an email to a Chinese friend who is starting in your school and giving her/him a list of materials that the art lessons will require. An Interpersonal Listening and Speaking test could be a conversation with an interviewer in a pre-recorded video in which the test-taker answer a series of questions such as '我早饭喜欢喝粥。你早饭吃什么?'

The ACTFL and CEFR standards have been the two major frameworks for learning, teaching, and assessing foreign language skills. Since 2010, the ACTFL and the American Association of Teachers of German have organised the ACTL-CEFR Alignment Conferences to establish an empirically researched-based

38 *Framework-based assessment of L2 Chinese and a CFL model*

alignment between the two guidelines and the tests based on the construct definitions drawn from the ACTFL Proficiency Guidelines and the CEFR standards (ACTFL, 2016). The conferences have produced a series of studies and publications on both frameworks and the relationship between the standards. The most noted is the CoE funded research on the alignment of ACTFL reading and listening proficiency tests in five languages with the CEFR descriptor scales, which has produced an *Official Correspondences between ACTFL and CEFR Ratings and ACTFL Assessments* (ACTFL, 2016: 4). The alignment proposed two one-directional correspondences for reading and listening, and speaking and writing (see Table 2.3).

The NCSSFL-ACTFL Can-Do Statements published in 2017 are established in correspondence to the CEFR standards in similar terminology. The CDSs are based on the Guidance and Descriptors and organised by the ACTFL modes of communication—interpretive, interpersonal and presentational—in consideration of the 'World-Readiness Standards' as benchmarks and indicators of proficiency and performance in different contexts. Furthermore, the CDSs are proposed with a learning-centred approach similar to the CEFR *Self-assessment grid*. As a result, the CDSs have become (1) the criteria to assess what learners can do consistently over time and help them set learning goals when progressing along the proficiency continuum; (2) learning objectives that can be adapted for school or post-secondary curricula and independent learning goals for performance-based assessment (ACTFL and NCSSL, 2017). There are also self-assessment questions for each specific level in different communicative modes on different domains. The one for

Table 2.3 Correspondences Between ACTFL Tests and CEFR Rating

One-Directional Alignment (Receptive Skills—Reading and Listening)			One-Directional Alignment (Productive Skills—Speaking and Writing)		
Rating on ACTFL listening and reading tests		Corresponding CEFR rating	Rating on ACTFL speaking and writing tests		Corresponding CEFR rating
Distinguish		C2			
Superior		C1.2	Superior		C2
Advanced	High	C1.1	Advanced	High	C1.2
	Mid	B2		Mid	C1.1
	Low	B1.2		Low	B2
Intermediate	High	B1.1	Intermediate	High	B1.2
	Mid	A2		Mid	B1.1
	Low	A1.2		Low	A2
Novice	High	A1.1	Novice	High	A1
	Mid	0		Mid	0
	Low	0		Low	0

the Intermediate Low level in presentational mode is 'How can I present information to give a preference, opinion or persuasive argument?' In response, the CDS provides the competence description, which is 'I can express my preferences on familiar and everyday topics of interest and explain why I feel that way, using simple sentences' (ibid.: 12).

The ACTFL Guidelines and Descriptors differentiate the constructs of language proficiency and performance for norm-referenced and criterion-referenced assessments. The Guidelines can be applied for defining constructs for assessing proficiency. The Descriptors, on the other hand, are useful and practical to those who develop CBA for formative and summative purposes. The ACTFL approach for defining constructs for assessment unifies the task-centred, interactionist and socio-interactionist approaches with trait-based elements such as language control in vocabulary, functions and text types, communication strategies and cultural awareness. The established correspondence with the CEFR standards has improved the transparency and potential for broader applications. More importantly, the unique features of the Chinese language are considered by the rating of the ACTFL Chinese tests. Therefore, Everson (2011b) strongly recommends that the CFL programmes in American schools and universities standardise teaching and assessment with the ACTFL guidelines. However, as a general language framework, the ACTFL proficiency and performance description could not deal with thoroughly the unique features of the Chinese language and the intricacies to assess L2 competence. Therefore, it is a language-specific guideline inclusively dedicated to learning and assessment of L2 Chinese that we need to consult for defining the construct for assessing L2 Chinese.

2.4 ICCLE-based assessment of learners' competence in L2 Chinese

The Centre for Language Education and Cooperation, previously the Office of Chinese Language Council International (Hanban, hereafter) and affiliated with the Chinese Ministry of Education, was established in 1987 to promote learning of the Chinese language and knowledge about the culture. Hanban has also been the authority for drawing up benchmarks and standards for CFL curriculum development, teaching and assessment. Amongst the many published documents by Hanban, the most known is the *Chinese Language Proficiency Scales for Speakers of Other Languages* (CLPSSOL hereafter Hanban, 2007); the *International Curriculum for Chinese Language Education* (ICCLE hereafter Hanban, 2008; 2014); and *The Graded Chinese Syllables, Characters and Words for the Application of Teaching Chinese to the Speakers of Other Languages* (Hanban, 2009). This section mainly introduces the ICCLE and discusses its language-specific features as a comprehensive benchmark for teaching and assessing CFL learners' language competence.

The first edition of the ICCLE was published in 2008 and has been translated into 45 languages. When the guideline was being drafted, Hanban consulted extensive research and 300 CFL experts and teachers from schools, universities, language educational agencies or testing organisations inside and outside of China (Hanban, 2008). The ICCLE aims to standardise the teaching objectives for CFL curricula and provide teachers with a framework for teaching and assessing CFL learners' progress. The revised edition (Hanban, 2014) changed the original five levels of competencies into six and aligned them with the six levels of the HSK tests. It also updated the graded lists of characters, lexical items, grammar, topics/themes and language knowledge for each level. For practicality and teacher training, the revised ICCLE also added appendices of recommended classroom teaching plans, model samples of lessons and a teaching evaluation form. The modified structure of Chinese language competence (see Figure 2.2) is presented, too, for consistency between teaching and assessment. Flexibility when applying the guideline is encouraged for different learning contexts. Media, online and digital resources are also recommended to widen the scope of learning and strengthen language skills for the internet era.

The ICCLE (Hanban, 2014: 2–3) claims that the framework was intended to be scientifically valid, practical, purposeful, flexible and applicable to most learning contexts. It is grounded on theoretical background for communicative language competence, related research and successful teaching experiences achieved at home and abroad. Furthermore, Hanban claims that the framework is modelled

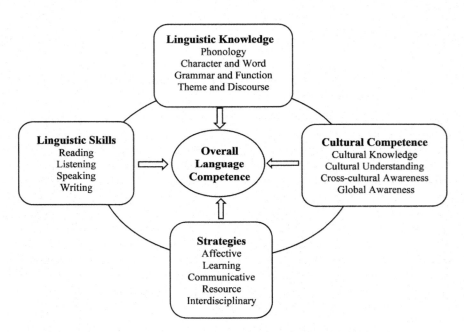

Figure 2.2 The ICCLE Structure of Chinese Language Competence (Hanban, 2014: 5)

after the merits of the CEFR and other influential language frameworks. The four components of overall language competence are, though independent, interdependent, interacting and relying on each other. The first two, *Linguistic Knowledge* and *Skills*, are the 'basics' of the overall language competence. *Strategies* are important for increasing the efficiency of communication and improving learning autonomy. On the other hand, *Intercultural Awareness* helps learners to achieve pluricultural visions in intercultural communication, which is critical to improving the appropriacy of language use in different social contexts.

As mentioned earlier, the ICCLE benchmark defines six proficiency levels in correspondence with HSK Level 1 to 6, termed as *stages*. For each stage, an overall 'criterion' is provided, which resembles the CEFR's global scales, and the criteria for measuring the competencies are expressed in CDSs. The following is the criterion for Stage 3, an equivalent of HSK Level 3 and CEFR B1:

> The learners within Stage 3 of ICCLE can learn and understand the language related to the daily setting and use comparatively complex grammatical structures when talking about familiar topics in interaction and providing descriptions in simple discourse. They are confident and interested in learning the Chinese language and can apply strategies for learning and communication. They are capable of using learning resources and carrying out interdisciplinary studies. They also have basic knowledge about Chinese culture and can communicate with cross-cultural awareness and international perspectives.
> (Hanban, 2014: 11)

Following the overall competence description for each stage are the learning objectives and expected learning outcomes of the four competencies. The following are the condensed lists of the CDSs and learning objectives for those studying for Stage 3 (Hanban, 2014: 11–16):

1. *Linguistics skills*:
   - Can understand conversations and presentations of ideas on simple and familiar topics encountered in everyday life and study and tell simple ideas, stories and needs in those contexts
   - Can comprehend texts on less complex themes for gist and specific information and write short texts in paragraphs with written expressions, basic structures and vocabulary on topics closely related to personal life

2. *Linguistic knowledge:*
   - Can speak with overall accurate pronunciation and tones and master 600 high-frequency Chinese characters and 600 lexical items related to daily life, study and work
   - Know the differences between the components of characters and radicals and able to identify the iconicity, semanticity and phoneticity of characters

- Can correctly apply the compound (e.g. attributive, adverbial) and unique (resultant complements) sentence structures
- Can use the expository, descriptive and narrative functions in daily life, study and work contexts on themes such as hobbies, surroundings and cultures
- Know the differences between the discourse styles in L1 and L2 and can understand meanings in-depth and can use comparatively simple rhetorical devices

3 *Strategies:*

- Can overcome difficulties in the study with increased motivation, interest in the language and culture and consciously use learning strategies (e.g. critical thinking, note taking, expressing meanings with visual aids and body language).
- Can plan, self-monitor, and assess own learning through communication with teachers and peers
- Can use gestures, facial expressions and necessary Chinese etiquette to improve the efficiency of interaction
- Can obtain information by using libraries, provided learning resources, the internet or from people, organisations and communities
- Can expand the range of obtained knowledge in the culture and engage with interdisciplinary activities in history, arts and customs

4 *Cultural competence:*

- Know the achievements and contributions made by China to the arts, history, science and education and Chinese idiomatic expressions, traditions, etiquettes and customs, family and interpersonal relationships and act accordingly
- Start to know the relationship between language and culture and the need to learn Chinese culture and consciously transfer cultural knowledge into communicative competence
- Understand cultural diversity and the similarities and differences, and under the teacher's guidance, start to appreciate, compare and discuss the local culture and improve intercultural competence

It is evident that the ICCLE guideline has contributed significantly to the construct definition for assessing L2 Chinese with the following characteristics:

1. L2 competence in Chinese is viewed as consisting of multi-componential trait-based elements of linguistic knowledge, skills, general knowledge of topics and themes, communication strategies and intercultural competencies, which departs from the traditional approach for construct definition (e.g. CLPSSOL) and is aligned with influential language frameworks such as CEFR and ACTFL.
2. The comprehensive and all-inclusive competence descriptions and learning objectives (e.g. grammar, discourse knowledge and intercultural competence)

are provided for a full range of proficiency levels in L2 Chinese with the corresponding graded lists of characters and lexical items.

3   Phonological competence (PC) has followed the CEFR approach and consists of the intelligibility of sounds and tones, control of prosodic features and the use of Pinyin for dictionaries of both paper and digital devices. Only beginner learners can write words and sentences in Pinyin for learning the Romanised phonetic system (see Table 2.4). At higher levels, the learners are also required to understand the regional accents of Mandarin Chinese.

4   Character and word (字词) competence instead of the sinographemic competence proposed by the EBCL project, which includes knowledge about the script and mastery of the graded characters and lexical items. Orthographic competence (OC) is defined as one of the writing skills (see Table 2.4).

5   A variety of resources is attached for teachers or test developers—for example, the graded lists of characters, lexical items, grammar, topics and themes, samples of teaching plans and classroom activities and suggestions for assessment.

As a benchmark and guideline for CFL curriculum development, ICCLE is, to a great extent, much more comprehensive in scale and inclusive of the unique features of the Chinese language than the other frameworks. It provides distinctively

Table 2.4 The ICCLE Learning Objectives and Targeted Skills for Phonological and Orthographic Competence at Stage 1 (Hanban, 2014: 1–2)

Knowledge and Competence	ICCLE Learning Objectives (LO) and CDSs at Stage 1
Pronunciation (语音)	**LO of Pinyin:** a. master and pronounce Pinyin correctly b. differentiate Pinyin of characters c. understand the tonal language and the tones **CDSs for reading and writing skills:** a. can use Pinyin to look up the unknown characters in dictionaries b. can write basic words and short sentences in Pinyin
Character and Word （字词）	**LO of vocabulary:** a. fully acquire 150 characters and 150 basic words on everyday topics b. distinguish basic elements, components and radicals of characters c. understand the relationship between characters and words d. know the basic strokes and stroke orders of characters **CDSs for writing skills:** a. can copy characters learned correctly b. can write by hand characters with correct stroke order c. can write by hand correctly the lexical items and the basic formulaic expressions for social contexts

defined language competencies in L2 Chinese and subcomponents (e.g. linguistic, skill, strategic and cultural) with a competence descriptor of a full range of the linguistic knowledge (e.g. the graded lists of characters, lexical items, grammar, discourse in graded topics and themes). As a result, teachers would find the guideline transparent and resourceful for their CBA to assess learners at various development stages. Test developers can also consult it when defining the constructs for competence at various levels of proficiency.

Unquestionably, the benchmark and the attachments inform the learners of the expected learning outcomes and criteria for independent learning and self-assessment at the different stages of studies. For example, when learning to achieve Stage 3, the learning objectives and language skills expressed in CDSs can guide them with explicit and detailed goals for planning and monitoring their progress (see the CDSs and learning objective introduced earlier). Especially for those studying to achieve Stage 1 who are concerned with the learning outcomes of Pinyin and characters, the details presented in Table 2.4 inform them that the learning objectives for Pinyin emphasise the importance of phonological control (e.g. abilities to pronounce different sounds and tones correctly, using Pinyin to increase vocabulary). They must know the script and the vocabulary and have the competence to write the characters they learn. Moreover, they are informed that writing the script is compulsory and writing in Pinyin is not accepted for written production in Chinese.

The ICCLE has been mainly followed by the CFL programmes in China and the Confucius Institutes outside of China for curriculum development, teaching and assessment. The former enrol thousands of learners from overseas, many of whom are sponsored by Chinese scholarships for language or degree courses. The latter, on the other hand, are reportedly teaching about 1.85 million learners in 1,193 Confucius Classroom all over the world (Confucius Institutes, 2018). Thus, the ICCLE approach for construct definition needs scrutiny for its great impact on most of the CFL learners on the CFL programmes in China and the Confucius Institute courses. The first issue is that the benchmark has not fully addressed the co-constructed nature of interactive spoken language in assessment and dealt with learners' interactional competence. The CDSs for Stage 3 on language skills introduced earlier (see P. 41–2), for example, are for activities or tasks in receptive or presentational mode. The CDSs for interactional competence are seldomly observed amongst speaking skills. Further, the CDSs for competencies in applying language functions and discourse devices focus mainly on linguistic knowledge, e.g. 能有效地表达情感、态度和意见等 (Can express emotions, attitudes and views effectively). Such an approach is different from the related CEFR and ACTFL-NCSSFL CDSs for interactive spoken production that emphasise the competence to 'exchange, check and confirm information, deal with less routine situations and explain why something is a problem' (CoE, 2018: 88). The absence of competence descriptors for interactional competence is concerning as the construct for assessing interactive discourse is co-constructed and contributed by all participants.

Secondly, the ICCLE concept for strategic competence is different from those defined by the CEFR and the ACTFL Performance standards, which embrace the strategies of planning, execution, monitoring and repair in various modes of language activities. Specifically, they are the bottom-up/top-down processes in reading comprehension, planning, monitoring and repairing during speaking and writing tasks, asking for clarification and confirmation in interactive discourse, explaining and simplifying a text or concept, etc. The ICCLE CDSs of strategies, on the other hand, are related to affective learner factors in communication, learning skills, using resources and interdisciplinary cognitive skills (see P. 42 for Stage 3), which are not the communicative strategies that 'provide a cognitive management function in language' (Bachman and Palmer, 1996: 70). Therefore, it seems that the ICCLE approach for defining the construct of language competence for assessment has not successfully integrated the cognitive processing and communicative strategies for language use in the contexts provided by the tasks.

Thirdly, as observed, the linguistic skills defined by the ICCLE overlap extensively with the linguistic knowledge proposed as learning objectives, as Table 2.4 shows. The ICCLE defines linguistic skills as an 'essential component of the competence that operationalises the comprehensive language use' (Hanban, 2014: v), on which Bachman and Palmer (2010: 220) may disagree and argue that '"language skills" (listening, reading, speaking, and writing) are not the constructs to be assessed'. They are 'language use activities' because (1) skills alone are not sufficient to represent all the elements involved in a language-use task; (2) skills can hardly be defined as an independent element for assessment because performance on tasks demands more than one language skill and (3) the performance of skills cannot be separated from language knowledge. Thus, precaution is necessary when applying the ICCLE CDSs to assess competence in receptive, productive or interactive mode as the designed test items or tasks could engage more knowledge and abilities than what is intended. Otherwise, the construct validity of an L2 Chinese test may be at a risk.

To conclude, the review of the construct definitions by the language-specific benchmarks for L2 Chinese competence, EBCL and ICCLE, has revealed that they have optimally reflected the Chinese language's unique features with specific and full scales of competence descriptors. The EBCL benchmark, as part of the CEFR's development for standardising language education and assessment, has followed the action-oriented approach and distinguished language knowledge, competence and accompanying strategies for language use. The ICCLE guideline has integrated the merits of the guidelines or frameworks and become the most comprehensive and embracing benchmark for learning and assessing L2 Chinese. Nonetheless, both language-specific benchmarks have inconsistencies in conceptualising the components of L2 competence in Chinese, which has created confusion and may mislead the CFL learners and teachers. The following questions are therefore raised concerning construct definition for L2 Chinese competence based on language-specific benchmarks:

1   How should the construct definition for assessing L2 Chinese take advantage of the general and non-language-specific frameworks to identify and formulate its various components?

46 *Framework-based assessment of L2 Chinese and a CFL model*

2   How should the construct definition for assessing L2 Chinese take the advantage of language-specific guidelines to differentiate and describe the competencies with the phonetic system and script?
3   How can the EBCL project's notion for PRWC and the assumption about language skills by the ICCLE be re-defined to be theoretically and empirically viable?
4   Provided that the Chinese language has some challenging characteristics for learning, teaching and assessment, should the construct definition identify the core competencies that generate the overall communicative competence? If so, what are these core competencies?

2.5 A CFL model for construct definition for assessing learners' L2 competence in Chinese

In response to the questions raised previously, a *CFL Model of Construct Definition for Assessing Learners' Competence* (CFL Model hereafter; see Figure 2.3) is proposed in consultation with the recent research on the nature of language performance and proficiency and the second language acquisition of Chinese.

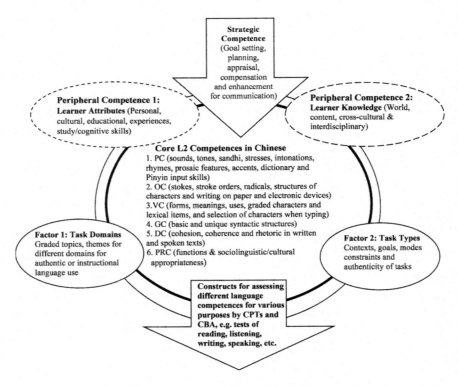

Figure 2.3 A Model of Construct Definition for Assessing Learners' Competence in L2 Chinese

The model is primarily intended for the summative and formative CBA as learning and developing competence in Chinese mainly occur in the classrooms on language programmes. The model informs the CFL teaching professionals of the distinctive and specific components of competencies in L2 Chinese, the relationship amongst them and the factors critical to the performance on an assessment. It also helps the CPTs with an updated interpretation of competence and proficiency in L2 Chinese, providing information to improve their tests' coherence in terms of construct validity.

The CFL Model identifies three types of constructs for assessing L2 competence in Chinese—the *core*, *strategic* and *peripheral* competencies—and two *factors* influencing construct definition for assessment of L2 Chinese. The core competencies are the 'underlying enabling subskills' for communicative language use (Jones, 2012: 250) which earlier research (Bachman and Palmer, 1982; Harley et al., 1990) explored also as the general language proficiency factor consisting of mainly grammatical/pragmatic/sociolinguist knowledge. Recent empirical research on the nature of language proficiency has agreed to such a finding and highlighted that L2 learners' communicative competence comprises mainly linguistic elements. For example, Hulstijn (2011a, 2011b, 2011c), Hulstijn et al. (2009) and De Jong et al. (2012) applied an analysis of covariance structures and marking criteria of fluency and efficiency in receptive and productive speaking and writing tasks. The results showed that language learners' performance on speaking, writing and reading tasks has two distinctive elements: the declarative knowledge of grammar and vocabulary and the speed for processing linguistic information. Furthermore, when knowledge of grammar and vocabulary increases, so does the speed for processing because higher proficiency in linguistic competencies strengthens learners' cognitive skills that speed up processing the language input for output (e.g. in speaking tests, the test-taker's vocabulary knowledge and pronunciation alone explain 75% of the performance variance).

Therefore, Hulstijn (2011c: 239) concludes that studies have supported a model of language proficiency with the 'core components' consisting of basic or higher linguistic cognition (knowledge and speed) in the phonetic-phonological, morphological, morphosyntactic and lexical domains, and the 'periphery metacognitive components' of metalinguistic knowledge, knowledge of various types of discourse and strategic competencies. Bachman and Palmer (2010: 43) have endorsed such a conclusion and stated that learner characteristics (e.g. personal attributes, experience, general and subject knowledge, affective schemata and cognitive strategies) are the 'more peripheral attributes of language users'. They maintain that language competence can be considered a 'domain of information in memory' available for use when activated by language tasks in specific contexts to interpret, interact and produce in spoken and written discourse. On the other hand, the metacognitive strategies manage, assess and repair the process to control how language users utilise their attributes (e.g. language knowledge, general and subject knowledge, affective schemata) to interact with the characteristics of the language-use situation.

Also related to the construct definition as presented by the CFL Model, are the recent studies on the relationship between the CFL learners' Pinyin Competence (PC), Orthographic Competence (OC) and Vocabulary Competence (VC) with their overall proficiency and competence. The results of empirical studies, summarised as follows, indicate that the essential roles of the linguistic components must be recognised in the construct definition for assessing L2 Chinese.

- Challenging sounds for the CFL learners are the double or triple vowels (e.g. ie, üe, uo, üan, ün, ian, ing, eng, etc.), the retroflex, palatals, aspirated and unaspirated consonants, and sibilant consonants (e.g. ch, j, c, p, b, etc.) (Cai and Cao, 2002; Wang and Shangguan, 2004). However, tone accuracy decides the semantic meanings of words in communication (Ke, 2012; Chen et al., 2016), and the acquisition of tones has proved difficult, hindering interlanguage communication in Chinese (Zhang, 2013, 2018). Moreover, speaking with correct prosodic features such as word and sentence stress, rhythm and intonation is also an important part of PC and decided by acquisition of tones (e.g. Yang and Chan, 2010).
- For the development of OC, beginner learners should learn the script through a visual-orthographic learning process as it improves long-term retention of word form and meaning (Cao et al., 2013). During this process, if teachers prioritise teaching the high-frequency components and radicals of characters, it helps the learners to visualise the semantic meanings of characters and internalise the knowledge (e.g. Xiao, 2002; Shen and Ke, 2007). In contrast, Pinyin-dominated teaching methodology misleads the learners to perceive Chinese as an alphabetical language, which could delay their development in literacy (e.g. Huo, 2012; Leung, 2004).
- There is a strong connection between the CFL learners' OC for handwriting and their reading comprehension (e.g. Shen, 2010; Tan et al., 2005; Chang et al., 2014). Accuracy of handwriting can predict overall progress in learning Chinese (Guan et al., 2014) as repeated practice for handwriting characters strengthens the learners' OC, VC and PC (Guan et al., 2011, Chang et al., 2014).
- Because of the specific features of the script, the construct of VC in L2 Chinese differs from those in other languages, which consist of knowledge of the breadth and depth of form, meaning and use (Schmitt, 2010; Romagnoli, 2017). The construct definition includes knowledge and competence in the structure of characters, monosyllabic and compound characters, the derivation- and inflexion-like processes and the required amount of character and lexical items at different proficiency levels (Li and Ye, 2013; Ke, 2012; Jackson et al., 2003). The CFL learners' ability to associate characters with meanings, sounds and usage and writing the script is closely associated with their overall proficiency (Ling, 2007).
- Implicit grammatical knowledge in L2 Chinese strongly correlates with CFL learners' performance on reading comprehension tasks (Zhang, 2012). In contrast, explicit knowledge is a strong predictor of CFL learners' overall L2 proficiency (Li, 2017) and improves their performance on reading comprehension, short essay writing tasks and overall performance (Lu, 2014).

Framework-based assessment of L2 Chinese and a CFL model 49

The evidence provided by the studies suggests that the construct definition for assessing L2 Chinese needs to emphasise the importance of the basic attributes of language competence, PC, VC, OC and GC, which contribute to the overall development of the language. The CFL Model is proposed to reflect the findings and that Discourse and Pragmatic Competence (DC and PRC) are also the core competencies based on the component descriptions by Bachman and Palmer (1996, 2010; see Table 1.2). Furthermore, the model consulted the EBCL notion about SC and the ICCLE notions about PC, Word and Character Competence and the CDSs for OC. However, the following clarifies and explains further the constructs defined for PC, OC, VC and GC and their contribution to the CFL learners' overall competence in L2 Chinese.

1   Pinyin represents the pronunciation of Chinese characters and does not relate to the script phonetically and in writing. Unlike *Zhuyin* (注音) or the Mandarin Phonetic Symbols used mainly in Taiwan as a transliteration system, Pinyin is in alphabets rather than the toneless character-like syllables (e.g. ㄚ for *a* and ㄅㄚ for *ba*). It functions mainly in two ways for literacy in Chinese: assisting the speakers to pronounce the sounds and tones of the characters to make sense in the spoken language and acting as the input to know the meanings of unknown vocabulary from paper or electric dictionaries or to type characters for composing texts. Thus, the construct definition for PC by the CFL Model has abandoned the ECBL's notion for PRWC (see 2.2), following the concept of the CEFR standards for Phonological Control (CoE, 2018) and the ICCLE's descriptions of phonological competence (Hanban, 2014). It comprises the subcomponents of phonological control of the elements stated in Figure 2.3, using Pinyin for dictionaries and typing texts on electronic and digital devices; accomplishing necessary stresses, intonations, rhymes and prosaic features; and understanding the regional accents of Mandarin Chinese at higher levels. Typing Pinyin to compose is identified as part of PC in that it is an ability due to knowledge of and competence in the phonetic system, though it certainly overlaps with VC.

2   Writing characters configured with strokes, radicals and components in prescribed structures involves a process during which the related visual and motor systems work together (Guan et al., 2011). OC in Chinese, therefore, is fundamentally different from that in alphabetical languages which is to write the phonological elements of a word. In Chinese, it depends on an awareness of spatial literacy that recognises and realises the spatial relationships between strokes and the length of each stroke in terms of its proportion (Han, 2017). Therefore, the model follows the proposal of GOC by the EBCL project, modifies the CEFR description of orthographical control and adopts the components of Character and Word knowledge established by the ICCLE. In consideration of the fact that nowadays, writing in Chinese is not all on paper, OC also includes writing on the screens of electronic and digital surfaces (see Chapter 7.1 for the construct definition of OC).

3   VC in L2 Chinese, as presented by the CFL Model, focuses on the breadth and depth of the form, meaning, use of vocabulary and the acquisition of the graded lists of characters and lexical items (for details, see Chapter 5.1). Such an approach is consistent with that for defining PC and OC, which attempts to distinguish those competencies to improve the clarity of test specification and rating criteria. Amongst the constructs of VC for the forms of vocabulary are those including knowledge of the root and compound characters, the monosyllable and compound words, radicals, components and the construction of characters. It also involves the learners' phonological and grammatical control for using vocabulary in their specific meanings, concepts and associations accurately and appropriately. Furthermore, another characteristic of the Chinese language is the grammaticalised lexis rather than a lexicalised grammar as in English (Xing, 2015). Therefore, the construct for assessing the competence to understand and apply the inflexion-like affixes, markers and particles, reduplication, etc. often intersperses with that for assessing GC. Finally, the ability for selecting the characters when typing Pinyin to compose texts is identified as one of the components of VC as knowing the meanings of the characters with the same Pinyin without tones is a vocabulary ability.

4   GC addresses the competencies for applying the syntactic structures in Chinese categorised as the basic and unique structures in both spoken and written discourse (Xing, 2006), in correspondence to the unique typological parameters of the Chinese syntax (Li and Thompson, 1989) and the linear word order (Li, 2014). Such a construct definition for assessing GC might be observed as critically different from those for other languages consisting of the phonological, graphological, lexical, and morphosyntactic forms and meanings (Purpura, 2004). This is to address the nature of the grammaticalised lexis resulting in the specific features of word forms (e.g. compounding of characters and words) and the morphological characteristics (e.g. deviation- and inflexion-like processes and lack of tenses).

The notion of DC and PRC included amongst the core competencies has followed Bachman and Palmer's definitions (1996, 2010). DC is textual competence with the subcomponents of knowledge and ability for understanding and producing cohesive and coherent texts and applying appropriate rhetoric devices. Bachman (1990) explains that DC in spoken discourse is also comprised of conversational language use such as opening, maintaining and closing conversations, initiating and developing topics and interacting with interlocutors with speech acts or turns as called for by the co-constructed nature of spoken interaction. Thus, one of the components of DC is interactional competence, proposed by the socio-interactional approach for defining constructs for assessment (see Chapter 1.2). The notion of PRC also follows Bachman and Palmer's definitions (ibid.), including competence for applying ideational, manipulative, heuristic and imaginative functions and in sociolinguistic norms and cultural appropriateness (see Table 1.2 for details). The concept of *Strategic Competence* in the CLA Model is in line with the notion adopted by the CEFR, EBCL and ACTFL guidelines for the strategies in interlanguage communication. The competence includes a set of metacognitive strategies that manage how language users utilise their language knowledge, general and subject knowledge and affective schemata to interact with the characteristics of the language-use situation (Bachman, 1990; Bachman and Palmer, 1996, 2010).

Similar to the core language competencies, the two peripheral competencies, *Learner Attributes* and *Learner Knowledge*, are managed, monitored and adjusted by strategic competence when learners are performing tasks of different contexts, goals and domains. The two peripheral competencies are brought to assessment by the test-takers themselves, which, though not precisely linguistic by nature, definitely impact their performance. The impact could be positive or negative, because the characteristics of learners and their knowledge about the subject matter embedded in the test items and tasks can help or hinder their performance. Those are the concerns of the interactionist and socio-interactional approaches for defining the construct of language competence for assessment. Finally, the two *Factors* in the model, *Task Domain* and *Task Types*, are critical to the performance facilitated by tasks of various types (receptive, productive, interactive and mediation) and domains (general, personal, educational and occupational). Without the tasks designed with the intended application of specific language abilities, it is difficult to observe whether the test-takers can function in the target language in real-life situations on a continuum of authenticity to predict the learners' potential and allow the examiners and raters to judge their competence.

In conclusion, the CEFR and ACTFL guidelines have significantly influenced the learning objectives and assessment of a CFL programme and standardised the CPTs to a great extent. As a language-specific framework, the EBCL benchmark has made a pioneering breakthrough outside China with the proposed GOC consisting of SC and PYRWC and resolved some of the long-debated issues concerning construct definition for assessing the Chinese written language. However, as the benchmark was intended for CFL learners in Europe, a digraphia view of the Chinese written language has been applied to the extent that the competence to read and write Pinyin is considered part of orthographic control. Meanwhile, as the other language-specific benchmark, ICCLE provides comprehensive and distinctive competence descriptions and learning objectives for CFL curriculum development and pedagogy, settling issues with the construct definitions of PC and VC aligned with the CEFR standards and the characteristics of the Chinese language. Nonetheless, its construct definition of the four language skills and strategic competence has not successfully reflected the diverse and integrated nature of communicative activities and the critical role of strategies in interlanguage communication.

Thereby, the *CFL Model of Construct Definition for Assessing Learners' Competence* is proposed in this chapter, which consists of the core, strategic and peripheral competencies and two important factors on assessment performance. The model is conceptualised based on recent studies on the nature of language proficiency and L2 acquisition in Chinese, taking advantage not only of the non-language specific frameworks to identify and formulate the various components of competence in L2

Chinese but also of the initiatives and comprehensiveness of the language-specific benchmarks based on the unique features of the Chinese language. The constructs for PC, VC, OC and GC, though having followed the notions of influential language frameworks, are drawn with particulars of the features of the Chinese language and theoretical backgrounds for communicative competence. The model abandons some of the unsustainable notions of competencies in Pinyin and writing the script and adjusts the subcomponents of competencies in grammar and vocabulary. It also challenges the assumption that assessing L2 competence needs to embrace all the factors contributing to performance and identifies the core competencies as the primary contributors to performance, with the assistance of the two peripheral competencies and strategic competence to complete tasks of various domains and types.

Further readings

1 Chapter 3 in Han (2017) discusses how L1 (English) relates to the acquisition of L2 (Chinese) script, and Chapter 4 introduces a post-lingual pedagogical approach for teaching Chinese characters as a core competence.
2 Guan et al. (2015) discuss how the quality of writing predicts L2 development in L2 Chinese. The article also gives a comprehensive summary of research on the relationship between the ability to write the script and overall competence in Chinese.
3 Hulstijn (2007) discusses the issues of the CEFR in terms of the quantitative and qualitative dimensions of language proficiency. The article introduces the argument for core linguistic competence.
4 Weir (2005a) debates the limitations of the CEFR for developing comparable examinations and tests.

Reader activities

1 If you teach Chinese in Europe, the learning objectives established by your CFL programme are usually aligned with the CEFR standards. If this is the case, you can do the following:

- Examine the learning objectives in the textbook you are teaching and see if they relate to the Can-Do Statements at the corresponding level.
- Check whether the expected learning outcomes expected by your course are reflected in the *Self-Assessment Grid*.
- If you teach beginner learners (A1 or A2), determine whether the learning objectives for Pinyin and writing designed by your courses are similar to those proposed by EBCL. In the exams at the end of the instruction period, how do you assess PC and OC?

2 If you teach Chinese in North America, you can reflect on the following about the ACTFL guidelines:

- Compare the learning outcomes expected of the learners you are teaching with those of the same level as described by the *ACTFL Performance*

Descriptors for Language Learners (ACTFL, 2012b) for interpersonal, interpretive and presentational activities and see if your CFL programme can justify the differences.
- See the proficiency descriptions, the samples and corresponding rating rationale for the ACTFL Chinese LPT or RPT tests that you are interested in or at the level of the learners you are teaching on the ACTFL website. Compare the standards presented by the descriptions and rating rationale with those set up by your programme for the same level and assess if your learners can achieve the targeted proficiency in listening and reading when completing your course.
- Find the AAPPL Measure Score Report on the ACTFL website if you teach Chinese in schools and read the samples of the Score Description and Strategy and decide how many of your students have achieved the levels of performance described by the Score Description. Secondly, you should examine the Strategy and see if you agree with the recommendations and have also advised your pupils to apply those strategies to improve their Chinese.

3 If you teach foreign CFL learners in countries or regions where Chinese is an official language, you may be required to follow the ICCLE benchmark or the local guidelines. In this case, you can reflect on the following:

- Do you usually consult the guideline when preparing for exams for summative purposes? Which part of the guideline have you referred to most? Why?
- If the textbook used for your learners is standardised with the guidelines, can you see some discrepancies between the learning objectives and the competence description for the corresponding level? What is your decision regarding the discrepancies?

3 The CFL classroom-based summative assessment
Process, validity and reliability

Jones and Saville (2016) state that the recent attention to the approach of *learning-oriented assessment* has identified the concern of whether assessments have promoted more effective learning. Several terms have been used for this approach—for example, *classroom-based assessment, assessment for learning*, and *teacher-based assessment*—to distinguish them from *assessment of learning*, which 'focuses on proficiency, relating what is learned to ability in a "real world". It uses a strong measurement model ensuring comparable and interpretable measures' (Jone and Saville, ibid.: 11). In the CFL context, there have not been many studies on the approach of assessment for learning or classroom-based assessment (CBA) except that of Ke (2006) and Wang (2017), which have studied the effects of formative task-based assessment and self- and peer assessment on oral proficiency. Thus, this chapter first introduces the development of *assessment for learning* (AfL hereafter) and its advantages over standardised and external tests. As AfL in educational sectors has two purposes, summative and formative, this chapter focuses on the summative assessments developed through CBA for learning CFL. The next chapter will focus on formative assessment, which is characteristic of the assessment information used by both teacher and learner to modify their work and make it effective (Black, 1993). The contexts, purposes and consequences of CBA and the specific features of CFL will be introduced and discussed in the second part of this chapter, which provides the background information for the practice recommended for developing summative CBA. The third part discusses the process for developing summative CBA, its principles and practice for the different stages. Finally, the concepts of validity and reliability will be introduced and explored for assessing L2 Chinese competencies. Good practices will also be recommended to assure or improve the validity and reliability of the summative CBA that assesses CFL learners' knowledge and competence in the learning process.

3.1 Classroom-based assessment

As introduced previously, CBA is one of the terms that has been used for the AfL approach to educational assessments, which are different from assessing of learning which is norm-referenced by nature. Therefore, CBA has been and will be used instead of AfL for this book to signify a 'more teacher-mediated, context-based,

DOI: 10.4324/9781315167923-4

classroom-embedded assessment practice, explicitly or implicitly defined in opposition to traditional externally set and assessed large scale formal exams'(Davison and Leung, 2009: 395). Thus, CBA has been the assessment provided and administered much more often than the assessment of learning to pupils and students. However, it had been overlooked and taken for granted until the late 1980s, when the Assessment Reform Group (1989–2010, ARG thereafter) in the UK called for changes. The group's groundbreaking review of 250 studies on the assessment in several subjects in UK schools and elsewhere showed that attention to classroom-based formative assessment led to significant gains in learning (Black and William, 1998a, 1998b). ARG argued that the summative and formative CBA in an educational institute should create a process of seeking and interpreting information received by learners and teachers to find where the learners stand when working to achieve the learning objectives and what they should do to fulfil their potential as a learner. Meanwhile, in this process, teaching should nurture and support learning through adjusted teaching plans and strategies to motivate, mediate and enhance learning.

However, the comprehensive research conducted by ARG suggested that in many cases CBA had failed its goals and principles and worked towards passing national or international standardised examinations which did not usually correspond to the learners' needs and learning objectives in the syllabuses for the specific learning contexts (Broadfoot, 2005). Such practice, according to ARG, has a negative washback on learning towards the development of competence, which also raised concerns about the validity of CBA as teachers were not involved with the development of standardised tests (Broadfoot, ibid.). Furthermore, those external assessments were not based on the learners' needs, interests, strengths and weaknesses and would negatively impact students' intrinsic motivation for learning as well as on teaching and curriculum development (Harlen, 2005). In contrast, CBA or teacher-based assessments, according to Davison and Leung (2009: 40–402), are based on the AfL principles and have the following advantages:

- Scope: extensive range and diversity of assessment information is collected through much more opportunities.
- Authenticity: assessments are more authentic with less preparation that reflect genuine learner language competence.
- Validity: assessments are valid as they evaluate learning objectives based on learners' needs.
- Reliability: more reliable assessments can be developed by teachers because they know the learners better and with more opportunities to consult and reflect on the standards and syllabi.
- Fairness: fairer assessments are provided through negotiated and agreed learning processes, outcomes and standards, which are also communicated to other teachers.
- Feedback: constructive feedback is offered after assessments are administered, which improves learning with immediate effect.

- Washback: positive washback on learning encourages learners to realise study plans consistent with ongoing formative assessment aligned with teaching objectives.
- Teachers and learners: they are empowered by active involvement and participation during the assessment process.
- Professional development: teachers' assessment skills and knowledge are developed and improved.
- Practicality: practical assessments are incorporated with the language curriculum at a low cost and as part of everyday teaching without using valuable teaching time to prepare for external exams.

Bachman and Damböck (2017: 8) consider CBA in *implicit* and *explicit* modes. In the implicit mode, the CBA carried out is instantaneous, continuous and cyclical and as part of classroom teaching for formative purposes without learners' notice. In the explicit mode, the CBA activities, though also continuous and cyclical, are separated from teaching activities and mostly employed for summative decisions. In this mode, students know that they are test-takers, and their performance is being judged. The process will produce a grade or mark to be recorded for accreditation and certification. Ke (2006: 216) describes a successful. CBA in the explicit mode by a university CFL programme through task-based language assessment 'for diagnosis of progress and achievement' on the learning objectives standardised with the ACTFL guidelines. An example of CBA in the implicit mode is reported by Wang (2017), which allowed the students to play a significant role in the assessment process by engaging them with self- and peer assessment of oral presentations. The summative CBA is, therefore, the CBA in the explicit mode, which prioritises summative assessment of learning achievement and for placement or diagnostic purposes. The cycle and process for developing those summative CBAs must be regulated, and the principles and procedures for the process must be followed strictly to ensure validity and reliability. However, summative CBA of learning achievement is closely related to the unique features of the Chinese language and the specific characteristics of CFL learners, which may change the contents and techniques of assessments for different purposes to create positive consequences to learning.

3.2 The context, purpose and consequences of the CFL classroom-based assessment

The context

As observed by Han (2017: v), learning Chinese is commercialised in the West to attract investors as the market for businesses has incorporated into many countries' strategic plans, which has encouraged offers of Chinese language courses in schools and universities. For example, the UK considers Mandarin Chinese as a popular foreign language for schools to promote business and cross-cultural activities; the USA's strategy is primarily political for national security; and the

Australian government has taken Chinese language education as part of *Asian literacy* (Han, ibid.). Han also notes that the teaching of Chinese as a foreign language for the past three decades has adopted the same theoretical background as that for teaching English as a second/foreign language. This is problematic as the Chinese language is distinctively different from English. Such an approach has been challenging for generating a research framework for second language acquisition in Chinese, pedagogy and assessment of L2 competence and proficiency.

Another important factor for the CFL context is revealed by the statistics reported by the *Confucius Institute Magazine* (2018), the crucial role that the Confucius Institute (CI) plays in learning CFL outside of China. The Chinese Language Office (Hanban) had set up 548 CIs and 1,193 Confucius Classrooms in 154 countries and regions by the end of 2018. Those CI institutions are teaching 1.86 million learners face-to-face, 49.4% of whom are on credit-bearing CFL courses, with most receiving CI scholarships. These learners are taught by a prescribed course design and learning objectives drawn from the ICCLE standards through specific teaching methodology, constructs for assessment and techniques. Attached to this big group of learners is the impact of the large-scale HSK exams, the vigorous preparatory practice for the tests and the washback on learning and teaching. Reportedly, in 2018 the HSK tests had about 1,100 testing centres worldwide and a candidature of 680,000.

Additionally, the ACTFL has been increasingly influential to the CFL programmes in North America through both individual and organisational memberships, teacher training and the Global Engagement Initiative to provide a standardised assessment of proficiency and performance in L2 Chinese. There are also other internationally administered CPTs such as TOCFL produced by the Ministry of Education in Taiwan, the International Baccalaureate Mandarin Chinese (IB Chinese), the Cambridge IGCSE Chinese (Mandarin), the Pearson Chinese test, all having their shares in the fast-growing business for assessing proficiency in L2 Chinese. With such a background, the CBA by the existing CFL programmes, though mandated, structured and coordinated by educational institutions, have been affected and may have been subjected to the impact of those CPTs on their curricula, course designs and practice for assessments.

Furthermore, to the CBA in the CFL context, the teachers' knowledge and competence for assessment (KCA) and their beliefs in the value of assessment are other critical factors. As Borg (2003) points out, what teachers do in the classroom is motivated and realised not only by their knowledge of the content and pedagogic approaches but also by their beliefs in education and various approaches to teaching. The CFL practitioners, however, as mentioned in the Introduction, have not been provided with adequate training or input on postgraduate courses. They have largely followed either the principles and techniques of the PCTs or the practice of their schools or universities. As a result, it is uncertain if they have been capable of solving the dilemmas related to the challenges of assessing competence in L2 Chinese. In particular, dealing with the specific problems for assessing learners' competencies for the phonetic system and orthographic features, as discussed in Chapters 1 and 2 (for details, see Chapter 2.5), demands a high level of KCA, which again shows the CFL teachers' KCA is very important for their assessment practice.

Finally, the diverse linguistic backgrounds of CFL learners are another crucial factor in the context of assessing L2 competence in Chinese as they significantly affect the learners' competence in the written language. As mentioned in previous chapters, the Chinese script has been perceived as a great challenge, especially to those whose first or second languages do not have logographic features (here the first languages are the languages spoken at home and the second languages are those used in the learners' previous educational institutions). Moreover, the different Chinese language courses studied by the learners certainly have different expectations of learning outcomes. The following groups of learners have been identified for the CFL contexts.

1 *Learners from character or non-character background*: the former usually have fewer difficulties in learning the script, and the latter have more. For example, a Japanese or Korean CFL learner will find that the script of the target language is not as difficult as felt by those from non-character backgrounds, e.g. learners with first languages such as English, Italian, German and Arabic.

2 *Chinese heritage learners*: they are born or have grown up in countries where the official languages are not Chinese and are educated in the local languages. They speak Mandarin Chinese in accents or Chinese dialects at home. Thus, their spoken language, especially in listening, is much more advanced, and they learn speaking quickly and well.

3 *Cantonese learners of Mandarin Chinese*: they are from Hong Kong for secondary or tertiary education outside China. They are different from the heritage learners in that their listening comprehension of Mandarin Chinese (普通话) is advanced because it is one of the official languages in Hong Kong. However, most of them have not learnt Pinyin, having spoken at home and in schools Cantonese/Yue Chinese or Hakka/Kejia. Although those Chinese dialects are written in the traditional script (e.g. 愛 is written instead of 爱), they are different from Mandarin Chinese in phonology, semantics and syntax. Therefore, Cantonese learners have great advantages in learning reading and writing over the previous groups of learners.

4 *Learners on the Confucius Institute programmes*: as the agenda of CI is to promote the Chinese culture and Chinese language education, they are taught with a syllabus designed specifically for the learning needs and outcomes of the agenda. The purpose of assessment is often twofold: to evaluate learning achievement and maintain their interests in the Chinese language and culture.

5 *Learners who learn to write the traditional version of the script*: most of the CFL programmes now teach the simplified Chinese characters, though the courses in Taiwan, Hong Kong or other parts of the world may still teach the traditional version. As a result, when the learners change programmes and learn a different version of characters, the assessment criteria

need to be adjusted because of the higher or lower density of the traditional and simplified version.

6 *Learners on credit-bearing, major or minor Chinese Studies courses:* the CFL courses outside China are tailored for the Chinese Studies courses in colleges or universities. The syllabi, course designs, learning objectives, pedagogy and assessment are different from non-credit-bearing courses. Such courses have high standards and require the students to develop both competencies in the spoken and written language, often standardised with the influential language frameworks or benchmarked by the national standards. Thus, the construct definitions for assessment and standards are also different from those of courses for other purposes.

With the impact of the different groups of learners on teaching and learning, the CBA in the CFL context is illustrated in Figure 3.1, which includes the crucial factors introduced so far and demonstrates the dynamics amongst the factors. The figure also shows the author's views about how the different factors in the context affect the construct definitions and practice for both the implicit/formative and explicit/summative CBA for various purposes. The shaded areas are the theories and approaches for defining L2 abilities, the influential language frameworks and the CPTs. As observed, they might not have as powerful an impact as the factors in the blank areas, the institutional guidelines and practice and the teachers' cognition and beliefs. Such a situation will continue if the practitioners' KCA does not reach the required level to deal independently with the issues related to assessing the competencies in the written language due to the unique features of the script. This is not difficult to understand as it is the classroom teachers that make most of the decisions for CBA, especially for formative assessment that affects learning directly. Although in some cases, the high-profile language frameworks

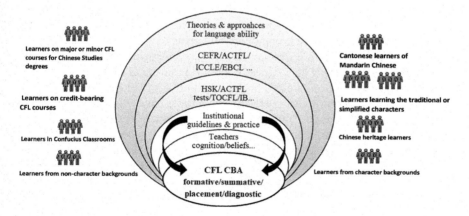

Figure 3.1 CBA in the CFL Context

and benchmarks such as CEFR, ACTFL, EBCL and ICCLE are the mandatory guidelines for a CEFL programme, the learning objectives and assessments are always catered for specific learning needs based on the linguistic backgrounds and the different requirements of the courses taken by the learners, as shown in Figure 3.1. The CPTs such as HSK, TOCFL or the ACTF Chinese tests may also influence the classroom teacher's views on L2 Chinese competence. However, we must address classroom teachers' 'implicit constructs', an internal criterion for the quality of student performance on assessment (Rea-Dickins, 2004; Teasdale and Leung, 2000). These implicit constructs concern the ideal performance, range of student performance, or the standards and criteria for judging learner performance and their relationship with the potential performance, which may not conform to the competence descriptions prescribed by the local and institutional guidelines for assessment. There are often discrepancies between the assessments developed by teachers and the requirements by the authorities and national or international benchmarks (Leung and Teasdale, 1997). Thus, educating and training the CFL teachers' KSC is essential to the validity and reliability of the CBA in the CFL context.

The purpose

Brown (2004: 42–3) argues that when embarking on a task to develop an assessment, it is critical that the test developer or classroom teachers know the purpose very clearly and reflect it in the test specification and through the test items or tasks, the marking criteria/rating scales selected or designed, and the feedback provided. Brown explains that only under such a condition can the validity and reliability of a test guarantee a fair assessment. This principle certainly also applies to the CBA by CFL programmes. Before working on an assessment, the CFL professionals must know the purpose.

In general, we assess language competence for five purposes: *proficiency, placement, diagnostic, achievement/summative* and *formative*. In the context of CBA, most assessments are not for proficiency or norm-referenced purposes. They are typically criterion referenced to examine the level of knowledge or performance on prescribed learning objectives achieved so that feedback can be provided for the progression of learning, and achievement is reported (Davies et al., 1999; Brown, 2004). In contrast to norm-referenced assessment, criterion-referenced testing is not interested in the distribution of students' performance across a continuum but whether the testing techniques have assessed the intended learning objectives (Brown, 2004). In other words, assessing language learning and competencies against a criterion or criteria is the principle for CBA whether it is for formative, summative, placement or diagnostic purposes. The assessment developed by testing organisations such as HSK, ACTFL Chinese tests or TOCFL is to measure the learners' language ability as it is at the time of testing 'regardless of any training they have had in that language' (Hughes, 2003: 11) or for 'gate-keeping decisions: immigration, access to employment and educational opportunities' (Green, 2014: 13).

According to Davies et al. (1999: 2 and 192), an *achievement* test is 'an instrument designed to measure what a person has learned within or up to a given time', and *summative* assessment refers to the evaluation of 'the outcome of a language programme for accountability purposes to provide a report to the external stakeholders'. Therefore, the contexts and aims of achievement assessment and summative assessment (SA) are different. SA has been defined as the *assessment of learning* (Black and William, 1998b) in a sense that it summarises learning outcomes of an instruction period to the public, though sharing the same characteristics as achievement tests in terms of purpose for assessment.

Undeniably, SA and FA are an indispensable pair to CBA in the explicit and implicit modes (Bachman and Damböck, 2017). SA assesses learning on entry or exit from a language course while FA is immersed in the learning process, and the purpose is to (1) identify the specific needs of individual students; (2) tailor instruction to meet these needs; (3) monitor the effectiveness of ongoing instruction; (4) understand and evaluate student performance in class; and (5) make decisions about helping students to reach the next level of instruction and optimise their learning (Genesee and Upshur, 1996). This means that FA could be implemented at the beginning of an instruction period when teachers are briefing the students about learning expectations and the forthcoming assessment, during the question/answer sessions, pair or group work and the pre- and post-reading or listening activities. SA is usually administered before or at the end of the instruction period. It is regarded as more important than FA by pupils and students as the results are recorded and reported to parents and authorities. These assessments conclude their performance for a period of learning or on a timed course.

For a language programme, *placement* and *diagnostic* tests are both necessary for different reasons. The purpose of a *placement* test is to identify the 'point' at which a learner could find the learning objectives and materials as either too easy or difficult at a specific level or streaming (Brown, 2004). The more accurate the placement test can locate the point, the more the learner will benefit from the language course she/he is taking. The most successful placement tests are usually tailor-made for a specific learning context and based on specific learning objectives. A *diagnostic* test, in comparison, is developed to identify learners' strengths or weaknesses during a learning process on certain expected outcomes (Hughes, 2003). Thus, it is used to see if learners have achieved certain learning objectives so that the original teaching plan should continue or be adjusted. Placement and diagnostic tests can be both summative and formative in nature. For example, at the beginning of instruction, a summative placement test will help the course directors or teachers to decide if a student who has studied in another institution can study a specific Chinese course that she/he has applied. A formative diagnostic test can be a gap-filling exercise given to the students after the teacher has taught the differences between 的, 得 and 地, and the students have done the prepared consolidation exercises. The results can inform the teacher of the students who have learnt the grammar and who have not. The teacher can also know which of the adverbs are more difficult for the students and whether they have understood or mastered the syntactic structures in which these words are employed. Based on the findings, the teacher will know better what to do to support the learners to learn this difficult grammar point.

The consequences

The introduction to the contexts and the purposes of CBA by CFL programmes indicates that assessments, whether they are formative or summative, involve decision-making. They are decisions for placing students on an upcoming course, adjusting teaching plans, and repairing and enhancing learning based on the result of formative assessment. They are also decisions on passing or not passing a student or how well the students have done on a course. As opposed to the common perception that only the high-profile proficiency tests are high-stakes, the decisions made for summative or formative CBA can also be high-stakes. The consequences could be serious and life-changing, too, as they affect the learners' motivation, confidence and self-assessment, which is crucial to their future learning.

Bachman and Damböck (2017) categorise the consequences of decisions by CBA into three types: low-stakes, medium-stakes and high-stakes. The consequences of high-stakes decisions can be life affecting and difficult to correct when the decision is about whether a student will pass a language course for the expected certification or qualification. The medium-stakes consequences occur when a student has been placed on a course due to overestimated or underestimated assessments of her/his proficiency level or competence. Not correcting the misjudgements in time will waste the students' time and fail to fulfil their potential for learning a language. The low-stakes consequences are mostly caused by decisions made based on FA activities in the classrooms (e.g. question-and-answer sessions, pair or group work) or through quizzes, short tests, and homework, which gather information on learning progress. Since most FA activities are ongoing during an instruction period and happening often in the interaction between teachers and learners, and learners and learners, most misjudgements can be recognised soon and rectified to avoid negative impact.

Nonetheless, classroom teachers all know that FA can also have high-stakes consequences because it is often done in the class in front of the learners' peers, where 'face' can be at high risk. For example, if a CFL teacher has asked students an inappropriate question (e.g. the type of question, poorly phrased, without consideration of learner characteristics or affective factors), it can discourage them to continue the learning process with interest. Furthermore, the *washback* of the consequence of CBA cannot be overlooked as it greatly impacts teaching and learning, which will be discussed further in terms of validity in the last part of this chapter. The next part will discuss how we can assure the quality of the SA CBA for validity and reliability so that wrong decisions are not made, and the consequences and washback are supportive and positive for learning and development of L2 language competence. Such efforts start with the process of developing CBA for summative purposes.

3.3 The process of developing CFL CBA for summative purposes

The process for developing high-stakes CBA in the CFL context, as in the contexts for teaching other languages as second/foreign languages, starts with a specific *purpose*, which can be summative, placement or diagnostic. The purpose depends on the situation that calls for assessment. Three common situations in the CFL context are described as follows:

> Situation A: a midterm speaking test is necessary for a group of learners from Hong Kong to assess if they have achieved the learning objectives for Pinyin on a twelve-week course. Based on the students' performance on the test, the teacher will adjust the teaching objectives, teaching materials or methodologies for the second half of the course.
> Situation B: an upper-intermediate class for reading and writing needs a test to divide the students into two groups, A and B, for the academic year. Group A is for the students from character backgrounds. Group B is for those from non-character backgrounds. As the CFL programme follows the ACTFL guidelines for proficiency (2012a), the learning objectives for Group A are aligned with those of ACTFL Intermediate-High, while those for Group B are with the standards for ACTFL Intermediate-Low so that the linguistic backgrounds of the students are taken into account.
> Situation C: a one-year course for the advanced learners will assess if the students have achieved the expected learning outcomes after a half year's instruction. It is a pencil-paper exam for two hours consisting of three sections: reading comprehension, grammar and essay. The CFL course has been standardised with CEFR B2. The results of their performance will be reported toward awarding a BA degree in Modern Languages with Chinese Studies.

For Situation A, the purpose is to diagnose the learners' strengths and weaknesses for having learnt Pinyin for six weeks. Can they accurately articulate the initials, finals and their combination? Have they learnt the tones and the sandhi of tones? Are the dialects they speak still interfering with their pronunciation in Mandarin? The student's performance on those constructs for competence in Pinyin will inform the teacher of the changes needed for the teaching objectives and materials for the second half of the Pinyin course. In Situation B, the purpose is to place the students interested in the upper-intermediate reading and writing course into two groups because the teaching materials, learning objectives and assessments will be different due to the different linguistic backgrounds. This is necessary for the fairness of CBA as, although all the students might have completed the same CFL course at the intermediate level, their linguistic backgrounds may benefit or hinder their learning in the written language course. If they are from the character background, e.g. the Japanese and Korean learners, the reading and writing course will not be as challenging as for those from America, UK or Italy. They will also perform much better in the FA and SA. In Situation C, an achievement assessment will provide the information for recording and reporting the students' performance on a CFL course with high-stakes consequences. In some cases, the results of the examination can contribute significantly to the overall performance to complete a BA or MA degree. In other cases, the situation could be the opposite. The examination also requires a much more comprehensive assessment, with three parts testing abilities for reading, writing and grammar aligned with the competence descriptors for CEFR B2. However, it is the quality of the tests requested by the three situations that will realise the purposes. The process to develop them is critical.

In consultation with the process for developing assessments described by Hughes (2003), Brown (2004), Green (2014) and Fulcher (2010), a process for developing SA in the CFL context is proposed (see Figure 3.2) in consideration of quality control and practicality. Language programmes do not usually have trained test writers, raters and sophisticated statistical procedures to investigate validity and reliability or conduct post-test validation studies. Therefore, the proposed

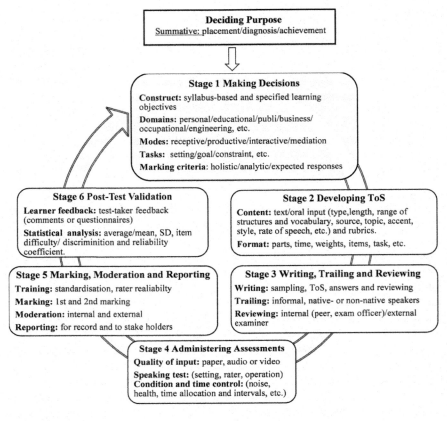

Figure 3.2 The Process and Cycle for Developing Summative CBA

process and cycle reflect the practical and realistic practice for developing SA through the CFL programmes.

Green (2014: 20) recommends that CBA should not be 'a one-off linear exercise' with assessment used just once and discarded or administered again without any improvement. It should be a cycle during which *planning, reflection, improvement, cooperation* and *evidence* are the basic principles for effective CBA on language programmes. Planning for the process described in Figure 3.2 is always the key to assessments of high quality. The more thoroughly the constructs, domains, modes, tasks and marking criteria are considered and securitised, the more valid and dependable the assessment will be. Comprehensive and in-depth planning will also help to draft the *Table of Specifications* (ToS hereafter) and write the test items. Reflection and improvement always interact closely when trailing and reviewing tests, marking performance and moderating rating. They are also critical to post-test validation because evaluating an assessment should be for improvement so that the next administration of an assessment can reflect more precisely the learners' achievement, state of learning and weaknesses and strengths.

We should certainly regard collecting evidence as essential when the markers or raters judge the test-takers' performance. Evidence is also important when planning an assessment for summative, placement or diagnostic purposes as information collected about the specific syllabus and learning outcomes can assist decisions on the constructs, domains, modes, tasks and marking criteria. Furthermore, evidence collected from the learners' responses and through statistical procedures will undoubtedly help us to reflect on and improve assessments through analysis and revision. We should also provide evidence if we say our assessments are fair, valid, and dependable, with positive washback on teaching and learning. To apply the principle of cooperation for the cycle of CBA, emphasis on teamwork is critical as it ensures sharing of ideas and criticism when planning, reviewing and improving an assessment (Green, 2014). Cooperation is important not only for internal and external examiners to review drafts and finalise the assessment before administration but also for the stages of marking, moderation and validation.

After the purpose is identified, in Stage 1 of the process we must first *define the construct* for assessment, which should be 'syllabus-based' (Bachman and Palmer, 1996: 117) and drawn from the specific learning objectives for summative CBA. In some cases, we make the decisions based on the mandated standards of a language framework, the national, regional or institutional benchmark. In most cases, however, the hidden influences are the theories of language learning and competence most familiar to the practitioners, especially their 'implicit construct' as introduced earlier. Therefore, cooperation is very important when teachers can share ideas about the assessment during planning to avoid the construct deviating from the learning objectives. The defined construct(s) for assessment at this stage should be described as observably and behaviourally as possible to help us to decide on the domains, modes, types of tasks and marking criteria that set standards for the expected responses or performance.

In Stage 2, the task is to write a ToS to provide a 'blueprint' for developing high-quality CBA for summative purposes. According to Cheng and Fox (2017), writing a ToS is the detailed planning of a test that can improve the quality and increase the credibility of the reference made on the learner's performance. A ToS can be either comprehensive or simple (see Table 3.1 for a comprehensive ToS and Table 3.2 for a simple ToS). The ToS presented in Table 3.1 is recommended for high-stakes summative CBA (Bachman and Palmer, 1996; Hughes, 2003; Fulcher, 2010), as the more comprehensive a ToS is with the information of the assessment, the less arbitrary the decisions are on the construct, input, tasks or items, expected responses and marking procedures. The advantage of a comprehensive ToS is that it can maintain the consistency of standards followed by a teaching team in terms of learning objectives and the targeted language competence. Furthermore, such a ToS will help the team to agree on the theory for language learning and L2 competencies established in their 'implicit construct' to align with the expected learning outcomes and purposes of assessment.

In addition, a comprehensive ToS is usually for the assessment of established language courses that are offered regularly. The assessments are high-stakes and will provide information for important decisions. Thus, reviewing those assessments in each stage of the development cycle, when reused, will improve the quality through the collaboration of teachers involved and the scrutiny of the internal and external examiners at the pre- and post- administration stage. Moreover, Cheng and Fox (2017) suggest that a *History File* should be attached with a comprehensive ToS to record the time it has been used, the revision made and the reasons, effects of and reflection about the revisions because a ToS 'evolves and improves over time and reflect changes in purpose, perspective, curricula and student needs' (Cheng and Fox, ibid.: 112). It is also the most important document for developing an assessment at all stages as it is the blueprint. Finally, the item/task samples provided are important because they set up the benchmark for the item writers' work.

Fulcher (2010) observes that comprehensive ToSs may restrain the test developer or item writer's creativity. They could create a situation in which teachers only teach the prescribed learning objectives expressed in the ToS and the learners are discouraged to learn more and develop their language competence depending on their potential. Therefore, Brown (2004) recommends the practical and straightforward specification consisting only of the outline of the test, skills to be tested, item and task types, the input and the format. This kind of ToS is, however, only appropriate for a test of specific purposes with low or intermediate stakes—for example, the Pinyin test demanded by Situation A (see Table 3.2 adapted from Brown, 2004: 52). For a high-stakes SA at the end of a course or instruction period, the information provided will not be sufficient for the test writer to ensure validity.

In Stage 3, firstly, the item writers, who are usually the classroom teachers in the CBA context, need to, based on the ToS, write the test items (e.g. multiple-choice, true/false, filling gaps, information transfer, error correction) and tasks (e.g. role play, writing a summary or essay, information gap, reading aloud), turning the learning objectives or the construct for assessment into operatable measures of

The CFL classroom-based summative assessment 67

Written Examination for Advanced (End of Summer Term)

Level: Level 3 (Targeting CEFR B2)	Time allocated: 2 hours	Weight: 40% for final grade

General Description:

This written exam administered at the end of the 3rd or 4th academic year measures the learning achievements of the students on joint degree courses (e.g. history, economics, politics, business and modern languages) with Chinese Studies. The exam takes 40% of the assessment for the semester. Other components are an oral exam (30%), a listening test (15%) and formative assessments (15%). This is a high-stakes assessment as 1/3 of the overall mark to pass the degree courses. The exam has three parts: reading comprehension, grammar and translation and short-essay writing. The constructs for assessment are presented as learning objectives.

Section	I. Reading Comprehension 30%	II. Grammar and Translation 30%	III. Essay Writing 40%
Learning objectives	1 Expeditious reading: can understand the main ideas and distinguish new information from the given 2 Careful reading: can understand the references intended by the formal written expressions, such as 为, 此, and can interpret meanings of the new compounds with learnt characters	1 Knowledge about and abilities to: use unusual structures for passive voice and related structures with 使 or 受 2 Can correctly use structures: 以 … 为 主, 所 attributive clause and 再 + adj. 3 Can express meanings and ideas with the previous structures in translation and the vocabulary learnt.	1 Can write effective expository or argumentative texts 2 Can convey information cohesively and coherently in text structure such as comparison, cause and effect 3 Can apply appropriate grammatical structures, vocabulary, and formal written expressions 4 Can handwrite characters accurately with required proportional components and compactness
Domains/ Topics	Learnt topic: 中国人送礼的习俗 and 中国人的爱情婚姻观	All sentences and texts are based on learnt topics.	Learnt topic: 过春节的传统 and 独生子女
Modes	Receptive written	Receptive and mediative	Productive written
Input (Texts and rubrics)	Part 1 (15%): an expository text within 600 characters Part 2 (15%): an argumentative text within 500 characters Adapted authentic texts from relevant websites with unlearnt compounds of learnt characters The structure and vocabulary are within the learning objectives and requirements for the proficiency level.	Part 1 (10%): 10 sentences consisting of commonly observed errors in passive voice and related structures Part 2 (20%): 4 short texts of two or three sentences in English	Two of the given topics: one is an expository text, and the other is argumentative. Instructions provide the information and opinions that must be provided in writing.

(*Continued*)

Table 3.1 (Continued)

Item/Task	Part 1: 6 short-answer questions in English Part 2: 6 short-answer questions in Chinese Answers are provided in the answer booklet.	Part 1: error-correction task Part 2: translation task from English into Chinese Answers are provided in the answer booklet.	Students choose one of the two topics and must follow the instruction. The length of the essay must be at least 350 characters. Penalty for Pinyin applies.
Item/Task samples	Part 1: What are the two types of gift giving? Part 2: 西方人和中国人都希望有什么样的爱情和婚姻? Sample text: ……有的人在买年画，春联和各种各样的食品，有的在买首饰，名牌包，酒和香烟。大多数人是为了准备过年，薜旧迎新，但也有人买东西是为了送礼。……	Error correction: 中国人过中秋节的传统活动很被西方人喜欢。 Translation: Some Chinese people now celebrate the traditional festival away from home or abroad. Thus, they may not follow the tradition, especially the young people.	Topic: 我在中国过春节 Instruction: you must tell the readers when, why, where and how you celebrated the festival with a Chinese friend's family. Details about traditions and customs will be appreciated.
Expected response	Those for Part 1 show the ability to interpret the meanings in English. Those for Part 2 must be written in characters. Answers copied directly off the text provided are subject to a penalty.	Corrections involve only one part of the sentences. Extensive changes are not necessary. Answers to Part 2 are marked with a rating scheme.	The expository essay narrates the experience with details of the Chinese New Year traditions as required. The argumentative essay can convince the readers of the views presented on the topic given. Well-organised with cohesion and coherence. Accurate structures and appropriate vocabulary. Competent OC.
Marking	Expected answers and alternatives with allocated marks are discussed and reviewed before marking. Penalty for Pinyin applies.	Answers and alternatives for Part 1 should be provided in the Key and reviewed by the second marker. Marking criteria for translation: faithfulness to the source text; well-expressed target text and OC.	Analytic rating scale on Content (successful communication); Organisation (text and style); Discourse (cohesion and coherence); Language (grammar and vocabulary); and Presentation (OC and punctuation).
Specification supplement	Provide large-print text or extra time for students with learning difficulties.		

Table 3.2 Table of Specification: Diagnostic Pinyin Test for Students From Hong Kong

Pinyin Test (30 mins. in total)
Pinyin skills assessed: can correctly identify the combinations of initials and finals in tones when listening, can distinguish them in reading aloud and differentiate sandhi of Tone 3 in listening and reading **Input**: audio material, text of Pinyin and rubrics **Format**: two parts: (1) Listening (20 mins. 50%) consisting of two sections; (2) Interview: reading aloud (10 mins. 50%) **Tasks**: listening and writing Pinyin heard, listening and finding the mistakes in Pinyin provided; reading Pinyin provided for words, short phrases and sentences

knowledge and competence. To the trained item writers, such a task is also a great challenge and requires years of practice to implement the construct in test items or a task to facilitate observable behaviour that demonstrates a language competence. One of the challenges to the writers of summative CBA is sampling as it is difficult to create new samples as input for reading comprehension, grammar or translation questions, etc. (see Table 3.1). If in the new samples there are more learnt materials than necessary, the level of difficulty of the test items will be low, reducing the discriminability of the assessment. If there are too many materials that the learners are not familiar with, the purpose of the assessment may not be for testing learning achievement. Therefore, a balance must be kept well by integrating the learnt materials with an appropriate amount of unlearnt vocabulary and structures to maintain the validity and reliability of a CBA summative test.

Moreover, to carry out Stage 3 successfully entails not only the item writer's competence but also the cooperation between internal and external reviewers, and the item writers. Feedback from the reviewers is the objective information for the improvement of the draft exam papers, which the teachers should reflect and act accordingly on. However, the CFL programmes in North America or China or by the CI may not have the system of external examination. In such circumstances, before an exam is administered, more vigorous internal reviews and revisions are recommended. Trailing the completed exam papers is another challenge for a CFL programme. Different from the trailing by proficiency test developers, the CBA circumstances often do not allow for large-scale pre-test trailing with a significant number of non-native speaker learners. The potential leaking of a test is always a concern. As a result, informal trailing of items on a group of native-speaker students may be the only choice for the CFL courses, which, though is far from ideal, can be useful to know whether there are unexcepted responses and alternative answers. If a test is administered for the first time, feedback from such trials is important for revision for improvement. If it is reused the feedback from the post-test validation will be invaluable. At this point, however, the assessment is ready for administration.

Stage 4, administering assessments, is both physically and technically challenging as there are considerable factors that affect learners' performance—e.g.

quality of input, setting, human factors and time control. Especially when administering listening and speaking tests, the conditions are even more demanding for the quality of audio or video input, settings, time control, interlocutor effects and test-takers' physical and affective influences. Thus, the consistency and stability of the conditions for administration are part of the reliability of the quality of assessment, which will be discussed in full in 3.5 of this chapter. In Chapters 6 and 7, when the assessment of spoken and written language competence is discussed, administration reliability will be further explored in terms of training raters for speaking and writing tests (see Chapter 6.3 and Chapter 7.3).

Stage 5 is another critical process because whether the interpretation of the students' performance is reliable and truthfully reflects the test-takers language competence, to a certain extent, determines the success of a CBA. Firstly, before marking the keys and alternative responses to the test items such as multiple choices, cloze tests or true or false, answers should have been prepared and reviewed by the internal and external examiners; expected responses to performance on speaking and writing tests should have also been provided by the ToS (see the expected responses in Table 3.1). Secondly, training and standardisation sessions must be held after speaking or writing tests are administered so that inter- and intra-rater reliability can be improved (see details in 3.5; also refer to Chapter 6.3 and Chapter 7.3). During the training sessions, it is essential that the teachers fully understand the marking criteria and scales and reflect their own and colleagues' marking on the samples provided (usually in three batches: high, middle and low). Through standardisation, the teachers/raters should also know if they are more lenient or strict when judging the test-takers performance in the productive modes. Thirdly, the first and second markings need a thorough understanding of the criteria and cooperation of the two markers. The unsolved disagreements should be subject to internal moderation first, then, if still unsolved, be settled through the external examiner. Finally, when all involved are sure of the grades or marks given, the recording and reporting procedure should start.

For Stage 5, it is recommended that when first and second marking is completed, the internal examiner should spot check the marked papers and performance on speaking and writing tests. Internal moderation should be made before selected samples (representing high, middle and low performance) are sent to external examiners for inspection. When the external examiner's comments are given, there should be further moderation. However, officially hired external examiners might only be the practice for UK universities. Different practices for the moderation of assessment results are applied in other parts of the world. CI Chinese programmes may not need external examiners because usually, it is non-credit courses that are offered. Nonetheless, an independent and impartial external examination system is highly recommended as it provides informative comments about the fairness and consistency of assessment in line with standards and the operation procedures for assessment process. Such a system can also ensure the learning objectives and outcomes are comparable to those by similar CFL courses in other educational institutes.

The operation for Stage 6 is on two fronts. Firstly, Cheng and Fox (2017) recommend that collecting test-taker feedback through questionnaires is a valuable and worthwhile procedure as it provides the perspectives of the test-takers, which informs revisions for improvement of the administered assessment. On the other hand, statistical analysis of the marks or grades awarded can reveal further details of the learners' performance and provide evidence for the quality of assessments. The classroom teachers and educational institutes are often interested in the average overall scores of a group of test-takers or the average scores for other components of the assessment or each section in an exam paper. This is because *average scores*, also known as *the mean*, are 'measures of central tendency' in the test-takers' performance (Hughes, 2003: 220). For example, after the written examination, as presented by the ToS in Table 3.1, is administered and the overall scores and scores for each of the sections are finalised, the teachers or the CFL programme can find out the students' strengths and weaknesses by calculating the average scores of the written exam, speaking and listening test and formative assessment. Furthermore, the means of the students' scores obtained in the different sections of the written exam can also inform in which skills the students are more or less competent and which type of task(s) are more or less difficult for the students. Such information will provide evidence for exploring not only the performance of the students but also the performance of the assessment.

However, the mean does not provide all the information. Several other statistical analyses can also offer valuable evidence for reflection and improvement of the test administered for validity and reliability. Based on the recommendations by Cheng and Fox (2017), Hughes (2003), Bachman (2005) and Davies et al. (1999), Table 3.3 is a summary of the useful statistical analyses that the CFL teachers and programmes can apply in Stage 6 of the cycle for developing summative CBA for post-test validation studies. In the table, the purposes, the data required and the calculation procedure of four statistical analysis procedures are introduced. Moreover, the results expected and their indications are explained with suggestions for further actions. Those statistical procedures are recommended because they provide the basic but important information about the validity and reliability of a test or a test item/task. They can also reveal the relationship between different components of an assessment and between CBA and the related external tests. All the four statistics recommended in Table 3.3 can be operated in Excel or other statistical programmes, and the internet also provides examples and demonstrations. The training sessions organised by the CFL programmes should provide the input to develop the teachers' competence for analysing test results so that they can be confident to revise assessments before and after a test is administered.

This part has introduced CBA and its background and the contexts, purposes and consequences of the assessment of L2 in Chinese. The process for summative CBA in the CFL context should follow the principles of *planning, reflection, improvement, cooperation* and *evidence* during the six stages for good assessment quality. Every stage of the process is important because it can improve the consistency and reliability of content and form. More important are the stages after administration in that they are the procedures to ensure fairness and accountability. The following

Table 3.3 Useful Statistical Analysis for Post-test Validation of Summative CBA

Purpose	Statistics and Data	Results, Indication and Suggested Action
To know the typical distance/dispersion from the mean of a group of learners as an indication of variability of a test, item or task	Standard deviation (SD) Test-takers' raw scores from a test, task or item are calculated through formulas in an Excel spreadsheet.	The SD for achievement assessment is preferably smaller than those for diagnostic and placement tests. Investigations are suggested to see (1) why an SD is too far or too close from the mean for an SA and (2) why it is too close to the mean and makes it difficult to decide the placement of learners or for diagnostic purpose.
To know if an item or task is too easy or difficulty	Item difficulty (ID) The number of correct responses to an item and the number of test-takers The former is divided by the latter.	A value between 0 and 1. SA may need a higher value, e.g. 0.80–0.90, to indicate learning achievement. Those for diagnostic and placement tests should be lower to know what has not been learnt by a student or learners' weaknesses or strengths. Adjust the difficulty accordingly.
To know the capacity of an item to differentiate high from low performance	Item discrimination (ID Indexes) The correlation coefficient of the overall score and the score gained for an item Or the ID for high performing group is subtracted by that for the low performing group.	The higher the ID indexes are, the more discriminating the items are. Revise or discard the items with zero and negative indexes. Improve faulty items with very low positive indexes. Also, see if the items are assessing other abilities.
To know the relationship between different CBA tests and CBA with external tests	Correlation Coefficient Two sets of scores from two different assessments or assessments of different abilities Results can be obtained in an Excel spreadsheet.	The coefficients vary from +1 to −1, which indicates a positive and negative relationship between two tests. 0 indicates there is no relationship. Interests are often in the relationship between an internal and external test, a listening test and speaking test, and a grammar or vocabulary test with other tests. Investigate if two tests are not positively correlated.

parts will introduce specifically the validity and reliability of language tests and some of the essential concepts of assessment practice.

3.4 The validity of assessing L2 competence in Chinese

Validity is the 'quality, which most affects the value of a test, prior to, though dependent on, reliability' (Davies et al., 1990: 221). Validity and reliability are closely interlocked as the former is about whether an assessment is testing what it claims to test and the latter is about how consistently a test is designed, written, administered and rated based on the intended construct of assessment. Construct definition is the main concern of validity as a test should test what it claims to test. Furthermore, the validity of a test must be evidenced through its *content, criterion, construct and consequence* (Brown, 2004).

Content validity of a CBA test is achieved if the topics, domains or themes involved are those that the test-takers have learnt on a CFL course. For example, if a group of CFL beginner learners are asked to do a role play in a speaking test—seeing a doctor—they should have at least learnt the vocabulary such as 医院，医生，挂号，药房，不舒服，吃药，打针 and the background knowledge about the medical system in China. As a result, this role play, whether for formative or summative purposes, is valid in content. On the contrary, if an exam paper developed by a large-scale standardised CPT is used as the achievement assessment for a group of learners at the end of instruction, the content validity of the summative CBA will be questioned because a standardised proficiency test is 'context-reduced' and assesses the language knowledge and competence of test-takers from different learning contexts. As the ACFTL Guideline (ACTFL, 2012b: 3) claims, proficiency assessment is designed to see how the L2 learners perform 'in real-world situations in a spontaneous and non-rehearsed context'. Thus, the construct definition for an L2 Chinese proficiency test is not syllabus based and does not cover the specific learning objectives and content of a CFL course.

The *criterion-related validity* of language tests is the extent of relatedness between two tests or two types of assessment techniques in terms of the information provided about the test-takers' competence (Genesee and Upshur, 1996). For example, if a group of test-takers has done very well in both a summative CBA and an ACTFL Chinese proficiency test of the same proficiency level, we can say that the two tests positively correlate because their standards and the construct definition may agree with each other and have produced the same results. Similarly, it is expected that the students who take the written paper as described by the ToS in Table 3.1 should perform well in both the grammar and essay section as those two language competencies are closely related, though the techniques of assessment are different. If the learners' performance does not relate at all, the method of correcting grammatical mistakes might need to be examined, or the sampling of input might be problematic.

There are two types of criterion-related validity: *concurrent* and *predictive*. A test's concurrent validity is supported by a positive relationship with a corresponding assessment taken at approximately the same time. The example given previously about test-takers' performance on a summative CBA and an AFTFL Chinese test at the same proficiency level shows that the CBA test is concurrently related in terms of standards with the high-profile L2 Chinese test. Predictive validity of a language test is demonstrated if it can predict a learner's performance on another test, which is often desired by placement, diagnostic, and proficiency assessments. For instance, two CFL learners had passed the ACTFL OPI at the Intermediate-High level before they came to a university in Germany and wanted to study an Advanced Spoken Chinese course. To ensure that the students were placed in a course suitable to their ability, the CFL programme asked them to take a placement test, which the students passed. After two weeks on the spoken course, the students have not felt that the course is too easy or too difficult. The teacher's observation is that they have been placed on the course appropriate to their competence. The evidence also shows that the placement test serves the purpose very well and it is positively correlated to the ACTFL OPI for the Intermediate-High level which has successfully predicted the student's competence to learn the spoken Chinese course. Most importantly, the decision made by the CFL course is correct and the students' learning progress has not been interrupted.

Construct validity 'has traditionally been defined as the experimental demonstration that a test is measuring the construct it claims to be measuring' (Brown, 2004: 9). It is a complex and multifaceted quality of a language test but 'a fundamental requirement for the effective operation of any assessment system' (Green, 2014: 81). Supporting evidence is critical for the construct validity of a test, which is provided through post-test validation studies. Summative CBA is criterion-referenced or syllabus-based and defines the constructs for assessment from specific learning objectives which may be aligned with language frameworks and institutional guidelines (Bachman and Palmer, 1996, 2010; Davison and Leung, 2009; Bachman and Damböck; 2017; Cheng and Fox, 2017). Therefore, construct validation study is a daunting task for teachers on a language programme, most of whom do not have the specialised knowledge and competence for such endeavours. Nonetheless, this does not mean that the teachers and CFL courses should leave post-validation studies to the testing professionals. The following are two feasible and common-sense methods to investigate the construct validity of a summative CBA as it is relatively high-stakes, and the validity must be examined to rectify mistakes to improve quality.

1 The content of any CBA must be checked for the connection between the construct for assessment and the domain, topics, themes and types of tasks (Brown, 2004). In other words, content validity is essential to the construct validity of a CBA. Therefore, actions must be taken when a reading comprehension test contains topics that the test-takers have not learnt and when a writing task for students at the intermediate level requires them to arrange characters provided into sentences.
2 Construct validity is the 'general, overarching notion of validity' which needs evidence for not only content validity but also criterion-related validity Hughes (2003: 26). The results from a CBA should also be compared to

those from the same group of learners on an 'independent and highly dependable assessment' to see the degree of relatedness (Hughes, ibid.). For CFL, such independent tests could be those developed by HSK, TOCFL or ACTFL. This practice is highly recommended as the CBA should share the same criteria with the corresponding independent test. For instance, if a student has done well in a CBA reading test standardised as CEFR B2 but failed to pass the TOCFL reading comprehension paper for Intermediate Level, the former needs to be examined for construct validity

It is comparatively easier to put the first recommendation into practice. To implement the second suggestion, however, would prove difficult because, as mentioned in both Chapters 1 and 2, there have been disagreements amongst the CFL academics and practitioners, and the CBA and the CPTs on the constructs for assessing L2 competence in Chinese, especially for assessing abilities in the written language. Specifically, the different answers to the following questions have significantly affected the construct validity for both CBA and CPTs in the CFL context.

1   Should the script be assessed as one of the two scripts along with Pinyin?
2   What composes OC, the ability to write the script? How should we distinguish competence in handwriting and composing through typing on electronic or digital devices?
3   Should written language be assessed after the learners have learnt the spoken language with lower levels of difficulty compared with those for assessing speaking and listening?
4   Is it justified that we assess less or at a much lower standard the written language of learners from non-character backgrounds?
5   What are the constructs for VC in L2 Chinese besides knowledge and competence of the form, meaning and use of vocabulary? Should we only assess whether the learners have remembered the graded character and lexical item lists for different proficiency levels?

The standardised CPTs, especially those with a high profile, have influenced the definitions of the construct for CBA supported by their post-test validation studies on criterion-related validity or predictive validity. Nonetheless, studies have shown that the construct validity of some of the CPTs may be in question as evidence has revealed a mismatched construct definition for assessing the written language between the HSK Level 3 and 4 tests and the summative CBA by both the UK and Russian universities (Lu, 2017). In the Northern American context, it has been reported that there are challenges to the construct validity of the ACTFL Written Proficiency Test (WPT) when it is administered as paper-pencil or computer tests or when the test-takers' production is in the simplified or traditional version (Liu, 2017). Ke (2006) also suggests that the predictive validity of the ACTFL OPI may be in question because of the weak correlation between the scores and the scores resulting from the monthly CBA speaking achievement tests awarded to 122 students in an American university's Chinese courses.

On the other hand, it is challenging for the teachers and the CFL programme to take initiative to improve the construct validity of CBA in two circumstances. The first is when practicality does not allow CBA to use authentic tasks that mirror life and indirect test items or tasks are employed instead to assess language competence or learning outcomes. To resolve this situation with the task-based approach for construct definition, McNamara (1996) has proposed that performance on the strong version of tasks measures learners' ability for a real-life situation, while the weak version assesses the underlying ability for real-life setting. Bachman (1990) also states that traits of language competence for real-life situations should be reflected in the construct definition, though authenticity for language testing can only be to a certain 'degree'. Yet it is a difficult task for classroom teachers who are not testing professionals to design the tasks in strong or weak versions regarding authenticity, although they can tell that the authentic tasks are listening to an airport announcement, reading signages in public places, talking with a Chinese about travel experiences, etc. Therefore, Brown (2004: 28) recommends the following to improve the construct validity of CBA tests developed by teachers for learners who are learning a second/foreign language in their own countries.

1 The language in the test is as natural as possible.
2 Items are contextualised rather than isolated.
3 Topics are meaningful (relevant, interesting) for the learner.
4 Some thematic organisation of the items is provided, such as through a storyline or episode.
5 Tasks represent, or closely approximate, real-world tasks.

The other situation where construct validity is at a risk is when the cognitive processes that the learners are undertaking are not in line with those elicited by the test items or tasks (Weir, 2005b; Green, 2014; Galaczi and Khabbazbashi, 2016). For example, the cognitive process elicited by the task of arranging provided characters into sentences is completely different from that for writing in the Chinese language, which includes the executive processes (goal setting, topic modifying, generating, organising and translating) and resources (language and content knowledge) (Weir, ibid.). The cognitive process for arranging provided characters into a sentence involves mainly applying known linguistic resources, translating the vocabulary and organising the sentences into syntactic structures. Moreover, the cognitive process for writing undertaken by the test-takers is both global (e.g. goal setting, topic generating, monitoring and revising) and local (e.g. applying the vocabulary and retrieving the relevant syntactic structures). As a result, such tasks for assessment of writing in L2 Chinese will be questioned for construct validity.

Consequential validity is another important quality of a test which is related to 'the effect of testing on teaching and learning' (Hughes, 2003: 1). According to Messick (1996), consequence validity has two dimensions: washback by an external assessment on classroom teaching and CBA and washback that occurs during the teaching and learning process. The former impacts the teaching materials, methodologies, content of curricula and assessment (e.g. Spratt, 2005; Davison and Leung, 2009). In the CFL context, when CPTs are sometimes used as the summative CBA, the classroom teachers tend to teach the contents of the mock or past papers, graded lists of characters and lexical items published by the testing organisations, overlooking the learners' needs, interests and learning contexts. Therefore, teaching would not be adapted to the learners' strengths and weaknesses. The latter, on the other hand, refers to the washback resulting from teaching that affects learners' motivation, independent learning, performance, study habits and attitudes toward their studies (Brown, 2004). This means that teachers' practice in the classroom, during the interaction with learners and for assessment, could all influence learning. Especially, 'the validity goal in classroom assessment is to meaningfully and accurately interpret assessment information', such as the grades, scores or the teacher's comments made in the assessed coursework or exam papers (Cheng and Fox, 2017: 65). Thus, the consequential validity of CBA will be ensured if the language course can adjust the impact of the external assessments and train the teachers for the recommended practice in the classroom.

3.5 The reliability of assessing L2 competence in Chinese

The second important quality of a language test is *reliability*, the consistency, stability and dependability of scoring and instruments used to reflect language learners' competence in a language. It depends on the consistency of test items/tasks, test-taker characteristics, rater's scoring, and stable administration condition, all aiming to implement the specific construct for assessment. To improve reliability, the standardised proficiency tests have applied statistical procedures (e.g. reliability coefficient, split-half, repeated administration) and other measures (e.g. rater standardisation, consistency of administration condition). Under the condition of CBA, different approaches are applied for the factors related to reliability, which are the *student-related reliability, administration reliability, test reliability* and *rater reliability*.

S*tudent-related reliability* refers to the consistency of the factors due to test-takers' characteristics such as physical, physiological, psychological and experiential characteristics (O'Sullivan, 2012). Physical characteristics include age, gender, long- or short-term health, disabilities, etc. Psychological characteristics refer to test-takers' personalities, memory, cognitive styles, concentration span, motivation, mental health, etc. Test-taker cultural and social backgrounds could also significantly impact their performance on test tasks. To reduce the variabilities caused by the physical and psychological test-taker characteristics, arrangements and assistance should be offered, e.g. allowing extra time or more breaks during exams and comforting anxious students. Individual experiential characteristics are another source of variability, including linguistic and educational backgrounds, general knowledge and knowledge of specific subjects which would affect their performance in assessments. Understandably, the more similar characteristics shared by a group of test-takers, the more homogenous the responses that they would produce to the same assessment, and vice versa. More varying performance because of heterogenous test-taker characteristics has been considered a risk to the reliability of a test.

In the CFL context, many teachers and programmes have been concerned with the advantages of learners from character backgrounds when assessing competencies in reading and writing and heritage learners or learners from Hong Kong when assessing competencies in the spoken language. In comparison with learners from non-character backgrounds or those who have not been in contact with the target language in their social and educational settings, they can perform much more satisfactorily with much less effort. Therefore, in certain cases, the CPTs or the CBA of the CFL programmes are perceived as unfair because they may assess the abilities that some learners are inherently weaker than those from advantageous backgrounds. However, similar to courses and proficiency tests for other languages, it is not practical and realistic to offer assessments based on learners' linguistic, cultural and educational backgrounds. As a result, some CFL teachers have found it an 'impossible mission' to develop the summative CBA with high stakes which can be fair to all learners. Therefore, measures should be taken to assure that the teachers are competent to balance the learners' strengths and weaknesses when developing CBAs so that test-taker reliability does not pose risks to overall reliability.

Administration reliability refers to the consistency and stability of the condition in which the assessment is administered to test-takers. For example, audio and video input for listening or integrated spoken language tests must be of good quality, and noise from outside needs to be dealt with. If time is given for reading the questions in a listening test, the amount of time given must be based on the learners' reading speed and the same for all of them. This also applies when time is given to handwriting answers in paper-and-pencil tests. For the speaking tests, administration reliability can be improved if the pre-test preparation time is the same for every candidate. The students who have not taken the test should not be allowed to have a 'chat' with those who have. If the conditions do not allow this, the oral exam should be designed to avoid such communication. Furthermore, oral examiners must provide a condition in which the test-takers can feel comfortable and relaxed. Thus, before the test administration, training and standardisation sessions for examiners, raters and invigilators are important to administration reliability.

Test reliability or 'instrument-related' reliability is the consistency of the methods or techniques applied for implementing the construct for assessment. In other words, the selected and created test items or tasks should effectively elicit the performance that provides accurate information about learners' progression or achievement of the learning objectives (Genesee and Upshur, 1996). The test reliability of an assessment will be in question when test-takers are provided with inappropriately employed methods so that they are confused about the specific requirements of a task; the test items or tasks are too easy, too difficult or too few; or they are given the 'freedom' to do what they can in a task in productive mode. Therefore, as the construct for CBA is based on learning objectives and criterion-referenced, the task reliability for a formative or summative CBA depends on whether the techniques used can reflect learning progress and achievement (Hughes, 2003). Again, as classroom teachers and language programmes are not equipped with sophisticated statistic procedures and the pre-test trials with substantial number of non-native speakers of the same proficiency level, a CBA needs to ensure its test reliability before administration. Hughes (2003: 44–8) recommends the following to teachers for this purpose:

1. *Designing assessments with reasonably more test items and tasks of a variety to elicit observable behaviours.* Research has shown that more items independent of each other will make a test more reliable. Therefore, there should be as many items or tasks in an assessment as conditions and resources allow, and they should not be the same type of items and tasks. For example, in a reading comprehension test, there should be at least two types of questions from a list of short-answer questions in the learners' first languages or Chinese and gap-filling, multiple-choice, or sequencing sentences based on the understanding of a text.
2. *Designing items and tasks with different levels of difficulty.* An exam paper should start with items of the lower level of difficulty and proceed with items with increasing levels of difficulty to distinguish the performance of higher levels from medium and lower levels. Example 3.1 is an example of how items of different levels of difficulty can be implemented in three gap-fill questions that assess abilities to use the comparative structures in Chinese. Item A) starts with the easiest, and Item C) finishes with the most difficult structure and vocabulary.

Example 3.1: Fill in the blanks in the following sentences with ONE character.
   A) 我＿＿＿她高很多。
   B) 她说汉语＿＿＿我一样流利。
   C) 他讲的故事是他们当中＿＿＿有意思的。

3. *Designing open-ended questions for performance in productive written and spoken mode with specific requirements to elicit the expected performance.* This is important for assessing writing through essay tasks, especially in L2 Chinese, as it has been observed that CFL learners often tend to avoid risks in paper-and-pencil writing tests by using simple grammatical structures and writing the lexical items learnt at lower proficiency levels. For instance, when the test-takers learning to achieve the proficiency of CEFR C1 are asked to write a short essay about 大学生活的一天 (a day in the university), if no specific requirements are given about the academic and social activities in universities, some of them would produce texts about their daily routines, which involves lower-level vocabulary such as 起床 (get up), 吃午饭 (have lunch), 跟朋友聊天 (chat with friends) or 写作业 (do homework) rather than what is included in the learning objectives such as 课堂讨论 (class discussion), 研究课题 (research subjects), 实验项目 (experiment project), 论文 (thesis),) and 学生会 (student union). These responses do not have

the attributes expected for the targeted proficiency level. Requirements for specific details would have ensured the test reliability of the writing task.
4   *Writing unambiguous instructions for answers to questions and performance on tasks*. Instructions should be clear, straightforward and written in a way that confusion is unlikely to occur. In Example 3.1, if 'ONE' is not in the instruction or not capitalised, the learners may complete the gaps with more than one character, which will make marking very difficult, and the construct intended for assessment will not be assessed. Since most CFL professionals' first language is Chinese, some CFL courses outside China have asked the local colleagues to proofread the drafts of their exam papers to avoid test-takers' confusion or misunderstanding because of inaccurate and flawed use of their first languages.

Rater reliability is the consistency of raters' or examiners' scoring performance for marking test-takers' responses to test items or tasks in receptive, productive or interactive modes. When marking multiple-choice questions, gap fillings, true or false questions, short-answer questions, etc., consistency of marking can be achieved without much difficulty if the expected responses and alternatives have been discussed and inspected by internal and external examiners. When marking the performance of tasks for speaking and writing assessment, however, it will not be easy for the raters and examiners to achieve consistency of rating. It is even more difficult for the oral examiners who have to interact with the test-takers and rate their performance at the same time or the raters who rate a large number of the learners' performance on the same speaking or writing task. Furthermore, different conditions for marking also affect rater reliability. For example, the oral examiners who interact with test-takers and mark their performance at the same time work under the most demanding conditions. Nonetheless, the raters' characteristics (cultural, linguistic and educational backgrounds, experiences in teaching and rating) and understanding of the expected performance on the construct(s) influence most *rater variability* and produce rater severity or leniency (Johnson and Gad, 2009; Taylor and Galaczi, 2011; Kim, 2015).

There are two types of rater reliability: inter-rater and intra-rater. *Inter-rater reliability* is the consistency of rating by all the raters who mark the same performance, whereas *intra-rater reliability* refers to the consistency of one rater marking the performance of different test-takers on the same assessment. Therefore, for a rater of performance on a speaking or writing test, the scores must be not only within an acceptable difference from those given by the co-raters but also consistent with the scores she/he has given to the other candidates. Rater reliability will be problematic when the raters do not agree on a score given to a test-taker's performance or when a rater is being 'erratic' and has awarded very different scores to similar performances. The resolutions for the standardised proficiency tests such as HSK or TOCFL, apart from the standardisation of raters, are statistical procedures (e.g. multifaceted Rasch analysis) to rectify the inconsistency.

Since CBA usually does not have the resources to conduct sophisticated statistical procedures, Hughes (2003) suggests that before a speaking test or marking learners' written work, a standardisation session for all examiners or raters should be held to (1) discuss the marking criteria and rating scales and the expected performance; (2) mark a set of performances in the higher, middle and lower ranges, discuss the different scores given and reach an agreement; (3) mark another set or, if the differences are large, several sets of performances in all ranges to find the harsher or lenient raters and resolve the inconsistencies; (4) conclude all the discussions and resolutions when all raters' marks are aligned with the marking criteria (also see Chapter 6.2 and 7.3 about training raters of speaking and writing tests). Rater training sessions can also resolve causes of intra-rater reliability problems such as tiredness, boredom and mood changes by sharing the methods that they use to deal with those situations when the rating workload is large.

Rater standardisation sessions can also deal with another risk for rater reliability, the inadequately defined marking scales or the 'instability' of the rater's understanding and application of the rating scales (Davies et al., 1999: 92). Thus, discussing the marking scales that have been selected or written is important as it is another chance to examine if they can reflect the learning objectives and differentiate the levels of performance on the purposefully designed tasks. One of the often observed instances of raters' unstable understanding and application of marking criteria is when they tend to compare a student's performance with others' rather than with the standards represented by the rating scale. At rater training sessions, those discrepancies and instabilities can be resolved to improve both inter-rater and intra-rater reliability.

In addition, during the training sessions, oral examiners and raters should also be reminded to detect if there is *interlocutor variability* that could influence their assessment of the learners' performance in speaking tests because it might result in problems with rater reliability. As discussed in Chapter 1 about the socio-interactional approach for construct definition (see Chapter 1.2), the co-constructed discourse of an interactive task often leads to indigenous assessment criteria for evaluating the test-takers' performance during indigenous and local assessment activities (Purpura, 2016). The training sessions can prepare the examiners and raters to notice and resolve the variabilities created by both the examiners and test-takers with indigenous assessment criteria (also see Chapter 6.3).

This chapter has introduced the backgrounds, related theoretical strands and advantages of CBA. The introduction to CFL contexts suggests that the learners with certain characteristics have specific learning needs, which teaching and assessment should adjust to support their language development in L2 Chinese. As CBA in the explicit mode is intended for summative, diagnostic and placement purposes with high or medium stakes, the validity and reliability of those assessments are paramount to the learners' motivation and interest in the target language, and in some cases, their future. CBA in the implicit mode is equally important, though they appear less intimidating because they also significantly influence their confidence, self-assessment and independence in the learning process. The introduction to the purposes and consequences of the CFL CBA has shown that the specific issues related to assessing the competencies of the unique features of the Chinese language would significantly impact learning and teaching. This chapter has discussed the process and cycle of summative CBA for CFL contexts and the various stages for developing high- or medium-stakes assessments. Planning, reflection, improvement, cooperation and evaluation should be implemented in those stages to improve validity and reliability so that the CBA summative assessments are useful and dependable with regard to content, construct, criterion and consequence, with reliability that accounts for learner characteristics, administration conditions, quality of test items and tasks and consistency of rater performance. This chapter has also introduced recommended practices for improving validity and reliability, which will help CFL professionals develop summative CBA. Nonetheless, formative assessment is what the CFL teachers have been practising daily. The next chapter will discuss the importance, strategies and impacts of FA on learning.

Further readings

1 Poehner and Lantolf (2005): 'Dynamic assessment in the language classroom' for a discussion of Vygotsky's sociocultural theory, the 'zone of proximal development' (ZPD) and its application for dynamic assessment.
2 Davison, C. and Leung, C. (2009) 'Current issues in English language teacher-based assessment,' for a detailed discussion on the advantages of CBA and the background and development of teacher-made assessment.
3 Chapter 4 in Cheng and Fox (2017) for an introduction and discussion on how to develop high-quality classroom tests.
4 Chapter 7 in Hughes (2003) on stages of test development.

Reader activities

1 Refer to Figure 3.1, CBA in the CFL Contexts, examine your teaching context and identify the following:

   a) The theoretical backgrounds you often refer to regarding language teaching, learning and competence in L2 Chinese. Which language standards (CEFR, ACTFL, EBCL, ICCLE or other standards and benchmarks) is your programme following? What is the benefit of such an alignment? Are there any disagreements between the standards and the CBA you develop for your students?
   b) Which CPT has your programme encouraged the students to take? Have you noticed the impact or washback on your teaching? Have your students or pupils reported any positive and negative feedback about the tests they have taken?

2 Refer to the advantages of CBA summarised by Davison and Leung (2009: 402) and respond to them with 'Agree strongly', 'Agree' and 'Disagree'. Then, you should share your answers with your colleagues or peers on the same training or postgraduate course.

3   Refer to Table 3.1, the ToS for the written exam for the advanced level, and do the following:
    a) If you do not have a ToS of the CBA at the end of the instruction of the CFL course you are teaching, write one yourself. It does not need to be as detailed as Table 3.1; however, it should have essential information such as learning objectives/constructs, input/text, tasks and response attributes.
    b) If you have had a similar ToS, please examine if changes should be made to the contents.

4   In the written exam you and your peer teachers have just completed, there are some multiple-choice questions. As they are difficult to write and will be used for the written exam next year, you need to investigate item difficulty and discrimination. Using and expanding the following table according to the number of questions and students who have taken the exam, you should find out if those items are at the appropriate difficulty level and capable of differentiating high-performing students from lower performers. 1 stands for a correct answer. 0 stands for an incorrect answer.

Student	Item 1	Item 2	Item 3	Item 4	Item 5	Item 6	Item 7	Item 8	Overall Marks (%)
Mary	1	1	1	1	0	1	1	1	85
Jack									
Amie									
Emma									

4 The CFL formative assessment and teachers' knowledge and competence for assessment

This chapter focuses on the CBA for formative purposes based on the social constructionist view of learning proposed by Vygotsky (1978), which the AfL approach applies for assessment. The Vygotskian perception of learning emphasises the social and collaborative nature of learning and the importance of the learner's zone of proximal development (ZPD), which has been supported and promoted by the research conducted by the Assessment Reform Group (ARG, 1989–2010). The first part of this chapter will introduce the nature, characteristics and theoretical backgrounds for formative assessment (FA hereafter) and the differences between FA and summative assessments (SA). The second part presents and discusses the recommended FA strategies and classroom activities. Most of the strategies and activities are not unfamiliar to CFL professionals, and they may have applied or used them often in the classroom. The question is whether they have been aware of and recognised their roles for FA. Therefore, the teachers' knowledge and competence in language assessment (KCA hereafter) are critical to their practice for FA, which the last part of the chapter will discuss. KCA, as mentioned in Chapter 3, is not only highly demanded by the process of developing valid and reliable SA but also by the FA practice.

4.1 Introducing formative assessment

As introduced in Chapter 3.1, Bachman and Damböck (2017) identify two modes of assessment, implicit and explicit. When CBA is in the explicit mode, it is SA separated from teaching activities and administered to measure and diagnose learning for administrative records and placement. And the students know that they are being assessed and there will be consequences for accreditation and certification. CBA in the implicit mode, on the contrary, is part of classroom teaching, and the learners do not know that they are being assessed. Black and William (2009: 6) define FA as:

> an assessment functions formatively when evidence about student achievement is elicited by the assessment, interpreted and used to make decisions about the next step in instruction that is likely to be better, or better founded, than the decisions that would have been made in the absence of the evidence.

DOI: 10.4324/9781315167923-5

Assessments in such a fashion emphasise the importance of evidence that demonstrates the success of learning elicited by the purposeful strategies or techniques—e.g. a dictation exercise that shows only half of the students are able to write the Chinese characters learnt in the previous week and the characters most students have mastered and those difficult for them. Based on the evidence, the teacher should examine the original teaching plan and make changes accordingly for effective teaching and learning. Without the elicited evidence, the teaching will either be aimless or fail to support learning. From the perspective of learners, FA is seen as the experience of participating in the classroom dialogues generated by pedagogic strategies to find evidence of learning achievement, reflect and assess themselves in comparison with their peers' state of learning.

Furthermore, Gardner (2006) summarises the ten ARG principles for assessment which describe the nature and characteristics of FA. ARG proposed that assessments should be as follows:

1 Be part of effective planning of teaching and learning
2 Focus on how students learn
3 Be recognised as central to classroom practice
4 Be regarded as a critical professional skill for teachers
5 Be sensitive and constructive because any assessment has an emotional impact
6 Take account of the importance of learner motivation
7 Promote commitment to learning goals and a shared understanding of the criteria by which they are assessed
8 Receive constructive guidance about how to improve
9 Develops learners' capacity for self-assessment so that they can become reflective and self-managing
10 Recognise the full range of achievements of all learners

According to Black and William (2009), the ARG's approach for CBA has embraced several strands of theoretical backgrounds about learning and education, namely *social constructivism and meta-cognition, cognitive acceleration* (Shayer and Adey, 2002; Adey, 2005) and *dynamic assessment* (Poehner and Lantolf, 2005). Amongst them, the most influential to AfL are the notions of cognitive acceleration and diagnostic assessment. Cognitive acceleration views learning as constructing knowledge based on the learners' experiences, in which the learner's participation assisted by pedagogic strategies can create cognitive conflicts that the traditional approach, providing answers to them, never could for learning. Therefore, classroom communication between teachers and learners, and learners and learners are vital media for teachers to provoke those cognitive conflicts necessary for learning and help learners to build their knowledge repertoire socially. Meanwhile, the learners can reflect on their learning and overcome the challenges set by teaching objectives.

Dynamic assessment (DA), on the other hand, derives from the sociocultural perspectives (Vygotsky, 1978) that define learning as activated by maturing mental functions through the social and collaborative activities during learning, when the 'zone of proximal development' (ZPD) is made clear to the individual learners. ZPD informs them of the achievement they have made and the assistance they need during the learning process so that learners are supported to work towards the learning objectives. Poehner and Lantolf (2005) identify two specific DA approaches: *interventionist* and *interactionist*. The interventionist DA is psychometric by nature for assessment and associates little with AfL. In contrast, the interactionist approach focuses on AfL in L2 development, which has been applied to online learning in the CFL contexts, incorporating mediation and support for students to know where they are in the learning process, where they should aim for and what they should do to achieve learning objectives. Such e-learning programmes have been constructed for reading and listening comprehension and Chinese grammar. Empirical studies have shown that they result in effective learning processes marked by actively engaging learners and enhancing their independence and autonomy when pondering over the different prompts provided and making their decisions (Poehner and Lantolf, 2005, 2013; Poehner and Lu, 2015; Shi, 2017).

The core of FA strategies and activities, according to Black and William (1998a), depends on the sequence of two actions. The first is how the learners perceive the gap between the learning objectives and what they can understand and do at present. The second is what the learners do to approach and realise the goal of learning. The outcomes of FA are the feedback produced by the learners' assessment of themselves, which helps them to adjust to learning. The teacher's role during the process is to organise the cognitive activities that provide feedback and adjust teaching (Black et al., 2004). In other words, the learners' agenda in this process is to explore, clarify, consolidate and finally go beyond the ZDP, while the teacher's agenda is to make the learning objectives available and accessible to the learners' ZDP and find out if the learners have achieved them and if the teaching needs to accommodate. In a way, FA is a process of discovery, mediation and decision-making, whereas SA is static and a less active process that records and reports learning at a specific time.

The five effective FA strategies and activities for classroom practice recommended by ARG are as follows (Black et al., 2004):

1   Sharing success criteria with learners
2   Classroom questioning
3   Comment-only marking
4   Peer and self-assessment
5   Formative use of summative tests

Black and William (2009) later updated the strategies (see Table 4.1) and explained the relationship amongst them in terms of the roles of the teacher, learners and their peers in the FA process. They also emphasise that there are three main goals in the process: (1) establishing where the learners are in their learning; (2) establishing where they are going; and (3) establishing what needs to be done to get them there. The five FA strategies by the teacher are applied to achieve those goals. For

Table 4.1 Aspects of FA (Black and William, 2009: 9)

	Where the learner is going	*Where the learner is right now*	*How to get there*
Teacher	1 Clarifying and sharing learning intentions and criteria for success	2 Engineering effective classroom discussions and other learning tasks that elicit evidence of student understanding	3 Providing feedback that moves learners forward
Peer	Understanding and sharing learning intentions and criteria for success		
Learner	Understanding learning intentions and criteria for success	4 Activating students as instructional resources for one another	
		5 Activating students as the owners of their learning	

example, the first strategy is used only when the teacher tries to inform what the learners are going to learn. The other four strategies are applied often at the same time to achieve the other two goals. The impacts of the five strategies are different, too, for a learner and their peers.

Carless (2012: 91) analysed the factors affecting the implementation of FA and claimed that the challenges are formidable because the teachers cannot assume that all students are motivated to engage themselves with the activities or perform effectively in the metacognition activities for the classroom as described in Table 4.1, self- and peer assessment. Therefore, apart from pre- and in-service training of the teachers, Carless (ibid.) proposes that teachers should learn planned and unplanned FA activities to serve the three main goals that Black and William (ibid.) have identified and to engage learners with FA. The planned activities are prepared or 'choreographed' by teachers before classes and presented on PPTs or handouts of exercises accompanied by a series of questions or answers to elicit student understanding of the new learning objectives. The unplanned FA activities are usually spontaneous and ongoing classroom exchanges between teachers and students, which aim to extend learning and reduce difficulties or misconceptions. Example 4.1 demonstrates an episode of a planned FA activity for a CFL class for advanced learners. Comments in italics highlight the FA goals and strategies.

Example 4.1:

Teacher: 好，藕断丝连，你们懂这个成语的意思吗？(Right, 藕断丝连, do you understand the meaning?) *Informing and sharing the learning objective through asking a question.*

Students: 不太懂。(Not really) *The teacher realises the first goal with the evidence that the students need further instruction, which is where they are in the learning process.*

Teacher: 没关系，先告诉我，藕是什么？看这儿。(The teacher shows a picture of a lotus with roots on a PPT and says, 'Don't worry. Firstly, tell me what 藕 is. Look here.') *With another question and visual*

88 *CFL formative assessment, teachers' knowledge and competence*

	aids, the teacher is creating opportunities for students' responses through which they can self-assess.
Student 1:	荷花的根。(Lotus root)
Teacher:	对。藕里有很粘的液体，切开的时候会有 . . ., 你们看。(The teacher shows a picture of a lotus root cut in half and says, 'Correct. The root has some quite sticky liquid in it. When it is cut there will be some . . . Look at the picture.'). *Acknowledging the correct answer, providing feedback to students for self- or peer assessment and trying to establish exactly where they are at the stage of learning.*
Students:	一些丝。(Some threads) *More students are activated, following the example of Student 1 and knowing more clearly what they need to do in the process.*
Teacher:	对。那么'藕断丝连'什么意思？(Yes, so what does 藕断丝连 mean?) *Providing feedback and helping students to conclude the learning objective.*
Students:	藕切开了，还有丝连着？(The root is cut in two but still linked with those threads?) *The teacher can see that most students are ready to move forward now.*
Teacher:	很好！如果我们用这个成语形容两个已经分手的恋人，是什么意思？(Very good! If we use this idiom to describe two ex-lovers, what do we mean?) *Activating learning toward a conclusion about the idiom as planned.*
Student 1:	他们不在一起了，但是男的还喜欢他的女朋友。(They are not together, but the man still likes the girl.)
Student 2:	也可能女朋友还喜欢男的，想跟他约会。(Maybe the girl still likes the man and wants to date him again.)
Student 3:	也可能他们都想再见面。(They both may want to see each other again.)
	The teacher has activated the students to learn from each other towards a more exact meaning of the idiom. At this point, they feel much more confident and that they own the learning process and objective.
Teacher:	你们都说对了！'藕断丝连'的意思是，两个人已经没关系了，但其中一个人或者双方还没有忘记对方。(You are all correct! 藕断丝连 means that one or both ex-lovers still can't forget each other.) *Providing feedback and concluding the learning episode.*

Carless (2012) recommends that effective FA practice should be a combination of planned and unplanned strategies. Heritage (2008), however, emphasises that both should be systematic because productive FA cannot rely on a series of unplanned events, and teachers must plan and design the questions, activities and learning materials based on specific learning needs. The reality is, as Harlen and James (1997) observe, that FA is often delivered less systematically than expected as the dynamics in the classroom are sometimes unpredictable and pupils or students approach new learning content in different ways. In Example 4.1, for instance, although the teacher prepared the picture of a lotus on PPT, she must react accordingly to the student's responses to the questions. The discourse shows that the teacher cannot predict the answers given and needs to adjust her/his speech to guide the exploration of the meaning of 藕断丝连. Thus, classroom teachers' competence in implementing effective FA strategies in classrooms has been considered critical to the quality and effectiveness of FA (Black and William, 2003; Leung, 2004; Carless, 2006, 2012). Further, FA activities, though seen as teaching activities, are instrumental to successful learning.

4.2 Teacher strategies for effective formative assessment

This section discusses and demonstrates the five FA strategies (FAS1, FAS2, FAS3, FAS4 and FAS5 hereafter) based on the proposals and updates by Black and William (2009) and Carless (2006, 2012). Some CFL teachers may feel that the strategies are common practice in their classrooms. The questions now for us, however, are whether the strategies have been applied as FA activities and whether they are applied purposefully to improve learning significantly. Thus, we must understand and know exactly how the five strategies are organised and conducted in the classroom during the teacher-learner interaction and assessment practices.

FAS1: clarifying and sharing learning objectives and criteria for success

Studies have shown that when learners are informed of specific learning objectives and expected learning outcomes, they perform better in classroom tasks and assess themselves more efficiently because they know better what they need to do to reach the targets and standards (Clarke, 2001). Most trained CFL teachers have been doing this as a routine at the beginning of an instruction period or a lesson. For example, teachers may tell their pupils or students, 'Today, we are going to learn the new characters for Lesson 6. By the end of the class, you should be able to understand their exact meanings in the dialogue and use them in sentences. Next Friday, we will see if you can write them in a dictation exercise.' Such episodes also occur when teachers are introducing the learning objectives of a beginner CFL course for Pinyin, the graded lists of characters or lexical items and the expected learning outcomes of the spoken and written language. However, the effects may differ when FAS1 is conducted with or without the teacher's awareness of it as a strategy for FA and the effective ways to organise such sessions. The following recommendations of techniques will help teachers to apply the strategy successfully.

1   *Introduce the learning objectives and criteria of success with explicit wording for descriptions of behavioural performance* (Clarke, 1998). Example 4.2 demonstrates the difference between the learning objectives as stated in the course document and the sharing and clarifying by a teacher to a group of students with greater impact.

Example 4.2:

> **Learning objective in writing:** to learn the use of the modal particle 了 to express change of state.
> **The wording used by the teacher:** we have learnt 了 to tell what has been done or happened. Now, you are learning another function of the word, what has changed or is different from before. For example, how do you say 'My father is getting old' in Chinese?

2 *Enhancing the information by encouraging learners to reflect on the learning objectives with questions* (Torrance and Pryor, 1998). For example, to inform the same learning objective about 了, the following questions will help learners to understand and remember it:

> Do you remember why 了 is used in the sentence, 我吃饭了?
> Can you say another sentence with 了? What is the meaning of it?
> Why is 了 used in 天黑了? Does it mean changes in time or that something has happened?

3 *When introducing the criteria for expected performance, teachers should provide examples of successful performance on test items or tasks in a summative CBA*. Students can also be invited to try the same questions and have their answers compared to the expected performance. By doing so, the students can know the distance between the criteria and their existing knowledge and competence (Carless, 2012). In a sense, the CFL teachers, mostly from an examination-oriented culture, may have used this strategy much more often than those from other educational and cultural backgrounds. Their task now is to reflect if they have applied the strategy for FA purposes rather than just to give correct answers to the questions. They must adjust the focus on helping learners to understand the learning expectations and find out what to do to narrow the gap between the target and their existing abilities, rather than training learners to know and remember the correct answers.

FAS2: activating productive classroom interaction through questioning and discourse strategies

This is the most important strategy because most of the FA strategies are initiated and realised by the teacher's questioning and discourse approaches during classroom interaction. The unplanned FA episodes Carless (2012) proposes also depend on teachers' use of questions to fulfil. For instance, when a teacher asks the students, 'Have you understood the meaning of "了" in those sentences?' it motivates *self-assessment* of the learning objective and criterion, and *peer assessment* is initiated, too, when some students respond to the question and the others are not able or prefer to keep quiet, which will provide feedback to all the students. The teachers' confirmation of the correct answers is the feedback to the learners. At the

CFL formative assessment, teachers' knowledge and competence 91

same time, the various responses by the students can help the teacher to adjust the teaching plan to assist those who have not achieved the learning objective. Thus, teachers' questioning skills and discourse strategies are critical to the scaffolding, mediating and collaborating in learning a language, which is often a social joint venture by the teacher and learners, and amongst learners and learners.

Figure 4.1 describes how questioning and discourse strategies facilitate and support the other FA strategies. FAS2, as shown in the figure, is differentiated into two categories, FAS2-A: Questioning and FAS2-B: Discourse. They are teachers' questioning and discourse strategies for FA, which are in the different forms of questions or discourse approaches, e.g. display or referential questions, and I-R or I-R-F. Those two strategies, as the arrows indicate, are applied to elicit and materialise the five FASs for specific assessment purposes. The outer circle that connects the five strategies means that FA, as an implicit assessment, is instantaneous, continuous and cyclical, impacting and interlocking with each other. The following is the introduction to the application of the strategies.

FAS2-A: teachers' questioning strategies for FA

Black and William (1998b) have famously illustrated that classroom teachers work inside a 'black box' where they have to manage complicated learning situations and take care of the students' personal, emotional and social affairs. They are occupied with not only the *input* that they pass on to the learners, the responses from

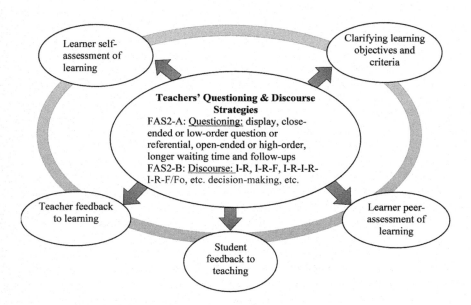

Figure 4.1 Core FA Strategies: Teacher Questioning and Discourse Strategies

learners, the institutional and parental demands and the requirements of internal and external assessments but also the *output* from the black box, the classroom, in terms of successful or unsuccessful learning. Thus, Black and William (ibid.: 141) emphasise that the teacher's responsibility in the 'black box' is to design and deliver 'an effective learning environment and the learner is responsible for the learning within that environment'. Such a desired condition is based on the interaction between teachers and learners in the classroom, showing that the teacher's questioning strategies are critical to both the input and output.

Studies have shown that certain types of questions are more productive for learning as they deepen the learners' cognitive activities (Stiggins et al., 1989; Black and William, 1998b, 2009; Burns and Myhills, 2004; Black et al., 2004; Hodgen and Webb, 2008; Walsh, 2011, 2013). Another view is that as questions are an essential and integrated part of teaching and teaching and FA are indivisible, as long as they serve the different purposes of FA, they are all effective questions that can lead to successful learning (Black and William, 1998b; Black et al., 2004). In other words, teachers should know the effect of the different types of questions and carefully plan the questions they ask in the classroom according to the purposes of assessment and the characteristics of their learners. As a result, they can discover the gaps between students' existing knowledge and the expected learning outcomes so that they can provide the information to the learners and assist them to narrow the gap. The studies mentioned previously have found mainly two types of questions and their impacts on L2 learning.

Question Type A: *display, close-ended* or *low-order questions*, which are the questions often asked by teachers to check whether the learners are following the instruction or have understood or remembered what they have learnt or for brainstorming or warming-up sessions. Such questions focus on the forms or meanings of the language structures and items. Although they serve the purposes of FA, they request narrowly defined correct answers retrieved from memory without much reflective and critical thinking. They do not usually generate much learner talk, which is very important for language learning. Thus, if a teacher intends to elicit authentic communication with creative use of the target language, they need to ask other questions rather than, for example, '中文怎么说 apple?' or 'What does 正在 mean?'

Question Type B: *referential, open-ended* or *high-order questions*, which engage learners effectively, elicit a broader range of student thinking and express detailed information rather than superficial, factual and one-word answers. They focus on content rather than on language forms, helping to develop the abilities in a target language to express inference, predication, verification and summary. The highly recommended referential questions are 'divergent' or 'open-ended' and not only require a higher level of thinking by learners but also resemble real-world communication. More importantly, they elicit much more learner talk than Type A

CFL formative assessment, teachers' knowledge and competence 93

questions. For example, '你们喜欢吃苹果吗？为什么?' 'Apart from "正在", are there other words that also tell something is happening?' Such questions explore the extent and depth of learning and provide teachers with details for adjusting teaching plans or moving forward beyond the intended learning objectives.

After the teacher asks the question, another two strategies should be used to ensure the outcome of the FA strategy.

1 **Longer wait time after questions are raised:** this seems trifling. However, many teachers may not do this so the questions may fail to achieve the purposes. A longer wait time is necessary because the learners need time to understand the question and think of their responses, or they are not certain about the answers and prefer to uphold responses. Wait time can be longer than usually given for the teacher to find the learners able or unable to answer the questions and what is the difficulty for some of them to respond. Such information can help the teacher to adjust the teaching plan for the next step of teaching. Insufficient wait time, on the other hand, engages less learner participation as there is not enough time to think and take initiative, which could result in passive learners just waiting for the teacher to give the correct answer so that little self-assessment is involved, depriving them the opportunity to find the gap between their existing ability and the expected learning outcomes.

2 **Follow-up activities after questions are raised and answered:** this practice is to expand students' understanding and learning by using both Type A and B questions alternatively to initiate accurate, extended and elaborated responses to their one-word or brief answers to the question. Follow-up activities include further questions probing the initial answers or inviting further information that motivates higher-order thinking and more learner talk in the target language. Often, they can elicit responses with more complicated linguistic forms and specific vocabulary (see Example 4.3 and analysis in brackets). They allow the teacher to see evidence of in-depth learning and breadth for decision-making on the next step of teaching and also serve as feedback to learners.

Example 4.3:

Teacher: Apart from 正在, are there other words that also express something is happening? (*Question Type A*)
Learner A: 正，在 and 着. (*This is a good and accurate answer, though the learner talk is less.*)
Teacher: Yes. Would you make a sentence with 着? (*Question Type B*)
Learner B: 他看着我，不说话。(*An answer in more complicated linguistic forms and specific vocabulary*)
Teacher: Good sentence!

FAS2-B: teachers' discourse strategies for FA

Classroom teachers' discourse strategies are equally important for FA to their questioning strategies when interacting with learners. The aim of the classroom discourse, according to Black et al. (2004), is to offer all learners the opportunities to think and demonstrate learning. Tsui (1989), in her seminal article on classroom discourse, challenged the powerful descriptive sequence of adjacency pairs (see 1 and 2, 3 and 4 in Table 4.2) in conversations described by Schegloff and Sacks (1973). She proposed that classroom discourse is typically organised by the three-part exchanges (see 5, 6 and 7 in Table 4.2), I-R-F, initially proposed by Sinclair and Coulthard (1975). The exchange consists of an initiation (I) from the teacher, followed by a response (R) from the learner(s) and feedback (F) that evaluates the response by the teacher. Sinclair and Coulthard noticed that the evaluative Feedback move is often upheld by teachers for different reasons, resulting in a frequent classroom discourse structure of I-R-I-R-I-R-F, with the feedback move existing much less frequently (see Move 1 to 7 in Table 4.2). Or the Feedback move is often a follow-up that responds to the learners' answers to questions or contributions to the classroom discourse (see Moves 10, 12 and 14 in Table 4.2).

For FA purposes, Torrance and Pryor (1998) and Leung (2004) suggest that teachers may need to avoid the 'evaluate' move in the I-R-F structure deliberately so that the interaction can be less threatening, and learners are encouraged to assess their responses to the question as in a natural conversation. This kind of interaction also encourages other learners to participate and contribute when the discourse can gradually transform from teacher-led to learner-centred. A teacher-led interaction is 'an unproductive interactional format' (Kasper, 2001: 518) at the expense of active student participation and less creative language use (Walsh, 2012). Therefore, effective speech modification by teachers for FA purposes is an essential element of classroom interaction that transforms the I-R-F classroom discourse structure to improve the condition and quality of learning (Walsh, 2011). The advantage of learner-centred interaction is that the teachers can observe successful and unsuccessful learning and adjust the planned FA activities to support learning and achieve the learning objectives.

In the classroom discourse shown in Table 4.2, we can see the intended modifications made through the teacher's strategies and the potential FA effects on learning. 'Move' in the table is an utterance or stretch of utterances with communicative functions in a conversation. It is one of the components in the hierarchical discourse structure as proposed by Sinclair and Coulthard (1975), namely *Lesson, Transaction, Exchange, Move* and *Act*. The follow-up move that does not act as feedback to the learners is labelled as Fo. In the table, FAS3 (activating students to self-assess and peer-assess learning) and FAS4 (providing effective feedback to move learning forward) are also listed when relevant, though they will be discussed later.

The episode of classroom interaction described here exemplifies the importance of scaffolding in the language classroom through teacher-learner and learner-learner interaction. Interactional scaffolding is the minute-to-minute

Table 4.2 Modified Classroom Discourse and Speech by Teachers for FA Agendas

Move No.	Move Type	Classroom Discourse	Teacher's Discourse Strategy	Potential FA Effect
1	I	T: Last Tuesday, we learnt that '正在' used before an action verb expresses an existing state or an action that is happening. Who can say a sentence with '正在'?	Briefing the learnt objectives and using a question to initiate student contribution	Sharing and checking prior learning; focusing on the further learning objective Effects of FSA1 and FSA2
2	R	L1: 她正在看电视。		
3	I	T: Can I have another sentence with the new words we've just learnt in this lesson?	Avoiding a Feedback move and target the new objectives	Setting up a new criterion Effect of FAS2
4	R	L2: 他们正在学唱京剧一个著名的京剧演员。		
5	I	T: 他们正在学唱京剧一个著名的京剧演员。	Avoiding Feedback move with repetition of the grammatically incorrect sentence to elicit corrections	Activating self- or peer assessment Effects of FAS2, FAS3 and FAS4
6	R	L2: Oh, sorry. 他们正在跟一个著名的京剧演员学唱京剧。		
7	F	T: Very good. You used '著名' and '演员'.	Performing a feedback move to confirm successful learning with specifics	A positive evaluation is given to highlight the learning criteria, eliciting self- and peer assessment. Effects of FAS1, FAS3 and FAS4
8	I	T: Any other words also express an existing state or action that is happening?	Expanding the topic for further learning through an open-ended question	Clarifying the next learning goal and collecting evidence to see if the teaching plan should be adjusted Effects of FAS1 and FAS2
9	R	L1: 在，在看书，在…	Avoiding the evaluative feedback move with follow-up moves in a rising tone to motivate more responses and maintain learner-centred discourse	Using simple initiating techniques to know the learners' existing knowledge Effect of FAS2
10	Fo	T: Yes (rising tone).		
11	R	L3: 在吃饭		
12	Fo	T: Yes (rising tone)		
13	R	L4: 正在，在，着？要？		
14	Fo	T: Uh-huh (rising tone).		
15	R	L2: 现在？		
16	F	T: Excellent! Quite a lot, aren't there? Now, let's see if we can find all you have said in the second conversation of Lesson 8.	Performing the evaluative feedback move and commenting on the responses	Offering feedback with encouragement, motivating self- and peer assessment and establishing the next learning task Effects of FAS1, FAS3 and FAS4

support that teachers should provide to their learners, which poses challenges because of the unpredictable dynamics in the classroom (van Lier, 2004; Many et al., 2009). Teachers, therefore, must be experienced in using the discourse strategies as supportive tools to help students to complete learning tasks like those presented in Table 4.2 (e.g. repeating incorrect answers, echoing/backchannelling responses, extending on topics or prompting the students to justify or lengthen their answers). Leung and Mohan (2004) propose a teacher FA discourse strategy for the students to make decisions during learning activities through analysing the classroom discourse based on the framework of Systemic Functional Linguistics (Eggins and Slade, 1997). They discovered three typical moves taken by both the teachers and students: *offer answer, reasons for/against the answer, respond to offer*. During such decision-making exchanges, the teacher assists the students to decide if they have answered the questions correctly or completed a task satisfactorily. Such a discourse approach, according to Leung and Mohan (ibid.), focuses on the process rather than the product. Scaffolding is also offered by both teachers and peers, acting as FA that motivates, facilitates and mediates learning.

FAS3: activating students to self-assess and peer assess learning

Self-assessment by language learners takes place during instruction and learning activities. Therefore, training pupils and students to assess themselves and others is an integral and critical part of FA as some learners do not know how to do purposeful and productive self- or peer assessment (Black and William, 1998b; Sutton, 1995). Wang (2017) reports that activities such as designing rubrics for a summative CBA oral exam, practising speaking tasks and observing and assessing their own and peers' performance can train the CFL advanced learners to conduct accurate and constructive self-and peer-assessment. The training improved not only the quality of the students' self- and peer-assessment but also their understanding of the standards and criteria. They also became able to reflect on their learning strategies and progress and critically analyse their work in consultation with the learning objectives. The following are a few of many activities that teachers can organise to train learners for productive self-assessment (Black and William, 1998b; Clarke, 1998; Sutton, 1995; Fulcher, 2010).

1 *Organising pair or group learning activities to motivate self-assessment*: peers' involvement can effectively enable learners to observe and assess their performance objectively. Peers' comments or criticisms are important complements to self-assessment as they are easier to be accepted because of the learners' equal social status. The effect is also much more lasting than the feedback from teachers or the results of tests and exams. Peers' involvement with self-assessment can also be done through organising pairs or small groups to mark each other's homework and responses to past or mock exam papers.

2   *Organising learners to assess their preferred ways of learning*: the activity can start with, for example, brainstorming on 'good' and 'not good' strategies and their advantages and disadvantages. The learners then can be asked to identify if their learning strategies are in the 'good' or 'not good' groups. Plans on improving their strategies should be made. However, such activities should be open-ended and acceptable to individual preferences.
3   *Discussing with the learners the different types of learning tasks and types of questions in assessments and asking students to assess their performance on the tests*: task types perceived as 'specific', 'typical' and 'new' should all be explained and clarified for learners to see if they have the metacognitive skills to tackle them. Learners can perform those tasks and answer the questions in pairs or small groups to compare performances, reflect and improve on the strategies that have been used.
4   *Organising learners to write marking criteria for the assessment of the productive skills*: this involves knowledge of the learning objectives and criteria for successful learning and the awareness of the observable behaviours for the expected performance.

Carless (2012: 152) considers peer collaboration and tutoring resulting from peer assessment as typical of the socially constructed nature of learning essential for successful learning. Peer tutoring during task-based language learning offers abundant potential for learning to progress beyond the ZPD. Though the roles of 'tutor' and 'tutee' are usually taken in turns, the students who understand the learning objectives and content usually play the tutor's role better than those who do not. Devitt and Liu's study (2017) reports that the beginner learners' experience of being the tutor and tutee produces successful learning and enhances learner autonomy and sense of responsibility. Their study suggests that 'collective scaffolding' (Donato, 2004) on the target language carefully planned by the teachers creates opportunities for co-constructing learning more efficiently than the learning activities without consideration of peer-assessment. For effective peer-assessment activities, the following are recommended by Genesee and Upshur (1996), Black et al. (2004), Topping (2005), Fulcher (2010) and Devitt and Liu (2017).

1   *Assigning drills and practice on newly taught learning objectives with a less demanding cognitive workload for pairs or groups* so that the learners can concentrate on the language forms or meanings and support each other. They should be also given opportunities for finding and correcting each other's errors and explaining why they are not correct so that peer-assessment could be provided more socially, and scaffolding is implemented as necessary.
2   *Organising interactive activities on learnt content with a more demanding cognitive workload*: such activities involve more joint effort, active

contribution and individual accountability to realise the communication goals. Therefore, peer assessment is particularly important for the process because both language competence and cognitive abilities are called for to meet the standards.

3 *Assigning peer tutoring projects or homework for learners to teach each other new input*: first, during such activities, the learners will feel less awkward interrupting the 'peer tutor' compared to a teacher to ask questions for confirmation and clarification. Secondly, they understand their peer's learning difficulties much better than the teachers, ensuring that peer tutoring is purposeful and can boost learners' confidence, motivation and sense of responsibility. Thirdly, peer tutoring demands that the learners know the new learning objectives thoroughly in advance, and the exchange of roles allows everyone to go beyond the ZPD and achieve the learning goals.

4 *Organising learners to share or assess portfolios of audio or video tasks intended to transform the learnt linguistic knowledge into competence in productive skills*: many CFL teachers and learners have been using the voice or video functions on WeChat as a platform for different homework, and the teacher's feedback and comments are given through social media too. To provide a socially less formal and threatening condition for peer assessment, the portfolios can be checked by peers instead of teachers, who on those occasions should act as the provider of correct answers and responses to inquiries about the criteria of assessment.

FAS4: providing effective feedback to move learning forward

FAS4 is usually implemented when the learning objectives that have been taught need consolidation to become a competence for language use. Nonetheless, learning a foreign language needs circles of practice, enhancement and improvement; therefore, it is essential that feedback is provided to improve performance. In Carless' view (2012: 10–11), five factors decide the quality and impact of feedback for formative purposes:

- The time when feedback is given
- The relationship between the feedback provider and receiver
- Whether the feedback focuses on the task and strategies
- How the feedback is given
- Whether the feedback is delivered privately or publicly

Recommendations have been made on providing effective feedback in consideration of the five factors.

1 *Providing feedback promptly and frequently after assessment activities*: specifically, feedback given within one week after students have learnt the new content improves learning most productively. Furthermore, feedback given after frequent and short tests offers more learning opportunities than

infrequent and longer assessments (Black and William, 1998b). The weekly or regular dictation exercise of the newly learnt Chinese characters, for example, is a good example of this recommendation. Such assessment does not involve a lot of content, and the feedback can be provided promptly by the teacher, learners themselves or their peers. Similar and more interactive or lively classroom activities could have the same FA function, which will need the teacher's creativity based on the learners' characteristics of learning. Although it is difficult for summative CBA to provide feedback soon after it is administered, two practices are recommended: providing written comments on the individuals' performance and arranging consultations during which the students can view their marked exam papers and ask for feedback.

2 *Providing feedback as a 'coach' with appropriate question types and discourse strategies*: Cheng and Fox (2017) observe that classroom teachers have two conflicting roles of being a 'coach' and 'judge'. When providing feedback for formative purposes, they should be the 'coach' rather than the 'judge', who can improve the strained relationship between the feedback provider and receiver. To do so, Johnson and Johnson (1990) suggest that teachers should apply appropriate question types and discourse strategies so that students are more willing to accept and follow the feedback. For example, referential, open-ended or high-order questions and discourse styles resembling natural conversation (see FAS2) can create a more relaxing condition for the learners to understand and consider the feedback given by the teacher.

3 *Providing constructive feedback with specifics that prioritises learning or assessment performance:* when giving feedback, most CFL teachers tend to say '很好', '对', '很棒', '太好了' ('Very good', 'Correct', 'Terrific', 'Excellent'), etc., or the opposite, '不对', '错了', '因该是 . . .' ('It's not right', 'Incorrect', 'It should be . . .'), etc. Some are also careful not to give negative feedback to protect learners' motivation and confidence. However, studies have suggested that such feedback as those mentioned is not effective feedback that improves learning significantly (Butler, 1987; Cameron and Pierce, 1994; Torrance and Pryor, 1998). In contrast, feedback with comments on the behavioural characteristics of learning and performance helps learners understand the essence of the criteria, especially when comments are accompanied by detailed descriptions, alternative responses and recommended strategies for a specific type of task. Therefore, Black et al. (2004) highly recommend comment-only feedback provided verbally or in writing.

Furthermore, studies on corrective feedback to language learners have shown that it has contributed significantly to FA. Ellis (2008: 12) advocates applying the sociocultural theory on corrective feedback (CF hereafter) as it regards learning 'as dialogically based; that is, acquisition occurs *in* rather than *as a result of* interaction' (italics in original). Ellis gives a figurative image of the ZPD in the experience of learning a language, the 'bud'. For the growth of the 'bud' or narrowing of the gap between present learning and expected learning, CF needs to interact with the scaffolding of learning and mediation between the engaged parties. Therefore, teachers' questioning skills and discourse strategies are critical for such learning episodes when the learners are digesting the feedback given to achieve the expected learning outcomes. It has been found that CF strategies neither too explicit nor too implicit provide learners with the most effective support and accelerates learning (Aljaafreh and Lantolf, 1994; Nassaji and Swain, 2000), for example, explicit correction, metalinguistic explanation, elicitation and paralinguistic signals (see the following examples). Those CF strategies will offer effective feedback for learners to overtake the ZPD and move learning forward with consideration of their affective characters and cognitive capacity.

Example 4.5: Explicit correction

Learner: 她一开心，想唱歌。
Teacher: 她一开心，就想唱歌。

Example 4.6: Metalinguistic explanation

Learner: 她一开心，想唱歌。
Teacher: Which word follows '一' when expressing 'as soon as'?

Example 4.7: *Elicitation*

Learner: 她一开心，想唱歌。
Teacher: 她一开心，what 想唱歌？

Example 4.8: Paralinguistic signal

Learner: 妈妈刚才吃饭。
Teacher: 妈妈 (pointing to the back to indicate the past) . . . ?
Learner: 妈妈刚才吃饭了。

FAS5: using summative or proficiency tests for formative purposes

Most summative CBA is achievement tests on the learning objectives developed by the classroom teachers or the CFL programmes. Some CBA, however, uses CPTs as a summative assessment due to institutional or national requirements. Thus, the application of FAS5 should be accommodated in two situations. In the first situation, the past papers are usually referred to during instruction and often used as examples of expected learning outcomes. In the second case, it is the published past papers or mock papers that are provided to learners for reference or trials to find the existing performance and the criteria for learning. Thus, the strategies of using summative or proficiency tests for formative purposes are important to help the learners to learn and perform better for the achievement test.

Four recommendations are given as follows to ensure that language learners can benefit most from the FA activities organised by teachers (Carter, 1997; Black et al., 2004; Carless, 2012; Cheng and Fox, 2017).

1   *Helping learners to familarise with the upcoming SA or the CPT to faciliate the learning process and connect the ongoing FA and the expected learning outcomes*: this can be realised by presenting and explaining to the learners how the expected performance by the summative assessment or the relevant CPT competence descriptions are related to the learning materials and objectives. The test items in the specific past papers of the SA or CPT should be provided to demonstrate this, e.g. taking one of the topics for the writing task to show the vocabulary involved and where they are located in the learning materials.

2   *Using the specific constructs of the language competencies implemented in the SA or CPT as information and data to identify the learners' strengths and weaknesses*: the diagnosis should be applied by the teachers to deal with learning difficulties through purposefully planned activities, for example, organising pair work to list the appropriate gifts for a Chinese friend, one of the components of the construct for assessing the interactive competence in the task '给中国朋友买生日礼物'.

3   *Allowing learners to take more responsibilities for learning through self- or peer-assessment activities*: learners are keen to know the format and content of the end-of-instruction assessment. However, some of them are not fully aware that they also need to be responsible for their performance when responding to the questions in the past papers of the SA or CPT. One of the activities to raise awareness is to select the relevant past papers and ask the learners to do them as homework and marked by a peer. The teacher then provides the keys and asks the pairs to discuss each other's correct and incorrect responses.

4   *Organising preparatory activities with emphasis on improving language competence rather than on test-taking techniques*: teachers should try to divert some learners' attention or interests in getting the correct answers rather than on how to obtain the abilities to provide the correct answers as they construct the language knowledge or competence expected by the summative and proficiency tests. One of the activities teachers can organise is, after the key is given, analysing the linguistic knowledge or components of competence necessary to achieve the correct answers and performance on receptive and productive tasks.

This part has introduced the nature and advantages of FA and recommended the activities and strategies to implement FA in the classroom and during interaction with learners. To collect evidence of successful learning or the gap between existing and expected learning, the teachers are required to organise planned or unplanned FA activities; apply explicit wording, the appropriate types of questions, discourse strategies and CF approaches; and organise various FA activities.

With such high demand for classroom teachers' competence for FA, it is never an overstatement that their knowledge and competence for developing and delivering CBA is critical to assessing L2 competence in Chinese. The next part, therefore, will introduce the teacher's competence in language assessment and its components and levels.

4.3 CFL teachers' knowledge and competence for assessing competence in L2 Chinese

Studies have shown that about 30% to 50% of language teachers' daily work is assessment related (Coniam, 2009). With CBA prioritised for developing L2 competence, it has been widely acknowledged that classroom teachers' *language assessment literacy* (LAL) cannot be overlooked by teacher training and professional development. At the frontline of language education, teachers' knowledge and competence for assessment (KCA, hereafter) is vital to the validity, reliability and washback of the CBA that they develop. Furthermore, due to the coexistence of CBA and CPTs in the learning context, the related CPT may have a greater impact on learning, so the teachers must be well-informed of the advantages and disadvantages of the standardised tests to resolve issues caused by the washback on their pupils or students. Therefore, the term KCA is chosen for this book instead of LAL because it reflects more fittingly the construct for the knowledge and competence required of the classroom teachers to develop and deliver FA and SA.

What does KCA consist of? Bachman and Palmer (1996: 9) proposed that it consists of the fundamental understanding of the issues and approaches and the ability to design, evaluate and use tests. After reviewing proposals made since the 1960s for the knowledge and skills demanded by the practice for developing assessment, Davies (2008) summarised that KCA compromises knowledge, skills and principles. Taylor (2013) regards LAL as developmental and multidimensional and profiles the competence as consisting of eight components. Furthermore, she proposes that all those involved with language assessment do not have the same level of competence. Recently, Kremmel and Harding (2020) conducted an empirical study of the different factors of LAL by using the eight components proposed by Taylor and added further details to the first two components. Table 4.3 presents the constructs of KCA as proposed by those mentioned.

Some professional language-education organisations have established standards, especially for classroom teachers' practice on assessment, offering training programmes, symposiums, workshops and webinars to improve the quality of CBA. One of the examples is the *Standards for Teacher Competence in Educational Assessment of Students* by the American Federation of Teachers, National Council on Measurement in Education and National Education Association (1990, the Standards hereafter). The Standards aim to help teachers to self-assess and identify needs for professional development, for teacher trainers to evaluate their courses for pre- or in-service teachers and for assessment specialists to update their knowledge on assessment for learning. In particular, the Standards encourage and

Table 4.3 The Components of KCA

Bachman and Palmer (1996)	Davies (2008)	Taylor (2013)/Kremmel and Harding (2020)

1 Understanding of the fundamental issues addressed when developing a new test or selecting an existing test
2 Understanding of the fundamental concerns with appropriate use of tests
3 Understanding of the fundamental approaches and methods for measures and evaluation
4 Ability to design, develop, evaluate and use tests appropriate to a given context and group of learners
5 Ability to understand the published research and information about published tests to make informed decisions
	1 Skills to apply appropriate methodologies for item writing and statistic procedures for analysing tests
	2 Knowledge of the theoretical issues about L2 acquisition, competencies, standards and benchmarks for language assessment
	3 Competence to apply the principles related to the appropriate use of large-scale proficiency tests for learners in different learning contexts
		1 Theoretical knowledge about language and language learning
		2 Competence to apply technical skills for:
		  a) language assessment construction
		  b) administration/scoring
		  c) evaluation language assessment
		3 Knowledge of the principles and concepts of language assessment
		4 Competence for language pedagogy
		5 Knowledge of the test impacts and sociocultural values
		6 Knowledge of local practice
		7 Personal beliefs/attitudes
		8 Ability to make decisions based on scores

guide teachers to assess their own or inspect other schools'/universities' assessments. The Standards' requirements for teachers are tailored to their daily jobs and tasks, which are to do the following:

1 Select and develop appropriate assessment methods for instructional decisions
2 Administer, score and interpret the results of both externally produced and teacher-produced assessments
3 Use results fairly and accurately to make decisions on individual students' progression and for teaching plans and curriculum development
4 Recognise unethical, illegal and otherwise inappropriate assessment methods and uses of assessment information

Nonetheless, evidence from recent studies has suggested that there is an overall lack of KCA, resources and professional training for classroom language teachers (Hasselgreen et al., 2004; Vogt and Tsagari; 2014, Tsagari and Vogt, 2017; Kvasova and Kavytska, 2014). As a result, teacher-made tests are observed of poor quality in some cases, confusion still exists amongst teachers on the nature of language learning and competence and the analysis of learners' strengths and weaknesses is inaccurate and mispresenting the actual competencies (Alderson,

2005). Most concerning is that the constructs for CBA or teacher-made assessment are found inconsistent with the learning objectives, influencing negatively on learning (Coniam, 2009). The studies also highlight the following as the areas for improvement:

1 Construct(s) for summative CBA are drawn directly from national and regional guidelines without consideration for specific learning contexts and objectives.
2 Standardised proficiency tests are used directly as CBA.
3 Pre- and in-service teachers are not trained to understand the difference between externally and internally developed tests, learning mostly from their mentors to implement the institutional practice which might have not been updated for years.
4 Some teachers are not confident and competent to organise FA activities such as self- and peer assessment and provide deficit-oriented feedback to learners which does not improve learning.
5 Most teachers have limited knowledge about different purposes for assessment, reliability and validity issues and basic and useful statistics to analyse the quality of assessments.
6 Teachers urgently need training for developing integrated tests, assessing intercultural competence, writing test items, acting as interlocutors in oral exams, using marking criteria and providing a reliable rating.

It is critical, therefore, that language assessment courses must be included in the training programmes for pre- and in-service teachers and students in the postgraduate courses for teaching CFL. The next concern is to what extent they should be competent for assessment. Should they be as knowledgeable and competent as the test writers, school/university administrators and professional language testers? Taylor (2013) answers this question with a conceptualised different levels of KCA for all involved with language assessment based on the scale from 0 to 4 proposed by Phil and Harding (2013). Table 4.4 presents the levels for test writers and classroom teachers as suggested by Taylor. In addition, the proposed levels for the CFL teachers are also presented in consideration of the demanding tasks of summative and formative assessments and the specific issues related to assessing L2 competence in Chinese. The proposed levels are also based on the fact that classroom teachers are the test writers of the CBA for different purposes.

As the table shows, in Taylor's view (ibid.) classroom teachers should be extremely knowledgeable and competent in language pedagogy, but they do not have to be so as the test writers in theoretical knowledge about language and language learning and in the technical skills for developing assessments. However, as the table shows, the standards expected of the CFL teachers are higher in several components of KCA than those proposed by Taylor. In specific, they should be extremely knowledgeable of Chinese linguistics and the theoretical background of L2 acquisition in Chinese so that they are confident and competent to develop summative and formative CBA based on the syllabus-based constructs. Secondly, they

Table 4.4 Proposed Levels of KCA of Test Writers, Classroom Teachers (Taylor, 2013) and CFL Teachers

Areas of KCA Taylor (2013)/Kremmel and Harding (2020)	Test writers (Taylor, 2013)	Classroom teachers (Taylor, 2013)	Requirements for CFL teachers
Theoretical knowledge about language and language learning	4	2	3
Competence to apply technical skills for: a) Language assessment construction b) Administration/scoring c) Evaluation language assessment	4	3	a. 4 b. 4 c. 4
Knowledge of the principles and concepts of language assessment	4	2	3
Competence for language pedagogy	3	4	4
Knowledge of the test impact and sociocultural values	3	3	3
Knowledge of local practice	2	3	3
Personal beliefs/attitudes	2	3	3
Ability to make decisions based on scores	2	1	4

Note: Explanation given by Kremmel and Harding (2020) for the rating:
0 = not knowledgeable at all; 1 = slightly knowledgeable; 2 = moderately knowledgeable; 3 = very knowledgeable; and 4 = extremely knowledgeable

should be extremely knowledgeable and competent to design, write and administer assessments and rate learner performance consistently. Thirdly, to resolve the concerns about the validity and reliability of assessing L2 Chinese, especially for assessing the competencies in the written language, they should also be well informed of the principles of language assessment to evaluate the tests they have developed and to solve any unwanted washback of the influential proficiency tests on learning. Fourthly, the CFL teachers should be extremely capable of using scores for decision-making as it is them who decide the scoring for performance on assessments, some of which are high-stakes. It is also the teachers who record and report the results to authorities for certification and accreditation, organise FA activities and make adjustments to teaching plans according to the evidence collected. As a result, for effective learning and assessment, the proposed levels of KCA for the CFL practitioners are as stated in Table 4.4, which disagrees with those proposed by Taylor (ibid.).

To conclude, this chapter has introduced the nature and principles of FA, the strategies and activities that classroom teachers should apply and organise, and the different components of KCA and the proposed levels to the CFL professionals.

As an indispensable part of summative CBA, FA aims to help learners to identify the ZPD during learning and to know what they need to do to achieve the learning objective. Therefore, teaching professionals must apply effective questioning and discourse strategies to raise learners' awareness and focus their attention on the gap between their existing knowledge and the expected competence and performance. The classroom discourse resembling the characteristics of natural conversations will support scaffolding and mediation for learning which also provides effective feedback by teachers, learners themselves and their peers. Furthermore, using SA and CPTs for FA purposes that prioritise language knowledge and competence can set up standards, nurture independence and enhance learning. Through FA activities, teachers also assess their teaching plans and effects on learning and make necessary changes based on the evidence collected. Assigned with both roles of teacher and assessor in the classroom on the CFL programmes, the CFL teachers' KCA needs to meet the standards for the knowledge, skills and principles that they should have for assessment practice. In the specific CFL contexts, higher levels of competencies have been proposed for the validity, reliability and impact of L2 Chinese tests for achievement and proficiency purposes.

Further readings

1 Walsh, S. (2013) *Exploring Classroom Discourse: Language in Action*, the Introduction, for an overview of the main discourse features of the L2 classroom interaction and the teachers' modified speech for different learning needs.
2 Hill (2017) 'Understanding classroom-based assessment practices: a precondition for teacher assessment literacy' for further understanding of CBA and guidance on how to analyse your own existing CBA practices.

Reader activities

1 Refer to the five strategies for FA introduced in the first part of the chapter and do the following tasks:

   a) You are meeting a group of beginner CFL learners for the first time. You need to explain the learning objective of Pinyin for the first three weeks and the expected outcomes. Make a note of the wording and examples you will provide.
   b) Record 50 minutes of your class. Identify the types of questions you have asked and see which types you asked the most. Then, you can analyse if those questions have achieved your FA agendas. If not, what should you do in future?
   c) Use the same recording for the previous activity and find the episodes in the discourse that you had to divert from your teaching plan according to what you discovered from FA strategies (e.g. self- or peer

assessment, feedback or explaining learning objectives and criteria). Is the adjustment well judged and worthwhile?

d) Review the ways that you have introduced the SA and relevant CPT to your students. What have you asked the students to do about the past or mock papers available? Make a note and assess them. What are the changes you should make?

2 Log on to http://wp.lancs.ac.uk/ltrg/projects/language-assessment-literacy-survey/ and respond to the survey *Language Assessment Literacy Survey Language Assessment*. As this is a comprehensive KCA survey with 71 questions on the different components of KCA, you can do the following:

a) Divide your answers into three groups:

1 Group 1: those you have answered 'very knowledgeable' and 'extremely knowledgeable'
2 Group 2: those you have answered 'moderately knowledgeable'
3 Group 2: those have answered 'not knowledgeable at all' and 'slightly knowledgeable'

b) Compare your answers to what is proposed in Table 4.3 for the levels in different components of KCA. What is the KCA in which you are strong? In what aspect are you weakest? Plan for improvement and professional development if necessary. You may need to plan for opportunities of in-service training or attend relevant workshops, seminars or conferences.

5 Assessing vocabulary, grammatical knowledge and competence in L2 Chinese

As the CFL Model (see Chapter 2.5, Figure 2.3) proposes, the CFL learners' knowledge and competence in Chinese phonology, vocabulary, orthography, grammar, discourse and pragmatics are the *core L2 competencies in Chinese*, or the 'underlying enabling subskills' for communicative language ability (Jones, 2012: 248). The following three chapters discuss how to assess those core competencies in the performance of tasks in receptive, productive and interactive modes for various themes and topics. The two sections in this chapter will first introduce the characteristics of the Chinese lexis and syntax and the main findings of the studies about second language acquisition of Chinese vocabulary and grammar. Previous research on assessing L2 Chinese vocabulary and grammar competence (VC and GC) will also be introduced, which is followed by the specific construct definitions for assessing VC and GC in L2 Chinese and the discussion of the measures and techniques for assessing the two competencies. Issues of validity and reliability involved with assessments of VC and GC will also be briefly discussed.

5.1 Assessing vocabulary knowledge and competence in L2 Chinese

'Words are the basic building blocks of language, the units of meaning from which larger structures such as sentences, paragraphs and whole texts are formed' (Read, 2000: 1). Nation (2013: 49) identifies three components of the vocabulary knowledge:

1. *Form: in spoken and written language and the word parts*, requiring learners to recognise the sound and spelling, pronounce and spell the word, and know and use the correct inflected and derived forms of the word to express meanings.
2. *Meaning: concept and referents and associations*, requiring learners to recall the meanings in context, produce the appropriate forms to convey meanings, understand and produce a range of uses of the word and its concepts and references and use synonyms appropriately.
3. *Use: grammatical functions, collocations, constraints on use due to register, frequency and modes*, requiring learners to recognise and produce the correct grammatical forms and collocations of the word, and use the word in the appropriate contexts.

Assessing vocabulary and grammatical knowledge 109

Defining the construct for assessing VC in L2 Chinese

The assessment of VC in an L2 varies with the morphology or specific features of the target language's words and word making, the relationships between words and meanings, and the grammatical structures. English words are spelt with letters and have either one or several phonetic units, and there is usually, orthographically, a space between words. Some words are free morphemes; some are bound morphemes. For example, 'mood' and 'moody' are both words; however, 'mood' is a free morpheme, and 'moody' consists of a free morpheme and a bound morpheme 'y', which changes a noun into an adjective. 'Mood', as a free morpheme and a word stem, makes sense by itself, while the bound morpheme 'y' does not, though it is a derivational suffix forming a new word with morphological changes. The morphological features of the Chinese language are, however, different. Firstly, there is no space between two Chinese characters; for example, 'mood' and 'moody' in Chinese are 心情 and 喜怒无常 which are words made of two or four characters without space between them.

Furthermore, the construction of 汉字 (characters of the Han) is not formed by the phonetic syllables but by the 'un-analysable' root or base, monosyllabic characters (Han, 2017: 27). Shen Xu, who lived in the Han Dynasty (202BC–220AD), complied *Interpretation of Words* (说文解字) with his peer scholars and summarised six principles/methods in which Chinese characters are constructed as follows, with the percentages of each type for the Chinese lexicon (Sun, 2006: 104–7).

1   Pictographic (日, 雨; the sun, rain): 3.9%
2   Indicative (上, 三; above, three): 12.3%
3   Ideographic (好, 休; good and rest): 1.3%
4   Semantic-phonetic compounds (洋, 进; the ocean, enter): 81.2%
5   Explanatory (考, 顶; exam, top): 0.07%
6   Borrowing (可口可乐, 比萨饼; Coca-Cola, pizza): 1.2%

偏旁, *radicals*, are the critical components of a character and contribute significantly to the construction of Chinese characters and their semantic meanings. They also make up most of the semantic-phonetic, pictographic and indicative characters. As most of the Chinese lexicon, approximately 20,000 words, are semantic-phonetic compound characters (Romagnoli, 2017), it has been widely acknowledged that knowledge of radicals is essential to L2 acquisition of Chinese vocabulary (Chu, 2006; Hayes, 1987; Ke, 1998). Some characters consist of only a radical or radicals and the 'un-analysable' root. For instance, 木, a radical and a monosyllabic character, means 'wood'. Two 木 together, 林, means 'woods', and three together, 森, means 'forest'. Furthermore, when compounded with other characters, semantic-phonetic words are produced, e.g. 树 (tree), 桃 (peach) and 桌 (desk) denote the objects that produce wood, grow on wood branches or are wooden. In those words, the radical, 木, carries the semantic meaning, and the other part may indicate the pronunciation of the character. Thus, *compounding* is an essential feature of the Chinese vocabulary.

110 *Assessing vocabulary and grammatical knowledge*

Compounding is a *derivation-like process* that creates *lexical items* (词) consisting of two to four *characters or morphemes* (字). The boundary between Chinese words is not clear because of the lack of morphological markers for tenses, plurals and cases of pronouns. Therefore, the compounding of monosyllabic characters produces unknown lexical items, sometimes with one or all of which the learners have learnt. For example, learners may know 心 (heart/mind), 中 (middle/centre), 楼 (building/floor), 上 (above/go up) and 宿舍 (dormitory). However, the compound words they form may have not been learnt by the learners, e.g. 心中 (in one's heart/mind), 中心 (centre), 上楼 (go upstairs)，楼上 (upstairs) and 宿舍楼 (dormitory building). This means that one of the important abilities for VC in Chinese is to increase the amount of one's lexical repertoire by knowing the compound words of two, three, four or even more characters already known. Such competence is also critical to reading comprehension.

As Sun (2006) states, when compounding happens between a verb and another word (e.g. verb, adjective, adverb, particles or markers), it creates four kinds of resultative complements: restrictive, non-restrictive, directional and attainment resultative (e.g. 解决/to solve, 听到/hear, 走下来/go down, 读完/have read). Furthermore, compounding through prefixes, suffixes and infixes, which are bound morphemes with free words or bound roots, create new words, which is the Chinese derivation-like process (see Example 5.1). This type of compounding often changes the grammatical category of the words (e.g. 饭/food，早饭/breakfast，吃饭/to have meals, 做饭/to cook).

Example 5.1: Derivation-like affixes

Prefixes: 学生, 学习，学会，学完, 看书，看着，看上
Suffixes: 大学, 心理学, 好学， 好看，翻看，细看
Infixes: 学得到，学不会，看出来，看不到

In addition to the deviation-like compounding, inflection-like compounding processes in Chinese with only suffixes creates words typically attached to free words, which rarely change the grammatical category of the original word (e.g. 他们, 看了, 看过，吃着). Those suffixes act as plural, perfective aspect, experiential and imperfective markers. Moreover, there are also *clitics*, *phrasal particles* and *reduplication* that lead to grammatical, functional and discourses changes, which is unique to the Chinese lexis and shows the close links between the form, meaning and use in Chinese vocabulary (Sun, 2006). Clitics are sentence-final or locative particles (see the underlined in Example 5.2); reduplication is the process of new words being formed by repeating a classifier, verb or adjective to express emphasis, informality or vividness (see the underlined in Example 5.3).

Example 5.2:

老王, 吃饭啦！又在网上玩呢? (Old Wang, dinner is ready! Are you having fun on the internet again?)

Example 5.3:

A: 妈妈，我能出去玩玩吗？ (Mum, can I go out and play?)
B: 天天就知道出去，老老实实在家待会儿不行吗？(Every day you only know to go out and play. Why don't you just stay home for a while?)

Finally, it is necessary to mention other two specific features of the Chinese lexicon. Firstly, the formal and informal vocabulary in Chinese can be very different from each other—for example, 妈妈 vs 母亲 (mother), 名字 vs 姓名 vs 姓氏 (name), 的 vs 之 (of), 如果 vs 若 (if), 是 vs 乃 (to be), etc. Thus, CFL learners need to know those words and use them appropriately for different contexts. Secondly, there is a large volume of homophones in Chinese morphology. As a result, Chinese people usually identify them by saying, e.g. '力，力量的力' (力, the 力 in 力量). Otherwise, they could be confused with other characters or words with the same Pinyin, *lì*. For example, in the ICCLE (Hanban, 2014) graded list of characters for Level 4, there are 历、丽、利、励 all pronounced *lì*, and in the corresponding list of lexical items, there are 经历，厉害，美丽，顺利，流利 and 鼓励. To learn those homophones, the learners must know the root characters in terms of constructions and radicals to distinguish the forms and meanings of the compound characters. Those two features further demonstrate that it is necessary to draw up the graded vocabulary lists of characters and lexical items for learners of different proficiency levels. Characters are the monosyllabic or root characters which build up the 'threshold' of a CFL learner's VC. The lists of lexical items, in comparison, provide the compounds of monosyllabic, disyllabic or multisyllabic words formed by the characters that learners must learn for a proficiency level. Therefore, the construct definition for assessing VC in L2 Chinese must account for the importance of the graded lists of characters and lexical items.

Romagnoli (2017) suggests that the construct of VC in L2 Chinese can follow Nation (2013) and Schmitt's (2010) notion which consists of three components: form (spoken, written and word part), meaning (concept and referent and associations) and use (grammatical functions, collocations and constraints on use). However, research and debates have called for a move from grammar-based to vocabulary-based instruction as the Chinese language consists of grammaticalised lexis rather than lexicalised grammar as in English (Li, 2014). More notably, the *Character-Unit Theory* (字本位) advocates that the basic unit for analysing the Chinese lexis is the character. Teaching vocabulary should focus on characters rather than words. It is the character that involves the interrelated facets of iconicity, semanticity and phoneticity, or the orthography, morphology and phonetics of the script, the salient features to CFL learners (e.g. Xu, 2008; Pan, 2006; Zhang, 2005). Shen (2010) also proposes that knowledge and competence in the form of the Chinese lexis, including characters, words, radicals, and compounds, are critical to VC in L2 Chinese. The following defines the constructs for assessing CFL learners' VC in accord with the Chinese vocabulary's specific features.

1. *Form*: knowledge of the root and compound characters (especially the semantic-phonetic compounds), radicals, constructions of character and parts of speech; mastery of the phonetic feature and competence for appropriately applying the knowledge in tasks of receptive and productive modes in specific contexts
2. *Meaning*: knowledge of meanings in first languages and the concept and referent; the compounding and the derivation-like processes of characters and the semantic meanings due to the iconicity, semanticity and phonetics of characters; and the competence for understanding, retrieving and using vocabulary and their associations accurately and appropriately
3. *Use*: knowledge of the inflection-like affixes of plural, perfective or imperfective and experiential markers and phrasal particles, reduplication and collocations, and the competence for understanding and producing correct grammatical forms within or beyond the morphonology level accurately and appropriately for various registers
4. *Quantity*: competence for understanding, retrieving and using characters and lexical items in *graded lists* in spoken and written language for receptive and productive tasks on the targeted themes, domains and functions corresponding to relevant proficiency levels

Techniques for assessing VC in L2 Chinese

There are usually two foci for assessing language learners' vocabulary, *breadth* and *depth* (Read, 2000; Nation, 2013). Tests of breadth examine the amount of vocabulary a learner knows, whereas tests of depth assess whether learners have a complete and in-depth understanding of the words in a target language. Based on the previous construct definition for assessing CFL learners' VC, tests of breadth are usually designed to assess the *Form* and *Quantity* as defined. On the other hand, vocabulary tests for depth focus on the comprehensive knowledge of the *Meanings* and *Use* of the characters and lexical items. However, tests of breadth to assess CFL learners' vocabulary have had a thorny issue: the graded lists for characters and lexical items vary significantly in quantity as prescribed by EBCL (2012b) and ICCLE (Hanban, 2014) and the high-profile CPTs (see Table 5.1).

The discrepancies in quantity have been challenging to CFL professionals and learners. The debate has been about how many words the learners know so that they can communicate in Chinese without major difficulties. The Chinese lexicon has about 60,000 words, 40,000 of which make up the general vocabulary, and 20,000 are the technical words. Certainly, CFL learners do not have to learn all of them as the learners of other languages. Ling (2007) proposes that a mastery of 2,000 active characters is sufficient as there will be more than 2,000 words resulting from the characters. This proposal has been supported by several studies suggesting that learning the active and high-frequency characters is critical to CFL learners' acquisition of vocabulary (e.g. Shen, 2009; Shi, 2000 cited in Romagnoli,

Assessing vocabulary and grammatical knowledge 113

Table 5.1 Graded Lists of Characters and Lexical Items Proposed by Benchmarks and CPTs

CEFR Level	EBCL Benchmark		ICCEL Benchmark		HSK	TOCFL
	Character	Lexical Item	Character	Lexical Item	Lexical Items	Lexical Item
C2	n/a	n/a	2,500	5,000	5,000	8,000
C1	n/a	n/a	1,500	2,500	2,500	8,000
B2	n/a	n/a	1,000	1,200	1,200	5,000
B1	n/a	n/a	600	600	600	2,500
A2	630	Written: 940 Spoken: 1,245	300	300	300	1,000
A1	320	Written: 940 Spoken: 589	150	150	150	500

2017). Most CFL programmes in China and the language classes by the Confucius Institute have followed the *Graded Chinese Syllabus, characters and words for the application of teaching Chinese to the speakers of other languages* (Hanban, 2009), or the ICCLE benchmark. The programmes abroad have followed either the EBCL benchmark or the textbooks used which usually comply with the regional or national requirements.

Another issue is the density of characters as the traditional version has more components and strokes and the simplified version has fewer of both (e.g. 汉 and 漢, 爱 and 愛). The concern is that the learners' performance on vocabulary, reading comprehension and writing tests is affected as the traditional version is more difficult to remember and time-consuming to write. Studies, however, have revealed mixed findings. Some suggest that learners recognise and read low-density characters faster and more accurately (Xiao, 2002). Others have found reading traditional characters does not affect reading comprehension performance (Hayes, 1987; Sargent and Everson, 1992). Regarding writing characters of high or low density, Jiang (2007) recommends that the impact on performance for assessment of writing be addressed with specific measures as it concerns the construct validity of tests. A common practice has been that both traditional and simplified characters are provided in exam papers so that test-takers can choose the versions they have learnt.

Vocabulary tests for breadth in the public domain such as websites (e.g. baidu.com, yellowbridge.com, arealme.com) are easy to access nowadays. For example, Nation's online *Vocabulary Size Test for Mandarin* (2018) uses multiple choices and matching questions (see Example 5.4) to evaluate how many Chinese words a test-taker knows. It converts the number of correct answers given into an estimated size of the vocabulary and reports immediately after the tests are completed.

Example 5.4: Choose the word matching the words in bold.

First 1,000: (1) see: They **saw** it.
a. 切 b. 等待 c. 看 d. 开始
Fourth 1,000: (3) candid: Please be **candid**.
a. 小心的 b. 同情的 c. 公平的 d. 直率的

114 *Assessing vocabulary and grammatical knowledge*

Fourteenth 1,000: (8) erythrocyte: It is an **erythrocyte**.
a. 止痛的药　　　　b. 血液中的红色的成分
c. 略显红色的白金属　d. 鲸家族中的一员

(Nation, Vocabulary Size Tests: Mandarin Version, 2018)

However, it is not clear where the samples of vocabulary are from or whether the standards are aligned with certain graded lists of characters or lexical items established by a benchmark or a CPT. In comparison, Example 5.5, a question to assess the vocabulary based on the ICCLE proficiency levels, is sampled from the 300 characters required for achieving Stage 2 (equivalent to CEFR A2). The difference between the two examples is that the former is only to assess the test-takers' breadth of vocabulary known, whereas the latter integrates listening and reading when assessing the targeted vocabulary for the proficiency level (热水，牛奶，茶，鱼，鸡，猫). Example 5.6, on the other hand, represents a widely used technique: multiple choices with visual input, to assess the breadth and use of the vocabulary of the CFL learners at post-elementary levels.

Example 5.5: Listen to the conversation and answer the questions by choosing the pictures.

Question 1: 小红喜欢喝什么？　　Answer: _____
Question 2: 她妈妈喜欢喝什么？　Answer: _____
Question 3: 她们要去买什么？　　Answer: _____

Figure 5.1 Favourite Drinks and Shopping

Figure 5.2 A Living Room

Example 5.6: Please choose the answers that best describe the picture.

1 房间里一個人 ____ 沒有。　　2 书架____ 有很多书。
A 就 B 也 C 些　　　　　　　A 里 B 放 C 上
3 沙发的前面有____ 猫。　　　4 沙发看上去不太____ 。
A 一个 B 一只 C 一条　　　　A 方便 B 随便 C 便宜

Assessing the depth of VC in L2 Chinese is different from the techniques for assessing the breadth and use of vocabulary as it entails the features of orthography, morphology and phonetics of characters. The techniques to elicit the performance of competence have been challenging, with only a few existing measures available for summative or formative CBA (e.g. Li and Ye, 2013; Shen, 2010; Jiang, 2007). The following examples demonstrate those techniques and measures.

Example 5.7: Fill in the missing information in the following table.

No.	Radical	Meaning of radical	Pinyin of word	Words with the same radical
熄		fire		
体	亻			你他们
村		wood		

Example 5.8: Guess the Pinyin and the meanings of the following characters. Write them on the line.

肿 Pinyin _____　拌 Pinyin _____　涨 Pinyin _____　喉 Pinyin _____
Meaning _____　Meaning _____　Meaning _____　Meaning _____

Example 5.9: Guess the meanings of the following characters and write them on the lines in English.

躬 _____　凸 _____
娶 _____　甬 _____
岔 _____　掰 _____

Example 5.10: You have learnt the two characters in the following words. Guess the meanings and put them on the lines.

心疼 _____　山头 _____
成全 _____　故人 _____

Example 5.11: Choose a character in A first and combine it with a character in B to form a new word. You can create as many as you can. Write the new words in C.

A　文 如 光 地 快 放	C
B　板 位 递 学 意 手	

116 *Assessing vocabulary and grammatical knowledge*

Correct responses to the questions in Example 5.7 require knowledge about not only the semantic meanings and pronunciations of the radicals/words but also the compound words they construct. Such questions emphasise the important functions of radicals for the formation of characters essential to VC in L2 Chinese for breadth and depth. Example 5.8 assesses the learners' knowledge about the pronunciation and meanings of the semantic-phonetic compound characters that are 82.2% of the Chinese lexicon. Furthermore, 77% of the phonetic components are valuable clues to the pronunciation, and 83% of the semantic components suggest the meanings (Wang, 1997). Thus, the competence to work out the approximate sounds and meanings of the unknown semantic-phonetic characters is vital to the CFL learners' VC. Example 5.9 assesses VC for guessing and understanding the meanings of the characters constructed based on six principles/methods introduced earlier. For example, 凸 is a pictographic character. The image indicates the meaning 'protruding or raised'. 娶 is a semantic-phonetic character meaning 'to marry a woman', with the top component meaning 'to take' and the bottom part meaning 'female'. 甭 is an indicative character, meaning 'not' or 'unnecessary'. Examples 5.10 and 5.11 both assess the learners' competence to understand the compound words with characters they have learnedt. For instance, as the learners have known the meanings of 心 and 疼, it is not difficult for them to understand the meaning of the two characters as one word, heartache'' or heartbroken.'' Similarly, if 文, 光 and 学 are known vocabulary, the learners can guess that 文学and 光学mean the studies for writing and optics. Those measures and techniques for assessing VC thoroughly reveal not only the learners' knowledge of the characteristics of the Chinese lexis but also their abilities to increase the amount of their vocabulary to improve reading and writing.

Example 5.12: Fill in the gaps with the words provided. You can use the words twice if necessary.

阳　朝阳　阳历　夕阳　太阳　阳光　阳台　阳面　阳性　炎阳　太阳能

我们家的房子在25层，太高了，但朝向很好，(1) ____充分。清晨在我的卧室里可以看到慢慢升起的 (2) ____，傍晚在爷爷奶奶的卧室里能看到落山的 (3) ____。我喜欢睡懒觉，有时候连早上八九点的 (4) ____ 都看不到，只能在爷爷奶奶卧室外面的 (5) ____上看日落。我家以前的房子一点不 (6) ____。自从搬到现在的房子，我的性格好像也 (8) ____了很多。

Example 5.12, on the other hand, assesses higher-level learners' knowledge about the various meanings of the character 阳, the meanings of the compound words with it, the associated meanings, concepts and referents. Specifically, this question demands the following knowledge:

- the construction of a character (阳 is of left-right construction)
- Components of a character/word (阳 has two components, the component on the left meaning 'hill' or 'capital' and the component on the right meaning 'the sun')

- type of character (阳 is a root and semantic-phonetic compound character)
- Pronunciation (yáng)
- Part of speech of the character/word (阳 is an uncountable noun)
- Meanings (阳 means 'the sun', 'brightness', 'light', 'positive', etc.)
- Concept and reference (warmth, light, optimism, hope)
- Associated words (阴, 光, 亮, 暗, 乐观, etc.)
- Derivation-like process (阳光, 阳面, 阳台 etc.)

Assessing VC for *Use* of vocabulary, as having been defined, is also testing vocabulary knowledge in depth. The measures for testing L2 Chinese vocabulary are different from those for other languages due to the inflection-like processes, phrasal particles, reduplication and collocation of Chinese vocabulary. VC for using the Chinese vocabulary involves not only retrieving, understanding and applying the grammatical features but also the competence for distinguishing the morphological changes and semantic variations, which is, though related to the syntactic structures of sentences, described as basic or unique (see the next part). Example 5.13 is an extended and adapted version of a multiple-choice question in a mock paper of Reading Test for Band B (TOCFL, 2019). The example shows the intricacies between assessing the breadth and depth of VC in L2 Chinese as lexical meanings and associations are entwined with the use of a word. In Example 5.13, for instance, to select the four choices in 1, the learner must know that, grammatically, a verb is needed to complete a sentence. Though amongst the four choices, three expectcp遊戲 (game) are all verbs, and only 打籃球 (to play basketball) is both grammatically and semantically correct and appropriate for the context prescribed by the text. 走路 (on foot) is not an activity for the weekend, and 打足球 (to hit/beat a football) is an incorrect collocation. A similar rationale for responding to the other questions in the example also applies, and both the breadth and depth of VC are necessary to decide on the use of the vocabulary.

Example 5.13: Fill the numbered blanks in the paragraph with the best answers provided by the multiple choices.

周末，我經常去____1，有時也去我家附近的一____2書店。這家書店的客人不多，____3書很多。書店老闆人很好，對客人總是很____4。去那裡不一定要買書，____5只是看看書。在那裡看書看累____6，還能在小咖啡廳裏悠闲____7喝点咖啡，跟朋友____8。

1	A 走路	B 打籃球	C 遊戲	D 打足球
2	A 座	B 張	C 家	D 條
3	A 有意思	B 又	C 感興趣	D 但
4	A 客氣	B 感激	C 客觀	D 感謝
5	A 你們	B 可以	C 他們	D 應該
6	A 過	B 了	C 著	D 的
7	A 的	B 得	C 地	D 很
8	A 聊聊	B 說話一會	C 聊一會天	D 說說

118 *Assessing vocabulary and grammatical knowledge*

Furthermore, the multiple-choice questions in Example 5.13, which combines with cloze tests to assess VC in L2 Chinese, is observed to be a versatile test item as it integrates much more than just the deviation-like or inflection-like compounding of the Chinese vocabulary. It can effectively assess not only meaning, form and use of vocabulary but also reading comprehension and grammatical knowledge. For instance, to provide the correct answer to 3, test-takers must achieve it through their reading ability to understand the logical relationship between the two sentences, 這家書店的客人不多 and ____ 3 書很多, to know that conjunction of contrast (D 但) should be used to complete the sentence. Moreover, to choose the correct answer for 7, learners need to know both the meaning of 悠閑 well and the lexical structure of the verbal compounds concerning the adjectives in the case of 的, 得 and地 to make the decision.

To summarise, assessing VC in L2 Chinese is noticeably different from testing that in other languages, which has been evidenced by previous research on the Word Association Test (WAT) for assessing VC in Chinese (Zhang et al., 2017; Hu, 2017). The studies have suggested that WAT, a technique that has been applied to assess thoroughly the vocabulary knowledge of Indo-European languages, is not suitable for the specific features of the Chinese lexis and affects the construct validity of the WAT tests for L2 Chinese. Therefore, the construct definition must acknowledge and integrate the features into the measures for assessing the CFL learners' VC. This part has followed such a principle, introducing specific features of the Chinese lexis and the constructs of the competence to communicate accurately in terms of the form, meaning and use of the vocabulary. A construct definition for assessing VC has been proposed to test the competencies in applying the grammaticalised lexis. Both the conventional techniques and newly designed alternative test items are introduced and discussed to ensure the construct validity and reliability of VC tests for L2 Chinese. The next part will inform the readers how grammatical competence (GC) in L2 Chinese is associated with VC and provide a tentative proposal of the construct definition to assess GC and introduce the methodologies.

5.2 Assessing grammatical knowledge and competence in L2 Chinese

Grammatical knowledge and competence have been considered the strong predictors of a language learner's overall communication competence (Ellis, 2008; Purpura, 2013). In the CFL classroom, a large amount of teaching time has also been spent on teaching grammar to improve learners' interlanguage development (Xing, 2006; EBCL, 2013). It has been a common practice of the CFL programmes that grammatical acquisition is assessed for formative and summative purposes. The construct defined is usually syllabus-based and tailored for specific learning objectives. In contrast, testing grammar has not been a priority for the influential CPTs. To Purpura (2013: 110), such '[d]isinterest in separate grammar assessment stems in large part from unsubstantiated beliefs that learners demonstrating "functional" levels of communicative effectiveness do not need to be assessed on the linguistic elements'. Nonetheless, classroom teachers cannot overlook that 'grammar and vocabulary (together with other building blocks of language competence such as phonology and orthography) are fundamental to all language use' (Green, 2014: 110). In the context of CFL, studies have also suggested that CFL learners' implicit knowledge of grammar is a strong predictor of their performance on reading comprehension tasks (Zhang, 2012); explicit knowledge of grammar is strongly correlated with their overall L2 proficiency (Li, 2017).

However, attention to GC does not mean defining the construct for assessing the ability has been clear and simple to CFL professionals as two unique 'typological parameters' related to the Chinese language's syntactic structures (Li and Thompson, 1989: 10) must be considered. The first is the basic orientation of the sentence in terms of 'topic verse "subject". The second is the word order. According to Li and Thompson, topic prominence is '[o]ne of the most striking features of Mandarin sentence structure, and one that sets Mandarin apart from many other languages'. In structure, the 'topic' always comes first in the sentence as it is assumed to be also known by the reader or listener, showing that word order in Mandarin Chinese is 'governed to a large extent by considerations of meaning rather than of grammatical functions' (ibid: 19). The three sentences in Example 5.14 all mean 'I have already read that book' and could be used in spoken or written text, depending on which preposition comes first to the speaker or writer's mind. In the last sentence, the absence of a subject is also an often-observed word order because, in specific contexts, the topic prominence is not who has read the book or that it is already known. In other words, the verbal phrase of a sentence in Chinese can be anywhere in a sentence depending on meaning rather than the grammatical structure or function.

Example 5.14: 我已经看了那本书。

Word order: I already read that book le.
那本书我已经看了。
Word order: That book I already read le.
已经看了那本书。
Word order: Already read le that book.

From a pedagogic standpoint, Xing (2006: 134–64) classifies the sentences in Chinese into three types of constructions based on word order, function and frequency in communication: the *basic sentence, unique sentence constructions* and the *nominal clauses* (see Example 5.15, 16 and 17). According to Givon (2001), Sun (2006) and Xing (1993, 2006), most of the sentential syntactic structures in Chinese discourse are basic constructions with the same or similar features as the learners' first languages such as English. The unique constructions and nominal clauses, on the other hand, are indispensable to Chinese texts for expressing specific meanings and for pragmatic inferences, which provide details important for communication. Some of the forms are also highly prolific though complicated—for example, the verbal-complement structures (Example 5.16 c). Furthermore, some of those unique sentence structures such as the nominal structures (Example

5.17) usually emerge in the earliest stages of CFL learners' L2 language development, which remain the learning objective because of the variations of the structure (Lu and Ke, 2018). Those unique structures and the nominal clauses, as Lu and Ke observe, have caused difficulties for the CFL learners' processing of the Chinese syntactic structures and potentially could delay their L2 development.

Example 5.15: Basic sentence constructions

> 明天他想去买一个文件包。(He wants to buy a briefcase tomorrow).
> Word order: Tomorrow he want go buy a briefcase.
> 据《人民日报》报道, 2019 年 1.4 亿中国人出境旅游。(*People's Daily* reported that in 2019. 1.4 billion Chinese went to travel abroad)
> Word order: *People's Daily* report, in 2019 1.4 billion Chinese go overseas travel.

Example 5.16: Unique sentence constructions

> a 他是五点钟到北京的。(It was at five o'clock that he arrived in Beijing).
> Word order: He is five o'clock arrive Beijing de.
> b 她已经把飞机票买了。(She has bought the air ticket).
> Word order: She already ba air-ticket buy le.
> c 他跑进屋子里去了。(He ran into the room).
> Word order: He run into room inside go le.

Example 5.17: Nominal clauses

> 她是我弟弟喜欢的那个女孩。(She is the girl that my younger brother fancies).
> Word order: She is my younger brother very much like the girl.

Purpura's *Model of Grammatical Knowledge* (2004, 2013) proposes that assessing grammar be based on the specific forms at sentential and discourse levels according to their associated potential meanings, such as ideas, information and pragmatic and sociolinguistic factors, including social status, formality and culture. Such a principle suits well the construct definition for assessing GC in L2 Chinese because of the grammaticalised lexis and the fact that the word order in a sentence is often decided by topics rather than syntactic structure. In addition, research on L2 Chinese grammar development has been mainly concerned with the acquisition of the unique structures at phrasal, sentential and discourse levels—e.g. prepositions, nominal structures, verbal complements, *ba* construction, relative clauses, temporal devices and aspect markers, who-expressions (Lu and Ke, 2018). This suggests that the assessment of CFL learners' GC should focus on the marked syntactic structures which they find different from those in their first languages and difficult to learn.

Thus, based on Purpura's model (ibid.), the assessment of GC should prioritise whether the learners can apply those unique forms to express the associated meanings embedded with the culture and sociolinguistic factors. In Table 5.2. are the proposed constructs for assessing CFL learners' GC at the sentential level in

Assessing vocabulary and grammatical knowledge 121

Table 5.2 Construct Definition for Assessing Forms and Meanings in L2 Chinese

Sentence Structure	Grammatical Form	Grammatical Meanings (Morphosyntactic and information management of meanings based on pragmatic and sociolinguistic factors)
Basic Sentence Structure	*Sentences with the same or similar structures as those in English or other languages*	Various meanings, functions and information provided based on pragmatic and sociolinguistic factors
Unique Sentence Structure	*Adjective predicate* No 'to be' word before an adjective	Describing the attributes of people, objects, status or situation, e.g. 她很<u>兴奋</u>.
	Ba sentence 把 followed by a nominal before a verb	Indicating a change or 'disposal' of an object, matter or status
	Topic-prominent sentences A noun, noun phrase or zero subject followed by a verb or a verbal phrase	Stating facts with an emphasis on the selected information or omitting those supposedly known to recipients in the discourse
	Focus construction 是 . . . (的) and 连 . . . 都 structure	Focusing and highlighting specific information in a sentence
	Nominal Structure Nominal clause + 的+ (head noun)	Providing specifics or highlighting a particular proposition in the sentence
	Verbal-complement structures Verbs complemented by another verb or adjectives, adverbs or direction words	Describing status (completion, resultative, directional, descriptive, potential, etc.) of action or explaining and commenting on a conducted action, e.g. 她听<u>得懂</u>
	Unique discourse devices or adverbials: e.g. 不但 . . . 而且, 虽然 . . . 但是, 如果, 既然, 只要 . . . 就/也, 即, 却, 而, 就, 也, 都, 当 . . . 时候, . . . 以前, 以后, 跟/像/同 . . . 一样/那样, 又 . . . 又, 越 . . . 越, 一边 . . . 一边, etc., used in fixed constructions	Giving referential links; clarifying condition, time, similarity, the consequence of an action; showing hedging, contradiction, exclusion, inclusion, cause and effect, concession, hypothetical or counterfactual situations, etc. in discourse, e.g. 他<u>一边</u>吃饭，<u>一边</u>看电视
	Adverbs or adverbials precede verbs or in the sentence-initial position	Informing time, location and attitudes in which an action is taken or the extent of it, e.g. 我很喜欢做饭；<u>去年</u>我没<u>在中国</u>学汉语.
	Negators 不，没，没有，别 used depending on time, types of sentences and verbs or aspects	Informing on events that did, have or will not happen in statements and imperatives, e.g. 2017年没能去那个音乐节，我今年也<u>不</u>能去。你<u>别</u>再提这事了.
	Question-word questions constructed with the constituent in question replaced by a question word	Asking for information or questioning for rhetorical purpose, e.g. 你喜欢听<u>什么</u>音乐？<u>什么</u>能使你高兴？
	Nominalisation with 的 placed after a verb or verbal phrase	Naming objects, materials and occupations in an informal tone, e.g. 我弟弟是<u>开飞机的</u>.
	Serial-verb constructions One subject has two or more verbs.	Denoting two or a sequence of actions conducted by the same person, e.g. 你该下楼去做饭，打扫房间了.
	Aspect markers: 了，过，在/正在，着，将，要 *used to denote perfective, experienced, durative and future actions*	Expressing events, actions and status happening at different times, e.g. 天要下雨了.

122 *Assessing vocabulary and grammatical knowledge*

consideration of the typological parameters of the Chinese syntax (Li and Thompson, 1989) and pedagogic practice (Xing, 2006). Two types of sentence structures are categorised, basic and unique, to distinguish the grammatical range and control that the test-takers can demonstrate in their performance. The construct definition does not include most of the grammatical changes caused by the deviation- and inflection-like compounding except the verbal-complement structures and verbal nomination with 的. They are included because of the structural changes that they make at the sentential level in spoken and written discourse.

Measurements and techniques for assessing GC in L2 Chinese

Purpura (2013: 117) identifies two types of measurements and techniques for assessing grammatical forms and meanings: *Selected-response Task* (SRT) and *Construct-response Task* (CRT). SRT examines recognition and recall, requiring learners to choose responses based on their detailed grammatical knowledge about forms and meanings. On the other hand, CRT aims to elicit language production on the relevant GC through two specific techniques: Limited-production Task (LPT) and Extended-production Task (EPT). LPT requires the learners to produce answers of a word to a sentence relying on their developing grammatical knowledge about forms or meanings, whereas EPT assesses GC with the input of a prompt demanding language production across several areas of knowledge simultaneously. Furthermore, three types of EPT techniques are identified: product focused, performance focused and process focused. Table 5.3 presents the test items and tasks often used or recommended to CFL CBA according to the classification of tasks by Purpura (ibid.).

In 2017 I conducted a small-scale online survey to investigate CFL teachers' perceptions and practices for assessing L2 Chinese. A number of 110 valid responses were received from the teachers mostly based in Europe. The results revealed that the top three tasks to assess GC for lower-level CFL learners are arranging given words in a sentence, filling gaps with multiple choices and translating sentences into their first languages. The top three for the higher-level learners are translating sentences and passages into Chinese, correcting errors and analysing a grammatical structure. Those tasks are either SRT or LPT, as shown by Example 5.18, 19, 20 and 21.

Example 5.18: Complete the following sentences with one of the choices.

我 ____ 去 ____ 上海和南京。
A. 没 . . . 过 B. 不 . . . 了 C. 没 . . . 了 D. 不 . . . 过

Example 5.19: Arrange the following words into a sentence.

去　　明天　　图书馆　　借　　她　　语法书

Example 5.20: Correct grammar mistakes in the following sentences.

1　你看的懂那本有关中国经济改革地文章吗?
2　你又忘得一干二净把交作业的事。

Assessing vocabulary and grammatical knowledge 123

Table 5.3 Test Items and Tasks for Assessing Grammatical Knowledge in L2 Chinese

Construct-Response Task (CRT)		Extended production (EPT)		
Selected Response Task (SRT)	Limited production (LPT)	Product focused	Performance focused	Process focused
• Noticing (recognise grammatical parts of a sentence) • True or false/agree or disagree • Judgment tasks (grammaticality acceptability, naturalness, formality, appropriateness) • Multiple choice • Error identification	• Arranging words into a sentence • Labelling/analysing • Gap filling • Cloze • Sentence completion • Discourse completion task (DCT) • Error correction • Translation into Chinese • Translation into first languages • Making sentences with given adverbials and connectors	• Essay • Report • Poster • Portfolio • Presentation • Debate	*Simulation* • Role-play • Improvisation • Interview *Recasts* • Retelling • Summary *Exchanges* • Information gap • Opinion gap • Problem-solving • Decision-making • Dialogue DCT	*Observation* • Checklist • Self- or peer assessment grid *Reflection* • Learning log/diary

(Adapted from Purpura, 2013)

124 *Assessing vocabulary and grammatical knowledge*

Example 5.21: Underline and label the subject, verb and object of the sentence. If there is a verbal complement, adverbials or nominal clauses, please circle them.

她终于慢慢地学会了以前觉得非常难的三声变调。

Example 5.18 is an SRT test item which assesses knowledge about negators (不 or 没), perfective (了) and experiential (过) markers. Test-takers are required to apply rather than to produce what they know about the words' grammatical uses and make the correct choices based on the contextual meaning provided by the incomplete sentence. Examples 5.19, 5.20 and 5.21 are all LPT test items that assess the learners' explicit knowledge of the different grammatical components in a sentence, during which they only need to copy or write a few characters. Those tasks are not of the EPT category because the learners' production in spoken or written language is limited through their GC to create meanings, ideas or information. Instead, the process involves mostly receptive language abilities.

Translation questions are also one of the LPT techniques applied to assessing GC in L2 Chinese, which the small-scale survey mentioned earlier shows that the CFL teachers have used for both lower- and higher-level learners. The difference is that translation into the first language is primarily for lower-level learners while translation into Chinese is for higher-level learners. Compared to the previous examples, the marking criteria for a translation task are much more complex, with scales for understanding or interpreting the original texts, realising the meanings in the target language faithfully in terms of meaning, register and style and expressively for readability. The language competencies entailed for translation tasks are not only grammatical but also vocabulary, reading comprehension and orthographic control if the target language is Chinese. Therefore, it is essential that when designing and writing test items for assessing GC, we must provide the expected responses and alternatives, and specific marking scales to improve the validity and reliability.

The findings from the small-scale survey also reveal that the CFL professionals who responded may not have been fully aware of the techniques for measuring GC through the EPT task types, whether they are the product-, performance- or process-focused tasks. The reason might be that those techniques have been usually employed for tasks in interactive or productive modes for assessment of speaking and writing for summative purposes when grammar is only one of the criteria for interpreting the performance (see assessing speaking and writing in Chapter 6 and 7). Another concern is that some CFL teachers may not have recognised the advantages of some of the SRT or CRT techniques (e.g. noticing and judgment test items, portfolio, report, checklist and DCT tasks) for their potential to facilitate self-and peer-assessment when learning basic and unique grammatical constructions. Learning grammar is a gradual process involving the mapping of form, meaning and use and the regression of progress with partially developed and erroneous structures in the learners' performance. Thus, the techniques should be applied cooperatively for summative and formative CBA of L2 Chinese grammar. The following suggestions will assist teachers to achieve this.

1 *Prioritising process-focused FA on grammatical knowledge:* as introduced in Chapter 4, sharing learning objectives and criteria is critical for effective

Assessing vocabulary and grammatical knowledge 125

and successful learning. Firstly, checklists, one of the process-focused observational tools for assessing GC, will help teachers to share the learning objectives of grammar with learners on both the basic and unique sentence structures. The checklists can be a self- or peer- assessment grid for an instruction period and assist the learners to monitor themselves for learning a specific grammatical form. Table 5.4 is an example of such grids on learning the nominal structure, in which the provided CDSs are drawn from the behavioural performance on the different types of tasks presented in Table.5.3. Some of the CDSs are for knowledge of the form and meaning of the structure, and some are for producing the form and meaning in productive language activities. The summary required by the grid will provide learners with opportunities to find the gaps between their existing knowledge and the learning expectations to move learning forward. Therefore, teachers should take advantage of those process-focused tasks when teaching the challenging unique structures listed in Table 5.2.

Table 5.4 Self-Assessment Grid for Learning the Nominal Structure

Student Name:						
The learning objective for grammar in the next two weeks is the nominal structure when you learn Lesson 5 in the textbook. You are asked to do the following for this self-assessment grid: 1 At the end of the two weeks, rate yourself on the learning objective. 2 The midterm assessment will test you on the grammar form and meaning in the oral written exams. After you receive the marks, rate yourself again on the learning objectives. 3 You should submit a summary of what you have and have not achieved in learning the grammar.						
Learning objectives for nominal clauses	*How have you been doing on the grammar form?*					
	In Weeks 1 and 2			*After Midterm Exams*		
	Not well	*OK*	*Very well*	*Not well*	*OK*	*Very well*
I can remember the structure, nominal clause + 的+ (head noun), e.g. 学汉语的美国人.						
I can understand the relationship between the nominal clause and the head noun stated or omitted, e.g. 学汉语的 and 美国人.						
If I am given two related simple sentences, I can put them in a nominal clause, e.g. 他是美国人and 他学汉语。						
I can understand the structure and meaning when reading.						
I can understand the structure and meaning when listening.						
I can use the structure correctly to express meaning when speaking.						
I can use the structure correctly to express meaning when writing.						

126 *Assessing vocabulary and grammatical knowledge*

Secondly, a learning log/diary as a compulsory portfolio is also a formative assessment technique to consolidate learning the complex syntactic structures over time. Research has suggested that the verbal-complement construction is a versatile but challenging grammar form for the CFL learners due to the many meanings it creates and the properties of the verbs in the structure (Jiang, 2009, 2017). Therefore, using FA to enhance the ongoing learning of the unique structure is a more productive methodology as keeping a weekly log for an extended instruction period could reinforce the grammatical input and help the learners to record the various verbs and related forms meanings they have learnt. In doing so, the learners are also assessing themselves. A more structured learning diary with the following questions as prompts for reflection, self-assessment and independent learning is highly recommended.

a) How many sentences of the verb-complement construction have you encountered this week in the learning materials and the teacher's instruction? Give five examples.
b) What are the verbs and their complements? Write them in pairs from the examples you have given previously.
c) What do the complements mean in the five examples you have given?
d) In the five examples, which part(s) in the verbal-complement structure is most difficult to understand and learn? Circle them.
e) Have you asked the teacher or your peers about the difficult points? If you have, briefly write their answers or explanations here.
f) How do you think you have been doing on the structure this week? Please provide the following:

- Two correct answers you have given in the class
- The ratio between the number of sentences that have used the verbal-complement structure in your homework and the correct sentences

g) Have you noticed some impressive use of the structure by your peers? Give three examples.

2) *Providing noticing, judgement and analysis tasks for FA and SA to assess GC*: noticing in second language learning mediates the L2 acquisition process and improves development as such cognitive activities are the first crucial step for learning the salient features of a target language (Schmidt, 1990; Mackey, 2006). Thus, it is worthwhile spending time in the classroom to engage CFL learners with activities to observe and notice the unknown or known grammatical forms and meanings. In addition to the FA strategies introduced in Chapter 4.2, teachers can also use the SRTs or LPTs tasks presented in Table 5.3 for learners at different proficiency levels. Example 5.22, for instance, is one of such noticing tasks to assess the learning of the particle, 了, by the learners at the lower-intermediate level (CEFR A2 to B1). The learners at higher levels (above CEFR B2) can do tasks such as Example 5.23 as they have learnt most of the basic and unique structures

and are able to notice and analyse the more complex language forms and meanings in spoken or written discourse. Furthermore, error identification/correction questions for assessing GC have also been a commonly used test item for CBA. However, the sampling of such questions should be based on substantial data from a learner interlanguage corpus or a collection of the learners' typical grammatical errors so that they could provide the evidence for self-assessment.

Example 5.22: Put the following sentence in three groups.

> Group 1: Actions or states that have completed
> Group 2: Actions or states that have changed
> Group 3: Neither Group 1 nor Group 2
> a) 我在中国三年了。
> b) 他不高兴了，我们别笑了。
> c) 很感谢，你帮了我很多忙。
> d) 你太辛苦了，休息一会儿吧。
> e) 她听妈妈的话，不抽烟了。
> f) 我没吃饭，只喝了点水。

Example 5.23: Examine the utterances in the short conversation and put the sentences into two groups. Group 1 are those that are not grammatically correct. Group 2 are those that are not usually used in spoken discourse.

A. 白酒我从来不喝，啤酒我喝一点。
B. 听说人从来白酒不喝比较胆小。
A. 谁说不喝白酒即胆小？
B. 谁不知道？
A. 好，我不相信这些。

3) *Develop discourse completion test (DCT) for assessing grammatical forms and meanings*: traditionally termed as cloze test (CT), this technique is 'cloze procedure reduces redundancy by deleting a number of words in a passage, leaving blanks, and requiring the person taking the test to attempt to replace the original words' (Hughes, 2003: 187). As Hughes states, CT has been an attractive procedure to teachers and test developers because it is easy to write, administer and mark. It has also been considered an integrative method that assesses underlying L2 abilities, which is supported by the high correlation between language learners' performance on CT and their overall performance on an assessment. Nonetheless, CT is an indirect measure, and its validity has been questioned. Therefore, Hughes (ibid.) suggests that CT should be complemented with other measures to produce reliable and useful tests. Regarding the specific formats of CT, he recommends that the *selected deletion cloze* and *conversational cloze* be constructed because, unlike the CT that deletes nth words (e.g. every seventh), words are taken out for intended constructs and specific grammatical structures and vocabulary included in the learning objectives. Most importantly, those two types of

128 *Assessing vocabulary and grammatical knowledge*

CT can be used to test the learners' abilities for both formal and informal written and spoken discourse in different contexts of communication. Given Hughes' recommendation, three types of CT for both written and spoken discourse are recommended for assessing GC in the CFL contexts (Example 5.24, 25 and 26).

Example 5.24: Fill in the gaps in the following passage by selecting the multiple choices.

前年冬天，马大卫跟我____(1) 爬长城。____(2) 天气很冷,____(3) 我听说 '不到长城，非好汉'，____(4) 没有坐游览车。登____(5) 长城以后，看____(5) 长城像一条龙，好像还____(6) 飞，景色太美____(7)。

(1) A. 来 B. 出 C. 近 D. 去　　(2) A. 虽然 B. 可是 C. 只要 D. 而且
(3) A. 如果 B. 但是 C. 既然 D. 因为　(4) A. 就 B. 也 C. 都 D. 才
(5) A. 下 B. 中 C. 上 D. 里　　(6) A. 到 B. 上 C. 来 D. 去
(6) A. 着 B. 了 C. 过 D. 在　　(8) A. 极 B. 了 C. 呢 D. 吧

Example 5.24 is an adapted DCT with multiple choices mostly intended for knowledge of discourse markers or verbal particles which frequently appear in some existing CPTs or CBA as the variety accommodates different levels of difficulty based on the proficiency levels of the test-takers. With the appropriate level of difficulty, learners can concentrate on the discourse's contextual clues and judge the grammatical forms and meanings necessary for the blanks. In comparison, Example 5.25 is also a typically selected deletion cloze based on written discourse. Without the multiple choices, such CTs are lexically more challenging than Example 5.24. Furthermore, the expected responses are not dichotomous answers. Marking such CT needs to consider alternative responses carefully. For example, the answers to (3) can be 但 or 可.

Example 5.25: Fill the blank with only ONE appropriate word.

现在在挑选楼盘____(1), 居室肯定是购房者考虑____(2) 一个因素。想买五居室的楼盘，____(3) 囊中羞涩，三居室就是许多家庭的目标。____(5) 三口之家或五口之家，三居室都____(6) 满足居住的需求，是当前比较____(7) 欢迎的户型。

Example 5.26: Fill the blanks in the following dialogue with ONE or TWO characters.

A. 妈妈，我要跟朋友去看电影了。
B. 午饭我还没做好呢。你 (1) _____ 不早说?
A. 对不起，忘了。我们想 (2) _____ 电影 (3) _____ 麦当劳吃饭。
B. 那你可不能回来 (4) _____ 太晚。
A. 不会的，七点以前一定回来。

Example 5.26 is conversational cloze DCT that involves understanding the interactive spoken discourse and demands the learners' competence for applying the grammatical forms to express meanings with pragmatic and sociolinguistic appropriateness and contextual acceptability, as Purpura comments (2004). This kind of DCTs is a reoccurring exercise in some widely used CFL textbooks (e.g. Liu et al., 2003, 2008, 2012). They help the CFL learners apply the newly learnt language forms for the meanings prescribed by the discourse. In this example, the forms of the question-word questions, serial verb structure and verbal-complement construction are the foci for assessment through the deleted words. The instruction that ONE or TWO words should be retrieved for the blanks increases the difficulty of the item, which is designed to elicit the performance of GC for more complex structures and meanings.

In summary, this chapter has introduced the specific features of Chinese morphology and syntax and the competencies necessary for the use and application of the forms and meanings. The construct definitions for assessing those two competencies are defined for breadth and depth of vocabulary knowledge and the mastery of the basic and unique grammatical structures. Furthermore, the components of competencies for VC and GC in L2 Chinese are discussed and identified in terms of the characteristics of the root words and derivation- and inflexion-like compounding of lexis and the special word order of the Chinese language. Furthermore, although some of the conventional techniques for assessing VC in other languages are still appropriate for L2 Chinese, innovation is important for the assessment of the unique features of the Chinese lexis. L2 Chinese tests have employed mostly the techniques for assessing GC in English, except that the word-order questions are used often. Amongst the test items and tasks recommended by Purpura (2013), those that will elicit self- and peer assessment effectively are recommended to the CFL CBA for summative and formative purposes, e.g. process focused, noticing, analytic and judgement. Suggestions for using the CT procedure are provided to emphasise the importance of discourse embedded in the contexts for language use. However, it cannot be overlooked that assessing VC and assessing GC actively interact with each other to the extent that sometimes they depend on each other. Finally, as the core competencies, VC and GC are the building blocks for the competencies in the spoken and written language, which are the subjects of Chapters 6 and 7.

Further readings

1 Read, J. (2012): Chapter 2 and 3 discuss the nature of vocabulary competence and introduce the research background for assessing vocabulary.
2 Li, L. (2017) discusses the relationship between CFL learners' grammatical knowledge and their overall proficiency levels.
3 Hughes, A. (2003: 186–98) introduces the cloze tests and advice on creating cloze-type passages.

Reader activities

1. Are your tests for the breadth of vocabulary sampled from the graded lists of characters or lexical items recommended by EBCL, ICCLE or the textbooks you use? Reflect on the techniques you have used, and tell the advantages and disadvantages.
2. Create and write three types of test items for assessing your learners' knowledge about radicals, the semantic-phonetic compounds and their competence for understanding the disyllable compound words. Share with a colleague or your peers on a CFL postgraduate course.
3. Check and monitor the spoken and written work your students have done, and find the five most commonly made grammatical mistakes. Use the information, and design two process-focused assessments to help your learners to study the unique structures of Chinese grammar.
4. Find in the grammar sections in the end-of-term written exam papers for the beginner, intermediate and advanced learners on your programme, and do the following:

    a) Categorise the types of tasks used (see Table 5.3) for the three proficiency levels.
    b) Investigate the type of tasks used most frequently for each proficiency level and decide if they are effective for assessing GC of the three groups.
    c) Improve the test items you find unsatisfactory.

6 Assessing Pinyin and spoken language competence in L2 Chinese

Competence in the Chinese spoken language consist of three components: Pinyin competence (PC) and competence in the receptive mode, listening comprehension, and competence in the productive mode, speaking. Speaking competence has two modes, presentational/monologue and interactive. As defined by the *CFL Model of Construct Definition for Assessing Learners' Competence* (see Chapter 2.5), PC is one of the core competencies in L2 Chinese and CFL learners' phonological control in both receptive and productive activities. Different from PC, listening comprehension and speaking competencies have more dimensions involving PC, VC, GC and discourse and pragmatic competencies. To achieve PC, learners must understand and correctly articulate Pinyin; the combination of phonetics, tones, changes of tones; and other phonological features. PC also includes the ability for using Pinyin as an input method for writing. Listening comprehension and speaking, on the other hand, engage much more complex cognitive activities and strategic competence and need the support of the two peripheral competencies (learner knowledge and attributes) to complete the test items and tasks. The three sections in this chapter, therefore, are concerned with assessing PC, listening and speaking in L2 Chinese. In each section, the specific features of Pinyin and the spoken language and research on the competencies will be briefly introduced first to define the constructs for assessment. Assessment measures and techniques will follow the defined constructs and be introduced and discussed for CBA for different purposes and proficiency tests.

6.1 Assessing Pinyin competence (PC)

Mandarin Chinese or 普通话 (*pǔtōnghuà*, Standard Chinese), which most of the existing CFL programmes are teaching, has been regarded as the standard speech of the Chinese language, also known as 华语 (Chinese speech) or 国语 (national speech). It is the dialect spoken by汉族人 (the Han people, 91% of the Chinese population) alongside the other dialects such as Yue, Haka, Wu or Xiang. Mandarin has been spoken since the Northern Song Dynasty (959–1126) in the courts of emperors and was known as 官话 (speech of officials). In 1958 at the Chinese People's Congress, Pinyin was officially established as the standard Romanised system to present the pronunciation of the Chinese language. In China and Taiwan nowadays, Mandarin Chinese is spoken in the educational and public sectors and by the media.

The Romanised phonetic system and acquisition of Pinyin and tones

Pinyin consists of *initials* and *finals*, or consonants and vowels as termed in languages such as English. They are called so for their positions in a syllable. For example, there are three initials in *pǔtōnghuà*, *p, t* and *h*, which are at the beginning of each syllable. There are three finals, *u, ong* and *ua*, which are at the end of each syllable. The finales can be of one, two or three letters. The initials, however, are mostly one letter except *for ch, zh* and *sh*. According to one of the widely used CFL textbooks, *New Practical Chinese Reader* (Liu et al., 2003, 2008, 2012), there are 21 initials and 38 finals which create over 1,200 combinations with different tones.

There are five tones, Tone 1, Tone 2, Tone 3, Tone 4 and the neutral tone, Tone 5 (T1, T2, T3, T4 and T5, hereafter). Their tone marks are respectively, ˉ ˊ ˇ ˋ. T5 does not have a mark. As the tones make lexical distinctions, a slight change in the pitch contour of a syllable can alter the meaning of a Chinese character without changing the phonetics (Xing, 2006; Ke, 2012). For example, when *di* is said with different tones, the characters can be 滴 (*dī*, a drop/to drop), 敌 (*dí*, enemy), 底 (*dǐ*, bottom) and 地 (*dì*, earth/ground/floor). If a learner intends to say '一滴水' (a drop of water) but pronounced a T4 for 滴, the meaning will be '一地水' (water all over the floor). Thus, the accuracy of tones is critical for CFL learners' spoken language in receptive, productive and interactional communication.

Tones also change in various conditions, which is known as *sandhi*. Sandhi of T3 is most frequent when followed by another T3 (changes into a half T3) or the other tones (changes into a short T4), though the tone marks do not change. In addition, 一 (*yī*), when followed by other tones, changes, and 不 (*bù*), when followed by T4, also changes. Example 6.1 shows all the sandhi in the Pinyin of a sentence:

Example 6.1: 我妈妈一直不看她 wǒ māma yìzhí búkàn tā (My mother never looked at her.)

- 我 (wǒ) changes into a half T3 because it is followed by a T1, 妈 (mā).
- 一 (yī) changes into a T4 because it is followed by T2, 直 (zhí).).
- 不 (bù) changes into a T2 because it is followed by a T4, 看 (kàn).).

The research on SLA development in Chinese phonology has revealed that: (1) learners acquire the finals earlier similar to those in English, e.g. *i, a, u, e*, than the finals in *lü, chi and ci* (Shi and Wen, 2009; Xie, 2015); (2) it is easier to learn the double or triple finals such as *ie, üe, uo, üan, ün, ian, ing, eng* (Cai and Cao, 2002; Xing, 2006); and (3) learners make more mistakes with the retroflex initials, *zh, ch, shi;* palatals: *j, q, x*; and *sibilants*: *z, c* and *s*, or the aspirated and unaspirated vowels, *p-b, k-g, t-d* (Wang and Shangguan, 2004). Worth mentioning is the large-scale

Assessing Pinyin and spoken language competence in L2 Chinese 133

study by Chen et al. (2016) based on a data of 90,841 utterances of words, phrases and sentences produced by 305 CFL learners of seven different first languages. The results about PC have shown the following:

1 Most phonetic errors are de-aspiration of the aspirated initials, e.g. $p \rightarrow b$, $c \rightarrow z$, $q \rightarrow j$, $k \rightarrow g$.
2 Most tonal errors are for Tone 3, with the lowest accuracy rate (58.8%), while the accuracy rate for Tone 1 and Tone 5 are 72.6% and 75.5%.
3 Phonetic-error rates are first-language specific, and the Romance L1 speakers (French, Spanish and Italian, etc.) made more mistakes than the Germanic L1 speakers (German, Dutch, Afrikaans, etc.).
4 Tonal-error rates are also first-language specific, and the tone accuracies of the Germanic L1 speakers are higher than those of the Romance L1 speakers.
5 More than 90% of the mispronounced tone pair is (3, 3) followed by (3, 2), (4, 4) and (4, 3).

Studies have also investigated the acquisition order of tones, which is 1, 4, 2 and 3 (Zhang, 2013, 2018). Tone 3 being the most difficult is due to two main factors: its acoustic similarities with Tones 2 and 4 and its multiple sandhi when followed by another T3 and the other tones. When tones are paired up, coarticulation of the two same or different tones causes difficulties for the learners. Comparisons of the accuracy rates produced by the native speakers of Japanese, Korean and English, Zhang (2013, 2016) confirms that, except T3-T3 being the most difficult, the acquisition order of tone pairs is T1-T1, T4-T4 and T2-T2. Furthermore, higher accuracy rates of T1-T3 and T2-T3 suggest that CFL learners may acquire such sequences earlier than T2-T1 and T2-T2 pairs produced with high error rates. Also critical to PC is the ability to produce prosodic features such as word and sentence stress, rhythm and intonation. Studies have shown that the inaccurate pronunciation of T3 and Tone 4 results in incorrect intonations for different questions (Yang and Chan, 2010). Intonation for statement sentences could also be problematic if T2 is inaccurately articulated. Those studies have suggested that the assessment of PC should prioritise the accuracy of Pinyin, especially tones. The summative and formative CBA should also consider the learners' L1 and develop PC tests accordingly.

The *Model of Construct Definition for Assessing Learners' Competence in L2 Chinese* proposes that PC consists of the abilities for articulating the sounds, tones, intonations and prosaic variations and understanding accents and Pinyin as input to use various dictionaries and compose texts on computers and digital devices (see Figure 2.3 in Chapter 2, the CFL Model, hereafter). This construct definition has followed the CEFR standards for Overall Phonological Control (CoE, 2018) and the benchmark of ICCLE (Hanban, 2014), excluding the Pinyin reading and writing competence recognised by EBCL guidelines (EBCL, 2012a). The difference between the constructs defined by the CFL Model and the language-specific benchmark, ICCLE, is that the latter has not defined the competencies for transcribing

134 *Assessing Pinyin and spoken language competence in L2 Chinese*

Pinyin for unknown vocabulary and using Pinyin for converted writing or keyboard writing. The ICCLE description of PC focuses on four components—abilities for Pinyin and tones, intonation and stresses, prosaic features and regional accents—which can be shown by its PC description for Stage 6 as follows.

1 Can communicate with fluent and natural Pinyin and tones
2 Can express fluently specific meanings through intonations, tones and stresses
3 Can understand the rhythm and prosaic features of the Chinese phonology fully
4 Can comprehend Putonghua with different regional accents

To implement the expected traits in the learners' performance on PC assessment, the following constructs of PC are identified and presented in Table 6.1. The competence for tones is emphasised in the definition not only because the lexical meanings in a tonal language are determined by the accuracy of tones but also because research has suggested that acquisition of tones, tone sandhi and tone pairs is critical to understanding and production of the spoken language. Even the prosaic features to distinguish question types in Chinese depend on the accuracy of tones for communication.

Table 6.1 The Construct Definition for Assessing PC

Components of PC Construct	Subcomponents
Production of sounds	Can accurately pronounce the initials and finals including those difficult, e.g. retroflex, palatals, sibilants, aspirated and unaspirated
	Can accurately pronounce the combinations of initials and finals
Production of tones	Can distinguish the differences between the five tones
	Can articulate Sandhi of tones, e.g. T3, 一 and 不
	Can articulate correctly the bi-tonal pairs with natural coarticulation
Production of intonation and Stresses	Can employ tones and tone pairs accurately to realise intended intonations, stresses or other prosaic variations in phrases and sentence
Understanding regional accents	Can understand Putonghua with regional accents without communication breakdowns
Transcribing Pinyin	Can accurately transcribe the Pinyin heard to find the meanings of unknown words
Converted writing	Can type Pinyin without tones for converted/keyboard writing on computers or digital devices

Tasks and techniques for assessing Pinyin competence

Currently, assessment of PC has not been the priority of the CPTs except for the Spoken Chinese Test (SCT) developed by Beijing University and Pearson (Beijing

Assessing Pinyin and spoken language competence in L2 Chinese 135

University and Pearson, 2014). It is mainly the affairs of the formative or summative CBA that has vigorously assessed beginner learners' learning of Pinyin to ensure that they will benefit greatly from the Romanised phonetic system for their future studies of the Chinese language. The teachers, especially in the first two months or so of a beginner's CFL course, have certainly applied some of the five formative assessment strategies (FAS) discussed in Chapter 4 to consolidate the input for Pinyin. The summative CBA, on the other hand, would usually include PC tests as part of achievement assessment, in which multiple-choice questions (MCQ) are often used to see if different sounds and tones can be distinguished (see Example 6.2). Dictation of words, phrases or sentences is also a popular method that teachers have been using to see if their learners can understand the Pinyin they have heard and correctly write the combination of initials and finals with the tones. Cloze tests have also been used for the learners to fill in the 'missing' Pinyin.

Example 6.2: Listen and select the Pinyin that you hear in each group.

1 A jù B qù C xù D zù
2 A shàng B shǎng C sháng D shāng
3 A piān B bǎn C tián D dàn
4 A zuòyè B zhuóyuè C cuòwèi D chuōwài
5 A xǎingshòu B xiǎngchū C qiǎngshǒu D qiǎngxué

However, the assessment of PC should always associate the Romanised phonetic system with the script as it is created to present the pronunciation of the written language. Examples 6.3 and 4 show how this could be achieved and that testing PC should also be integrated with listening, reading, reading aloud, grammar, vocabulary and speaking. Such an approach is to assure that assessment of PC has a positive impact on learning and the learners are not in any way misled that Pinyin and characters coexist as the script of the Chinese language. For instance, Example 6.3 requires learners to provide the Pinyin for the characters they have learnt, whereby not only PC but also VC is tested. Moreover, the ability for tones is highlighted, and the knowledge about the sandhi of 不 is also involved. Example 6.4 is designed for learners who have completed the Pinyin stage in their beginner courses, when they could recognise the incorrect pronunciation produced by others in terms of sounds and tones. The task also engages the learners sensitivity to what they have listened to and the competence to correct the mistakes in the pronunciation.

Example 6.3 Write the Pinyin on the lines for the words or phrases. You must mark the tones.

Words	*Pinyin*	*Words*	*Pinyin*
1 你们	_____	4 不是	_____
2 小宿舍	_____	5 饭店里	_____
3 有意思	_____	6 为什么	_____

Example 6.4: You have just heard the following sentences three times. Now, write on the line your corrections of the mistakes that the speaker has made in pronunciation.

The test-takers hear:

1 Míntiān tā máng bú máng, yǒu shíqiān má?
2 Wó wàipó shēntǐ bù sūfú, wǒ gēn tā qù yīyùn le.

Your answers:

1 _____
2 _____

One of the most practical and useful functions of Pinyin is that they provide the form, meaning and use of vocabulary. The ability to transcribe the Pinyin that the learners have heard is the first step to using it for unknown vocabulary and converted/keyboard writing. The tasks for assessing those competencies should prioritise authenticity to familiarise the learners with the tasks they will carry out when interacting with Chinese-speaking people. Examples 6. 5 and 6 are two examples of such tasks for the formative or summative CBA of the lower-level CFL courses. Although similar to Example 6.4, which assesses the learners' sensitivity and ability to capture the Pinyin they have heard, they integrate with the knowledge of the forms, meanings and usage of the vocabulary (Example 6.5) and GC and discourse competence for written text (Example 6.6). The two tasks are stimulations of the real-life tasks they will do most for communication in the spoken language. They can also be part of the summative CBA at the end of the instruction period to see if the learners have achieved the learning objectives using Pinyin as a resource for learning vocabulary.

Example 6.5:

The test-takers hear: 1 休息 2 便宜 3 火车站 4 动车

Instruction: Listen to the four words and provide the characters, Pinyin, meanings and the grammatical functions in the table. You can find the information from online or digital dictionaries.

Characters	Pinyin	Meaning(s)	Grammatical Function
1			
2			
3			
4			

Example 6.6:

The test-takers hear: 1 元宵节他和朋友去吃火锅了。
2 老师对我们很耐心，但也很严格。

Assessing Pinyin and spoken language competence in L2 Chinese 137

Instruction: You have learnt most of the characters in the two sentences. Listen and fill the gaps with the words you hear. You can find the words in your dictionaries based on the Pinyin you hear.

1 _____他和朋友去吃_____了。
2 老师对我们很_____，但也很_____。

Certainly, the other important function of PC is to assist and ensure accurate and natural pronunciation of Mandarin Chinese. Therefore, there are a variety of classroom activities provided by textbooks or learning materials, and teachers also design activities according to their students' learning needs, strengths and weaknesses in PC. Some of the activities are for consolidating the Pinyin input, and the others have served as formative strategies to evaluate learning and teaching. Those activities include reading aloud Pinyin—e.g. single characters, words, compound words, phrases, sentences or short passages—to assess the accuracy of produced Pinyin with correct tones, the changes of tones when required and the natural coarticulation of tone pairs. One of the often-used techniques applied to the summative oral exams for beginners is reading aloud a dialogue in Pinyin individually or in pairs, as Example 6.7 shows. In the example, there are nine instances of T3 sandhi and the difficult tone pair T2-T2. Those instances can be taken as the foci of the assessment and take a certain percentage of the total score for this task.

Example 6.7: Read the following dialogue in Pinyin with your partner.

A. Qǐngwèn, zhè shì zhōngwénxì de bàngōngshì ma?
B. Shìde, nǐ zhǎo nǎyíwèi lǎoshī?
A. Zhǎo jiāo wénxué de wánglǎoshī。
B. Duìbùqǐ, tā bù zài。Nǐ xiàwǔ liǎngdiǎn zài láiba。

Tasks in the receptive mode for assessing the competencies in applying stresses and intonations to words, phrases and sentences should be in characters rather than in Pinyin as meanings are expressed by the script in a language. The learners must make decisions regarding stresses and intonations after they have understood the written or spoken discourse. For instance, the written text for the dialogue in Example 6.8 is as follows, based on which the learners can decide that stresses should be placed on 中文系, 哪, 文学, 王, etc. and rising intonation should be applied for the first turn and falling intonation for the rest of the turns in the conversation.

A. 请问，这是中文系的办公室吗？ (Excuse me, is this the office of the Chinese Department?)
B. 是的，你找哪一位老师？ (Yes, who are you meeting?)
A. 找教文学的王老师。 (Teacher Wang who teaches literature.)
B. 对不起，她不在。你下午两点再来吧。 (Sorry, she has left. Would you come again at two o'clock this afternoon?)

Most of the tasks in the productive mode, however, should be implemented in speaking activities, and the standards are presented in the marking criteria. The rubrics often describe the PC performance as 'Accurate, fluent and natural Pinyin, tones, stresses and intonations' as the most satisfactory. 'Frequent mispronounced Pinyin with either unchanged or incorrect tones, stresses and intonation are misplaced, difficult to understand' as unsatisfactory performance. The third part of this chapter is about assessing speaking in L2 Chinese. PC as one of the marking criteria will be discussed further.

This part has introduced the characteristics of Chinese phonology and the acquisition of Pinyin and identified the constructs of PC for assessment. When the CFL learners can correctly pronounce the combination of initials and finals, accurate tones, changes of tones and the natural coarticulation of tones pairs, the meanings of utterances will be created for communication. The performance of PC in the receptive mode is also important as it is the other part of communication in spoken language. Therefore, test items and tasks should be designed to reflect the functions of Pinyin and integrate with VC, GC and reading for a language with a logographic writing system.

6.2 Assessing listening competence in L2 Chinese (LCC)

PC is the ability of phonological control of the Chinese language, which, as has been discussed, ensures that the other party of the communication can comprehend the speaker. Listening competence in L2 Chinese (LCC hereafter), on the other hand, is the ability to understand speech in Chinese, which is indispensable for face-to-face interaction in social, private, official or business contexts with Chinese-speaking people. However, testing listening, similar to testing reading, is not straightforward because 'we can observe neither the process of performing nor the product' (Brown, 2004: 117). This part introduces the cognitive activities and processes of listening comprehension in a foreign language and the impact of the specific features of the Chinese spoken language on the assessment of listening. The studies on listening in L2 Chinese and the assessment of LCC will also be briefly presented. The construct of LCC for assessment will be defined, and the measures and techniques will be discussed in the last section.

The characteristics of listening tests and construct for assessing LCC

The cognitive activities engaged in the listening comprehension process in an L2 differ greatly from those engaged in the speaking, reading and writing processes. Firstly, the *cognitive activities* for processing and understanding the spoken discourse are through 'internalising meaning from the auditory signals transmitted to the ear and brain' (Brown, 2004: 118). The activities experienced by language learners are in four stages, as described by Brown (ibid.119–20):

1   They recognise and retain the speech sounds in the short-term memory.
2   They make a spontaneous decision about the type of speech, its context and content.

3   They use their linguistic knowledge (bottom-up) or background schemata (top-down knowledge) to interpret the message heard and assign an intended meaning to it.
4   They retain the relevant and vital information in long-term memory without keeping the exact linguistic forms in which the information is originally received.

It is clear that the first stage is crucial to listening comprehension in any language, especially Chinese because the lexical tones determine the meanings of words. If a learner has misheard a tone and his/her short-term memory retains incorrect sounds, the decision about the type of speech, the context and content would be inaccurate too. Furthermore, unknown vocabulary and syntactic structures can also cause non-understanding or misunderstandings of the information transmitted. If the learners are familiar with the language domains and themes, they can work out the main information for long-term memory. If they do not have the access to top-down knowledge, the information retained will be either incomplete or incorrect. In a natural conversation setting, the listener can ask the speaker to clarify or confirm what they have said. The speakers' facial expressions and body language in person or on video will assist their comprehension. In most listening tests, however, the learners do not control the listening materials. As a result, there is a significant amount of *cognitive load*, and the four stages described by Brown (ibid.) have shown that the listeners' processing of the incoming information involves bottom-up and top-down knowledge and short-term and long-term memory within a very short time. The cognitive load for test-takers of a listening test also decides whether a listening test is easy or difficult to understand, interpret and respond to (Rost, 2015). The factors affecting the cognitive load experienced by the learners include the following:

1   *Length* (duration, information density, redundancy, restatement and elaboration of information)
2   *Complexity* (syntactic, directness and concreteness of meanings, pragmatic information such as L2 idioms and culturally specific vocabulary)
3   *Organisation* (e.g. unscripted conversations with greater redundancy and simpler syntax or the opposite, spoken texts, coherence, discourse markers, visual reinforcement and the position of information)
4   *Surface features* (speaker accent, hesitations and pauses, noise and distortion and speech rate)

Teachers and test developers must consider those factors carefully when planning and writing a listening test in consideration of the expected progress on the learning objectives and the learners' levels of proficiency. For example, the texts selected for the listening test for the learners to achieve CEFR A2 or ACTFL Intermediate Mid should be comparatively short, simple, relatively informal and with a low density of information that provides concrete rather than abstract information. The text should have more restatements and discourse markers to assist comprehension, and it should not be recorded by people who speak fast and with regional accents and use Chinese idiomatic expressions. In contrast, the texts selected for the learners trying to achieve CEFR C2, ICCLE Stage 6 or ACTFL Superior can be with the textual characteristics that native speakers can understand, e.g. natural speech rate and some local accents, at any length with linguistic complexity and density of information.

Speech rate is a critical issue for assessing listening as texts recorded with a speech rate much faster than what the test-takers can understand at their proficiency levels are challenging and even 'incomprehensible'. The average speech rate for British English is *four* syllables per second in conversations and interviews (Tauroza and Allison, 1995). As many words in English are more than four syllables, the test-takers will hear only one word in a second. However, because most Chinese words are monosyllable or disyllable, CFL learners will hear four or two words in a second. Often, four syllables in Chinese can be a sentence or formulaic speech with distinctive discourse or pragmatic functions—for example, 上课晚了 (It is late for class), 您夸奖了 (Your compliment is appreciated) and 不见不散 (See you until we meet again). As a result, the cognitive load demanded of CFL learners is much greater than that of learners of other languages, and they have to process faster the incoming spoken text and the information transmitted.

In addition to speech rate, the characteristics of Chinese spoken discourse may increase the level of difficulty for testing LCC, according to Xing (2006: 218–27). She summarises that there are five modes of the Chinese interactive conversation, *initiation, repetition, alteration, interjection* and *conclusion* (see Example 6.8), which are delivered very differently from CFL learners' first languages. Firstly, Chinese speakers organise their utterances with specific discourse markers (see the unique discourse devices or adverbials in Table 5.2 in Chapter 5). Secondly, they apply particular strategies to initiate topics, take turns and manage discourse, e.g. 1, 2, 3 and 5 in Example 6.8. Thirdly, language functions and pragmatics are expressed with specific linguistic forms and lexis, e.g. 4 in Example 6.8. Finally, in monologue discourse, topics are maintained with consecutive clauses without subjects but frequent word order variation. Therefore, the development of a listening assessment for L2 Chinese must consider those features of the spoken discourse in terms of cognitive load for the test-takers.

Example 6.8: Five modes of interactive Chinese spoken discourse

1 Initiation (to start a conversation):

   1a) 喂，老王在吗? (Starting a phone conversation: Hello, is Old Wang there?)

   1b) 哟，你去买菜了? (Starting a conversation with greetings: Oh! Have you gone to the grocery?)

2 Repetition (to express hesitation, confirmation, emphasis and speakers' attitudes):

   2a) 可以，可以，没问题。(Offering confirmation: OK, OK, no problem.)

   2b) 别说了，别说了，你就是错了! (Showing attitude: Don't speak, don't speak! You are just wrong.)

3   Alternation (to hold a turn and initiate a new topic):

   3a) 早闻您的大名，能问您个问题吗？ (I have heard your famous name long ago. Could I ask respected you a question?)
   3b) 不好意思，一会儿行吗？ (I'm really sorry. Could you wait a second?)

4   Interjections (吧, 啊, 么 or 呢 are used to solicit agreement, soften the tone, express insistence, exclamation, exhortation, assurance, etc.):

   4a) 行，就这样吧。 (Soliciting agreement: All right, that's it, OK?)
   4b) 你可不能再这样不听话了啊！ (Softening the tone: You'll have to listen in future, OK?)

5   Conclusion (different expressions are used to conclude an interaction)

   5a) 八点了，明天再说吧。 (Using time as a signal: It's already eight. We'll talk about it tomorrow.)
   5b) 说得很好，今天就到这儿。 (Using a comment to conclude a meeting or discussion: Well said. Let's finish for today.)

Given the speech rate, grammatical and discourse features of the spoken language, the suggestion is that the assessment of LCC by CBA or PCTs should first consider the '*default listening construct*' (Buck, 2001: 114), which prioritises assessment of the following behavioural traits. As we can see, such a construct definition focuses on the competence for understanding and processing the information provided with specific phonological, lexical, syntactic, discoursal and pragmatic features. Furthermore, the behavioural trait that demonstrates competence for understanding the inferred information or content is also included as part of listening competence in an L2.

1   Can process extended samples of realistic spoken language, automatically and in real time
2   Can understand the linguistic information that is unequivocally included in the text
3   Can make any inferences unambiguously implicated by the content of the passage

Specifically, Rost (2015: 198) proposes that the construct of listening competence consists of *phonological, lexical, syntactic, pragmatic* and *general knowledge*. General knowledge includes content, background and extralinguistic, paralinguistic, social, pragmatic and strategic knowledge. Pragmatic knowledge consists of the abilities to do the following:

1   Follow the flow of given vs new information
2   Infer speaker intention and motivation
3   Recognise intertextuality (cultural references)
4   Understand social and cultural conventions and relationships between interlocutors

Empirical studies on the assessment of LCC in recent years have been related to the construct definitions introduced previously. For example, factor analysis has found that listening abilities include recognising speech sound and information, comprehension and inference of the lexical meanings and contextual reasoning (Jin and Wang, 2012), which has evidenced the default construct proposed by Buck (2001). Furthermore, it has been reported that CFL learners awarded with higher scores in the HSK listening papers frequently apply metacognitive strategies such as planning, monitoring, selecting, predicting, inferencing and summarising, and those awarded with lower scores are likely to use translation and retelling strategies (Wu and Chen, 2006; Cai and Wang, 2013). Interestingly, research has also shown that vocabulary knowledge and competence in listening are positively correlated at 77.1%, which is higher than the correlation between word recognition speed and listening proficiency (Cai, 2015), suggesting that vocabulary may improve or hinder the performance on listening tests. Thus, Table 6.2 presents the proposed the construct definition for assessing LCC in consideration of the default construct, the specific components of the construct proposed by Rost (2015) and the revelations contributed by the recent research on the listening competence in L2 Chinese and the assessment of LCC.

Table 6.2 Construct Definition for Assessing LCC

Construct for assessing LCC	Subcomponents of competence
A. Competence in processing Chinese phonological system	Can recognise and retain the combinations of initials and finals of tones, sandi tone pairs and strings in short-term memory
	Can distinguish the Pinyin heard as characters, words and chunks in meaning units
	Can recognise and retain the stresses of words and sentences, intonation and prosaic features in short-term memory for syntactic processing
	Can recognise and retain the accent heard and process it in standard Mandarin Chinese
B. Competence in processing lexical and grammatical meanings	Can recognise and retain for syntactic processing the forms, meanings and use of the characters or lexical items heard as required by the graded lists for the specific proficiency levels
	Can assign the unique grammatical forms to the words and lexical items recognised and retained
	Can use the relevant linguistic knowledge (bottom-up) or background schemata (top-down) to interpret the message heard
C. Competence in comprehending Chinese spoken discourse and pragmatics	Can recognise spontaneously the features of the Chinese interactive spoken discourse and pragmatics expressed in Chinese and infer the relationship between the interlocutors, sequence and outcomes of events
	Can recognise the features of the monologue Chinese spoken discourse spontaneously and infer the intended information structure, context and content
D. Strategic competence for transferring full and inferred meanings in Chinese	Can follow and retain in long-term memory the flow of given vs new information, primary vs supporting and specific and general ideas for skimming or scanning purposes
	Can infer meanings unambiguously implicated in the context, goals of communication with social or cultural references
	Can predict and select forthcoming information and monitor and synthesise heard information according to the demands of tasks

Tasks and techniques for assessing LCC

Approaches for assessing listening can be discrete point, integrative or communicative by nature, depending on the construct identified for assessing a specific group of CFL learners and the purposes of assessment. However, it is critical for a listening test to avoid *construct-irrelevant variance* that assesses performance not related to the construct intended (Buck, 2001). For instance, if the intended construct for a summative assessment is to test a group of beginner CFL learners' competence for recognising and retaining the incoming specific features of Pinyin in short-term memory, Example 6.9 is one of the tasks to elicit the performance on the PC called for without the need to read and write the script. As the example also shows that listening tests engage other language abilities (e.g. reading, writing, grammar and vocabulary knowledge), measures must be taken to ensure that the indented construct for assessment does not become secondary. The different tones of 哪 and 那 and the recognition of the Pinyin of 了 and 要 in what the learners hear are the critical information for answering the question. Construct-irrelevant variance can also be due to the themes or content of the spoken text beyond the learners' general knowledge. Unknown vocabulary is certainly another difficulty for the test-takers to respond to the test items correctly. Thus, it is recommended that teachers develop their listening test based on the learnt themes, topics and vocabulary included in the learning objectives and materials. Test developers of CPTs should follow the graded lists of characters and lexical items established by the relevant guidelines and benchmarks. With the learners' competence and proficiency levels rising, however, an appropriate amount of unfamiliar language domains can be added to examine their abilities for the top-down process, skimming, scanning and understanding implicated information.

Example 6.9:

> Learners hear: 小李，你去哪儿了？
> Instruction: Choose the correct answer according to what you have heard.
> Question: Which one of the following should be a correct reply by 小李？
>
> a. 我没去那儿。 b. 我去图书馆了。 c. 我要去图书馆。 d. 我去哪儿？

Task characteristics or *types* are also important factors to item difficulty that impact the construct validity and reliability of a listening test. Buck (2001) claims that listening tasks vary in how the learners are requested to process the information provided. It is those requests that decide the types and characteristics of tasks. Brown (2004: 122–39) identifies four types of listening tasks—*intensive, responsive, selective* and *extensive*—which elicit test-takers to undertake different listening comprehension processes. Example 6.9 is an intensive listening task as the question focuses on the phonological and morphological elements of the listening text provided. The demanded information is in more than one position, to which the test-takers need to pay intense attention to distinguish the different sounds. Example 6.10 is a responsive task that creates interaction between the

144 *Assessing Pinyin and spoken language competence in L2 Chinese*

task and the test-takers—in this case, a well-wishing expression widely used by the Chinese during the Spring Festival. The question also requests the learners to write the response; therefore, not only PC but also VC, GC and pragmatic competence are demanded. This is a typical integrated test item for assessing LCC with increased item difficulty. Brown (ibid.) recommends that open-ended responsive questions are more authentic tasks compared to close-ended multiple choices.

Example 6.10: Listen and write down your response on the line to what you hear.

> Learners hear: 过年好！
>
> _____

Example 6.11: Listen and indicate on the picture where the different pieces of furniture are in the room.

> Learners hear: 我的房间很小，里面只有一张床，桌子，一个椅子和一个很大的衣柜。 床在窗户的对面，靠着墙。桌子和椅子在窗户的下面。衣柜很大，就放在了门的右边。
> Learners see:

The selective listening tasks are the tasks that require test-takers to provide specific information after listening to a limited quantity of spoken input. They include *cloze tests* with the required specifics taken out of the text and *information-transfer tasks*. The disadvantage of the former is that the tasks could demand more reading than listening. Thus, caution must be taken to ensure that the requested information is not difficult to obtain and focuses on only one type of detail, e.g. numbers, locations or varieties of food, clothes and books. Example 6.12 is an information-transfer task that requests the test-takers to retain the information heard and transfer them into a visual format such as tables,

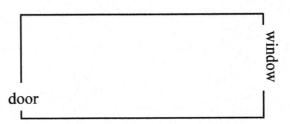

Figure 6.1 Drawing of a Room

diagrams, forms, etc. According to Brown (2004), the advantage of this type of task is that it reflects a greater extent of authenticity as people often carry out such tasks in everyday life and work with similar cognitive activities. It also has the flexibility to assess LCC from lower- to higher-level competencies

Assessing Pinyin and spoken language competence in L2 Chinese 145

because it is easier to adjust the contents, linguistic range and complexity of the listening tests.

Example 6.12: Provide the missing details in the brackets with the information given in the conversation you hear.

2018 年中国出入国游客人次	2.91 亿人次
( )	55.39 亿人次
2018 年中国游客最喜欢的国外旅游地	1. ( ) 2. 泰国 3. 美国 4. ( )
( )	1. 杭州 2. ( ) 3. ( ) 4. 云南

The extensive listening tasks are usually drawn from larger stretches of the spoken discourse of either conversations or monologues, including lectures or speeches. The main difference between the selective and extensive tasks, according to Brown (2004), is that the former is a listening process for scanning, while the latter is for understanding overall meanings and the ability to present them through dictation and note taking, retelling or summary writing. Although those tasks have a high degree of authenticity and integrate different competencies, scoring is not straightforward and requires a rating scheme consisting of several criteria. Therefore, the use of *interpretive tasks* is recommended, which 'extends the stimulus material to a longer stretch of discourse and forces the test-taker to infer a response' (Brown, 2004: 137). Short-answer questions are often used to achieve such a purpose (see Example 6.13).

Example 6.13:

> Learners hear: 今天早上起床晚了，不得不骑车去上课。骑到学校南大门的时候，你知道，路很窄，所以我不停地按车铃。一个女生带着耳机在我前面走，怎么也听不到我的铃声。我只能急刹车，但还是撞到了她。没想到她很生气，对我喊了起来。我只好不停地抱歉解释，可她好像根本听不懂，好像就是我错了。
>
> A. Instruction: Listen to what happened to 丽丽 this morning and answer the following questions.
> 1 丽丽每天都骑车去学校吗？
> 2 听她说话的人对丽丽的学校熟悉吗
> 3 丽丽觉得那个女生应该生气吗？为什么？
> 4 丽丽觉得自己错了吗？为什么？

The questions in Example 6.13 ask the test-takers to provide open-ended answers to reflect their interpretation of the audio input, a monologue. To do this, the learners need to understand not only all the involved vocabulary but also the zero-subject structure of sentences and the specific discourse devices. They will also make references from the narrative mixed with emotions indirectly expressed to answer all the questions, which demands the competence to infer information in the narration. Short-answer questions are in fact versatile as they can be applied to elicit answers that are intensive, responsive, selective or extensive. As a result, they have been a popular task type for both listening and reading tests. Especially when assessing whether the learners can infer meanings unambiguously implicated in the context and goals of communication with social or cultural references, short-answer questions can be used without much effort. However, Buck (2001: 147) has cautioned that although 'reference is at the core of language processing' and language learners need to comprehend beyond the literal meaning, measures must be taken to avoid construct-irrelevant variance. Referential questions must focus on the language competencies in understanding the main idea, the indirectly stated meanings or pragmatic implications rather than on subject matters, world knowledge or personal experiences.

Finally, here are a few suggestions for teachers to select audio or video input for developing listening assessments as input significantly affects the instrument reliability related to the length, speech rate, linguistic complexity, redundancy in the text and the structure of information of the texts selected.

1. If pre-recorded listening materials from broadcasters or the internet are selected, the contents and text characteristics may not fully comply with the learning objectives of a specific CFL course. Those materials must be adapted to suit the constructs defined and the levels of competence of the learners.
2. If texts are selected from other textbooks for CBA for their graded topics, levels of difficulty and the good quality of audio or video materials, precautions must be taken in case some of the test-takers may be familiar with the textbook.
3. Many teachers prefer to write the input themselves so that they can adjust the cognitive activities and load and the speech rate, length or linguistic complexity so that the listening test suits the learners' existing learning progress. Further, teachers know best the expected learning outcomes and the learners' general knowledge to avoid irrelevant construct variance. However, the disadvantage of such teacher-made input for assessing LCC is that it is not natural speech and the learners are familiar with the teacher's talk even if other teachers are invited to record the audio. However, as it is difficult to find spoken language input appropriate to a specific group of learners and learning objectives, *semi-scripted texts* are an alternative that are recorded or videoed with an outline of the content for the speaker(s) to make sure that the features of authentic and unplanned spoken discourse (e.g. hesitation, pauses, back channelling and self-corrections) could be retained (see Example 6.14). This alternative has been overlooked by most teacher-made listening tests, especially for higher-level learners.

Example 6.14:

> Subject: 熬夜不健康，但这个坏习惯很难改 (Staying up late is not healthy, but this bad habit is difficult to change.)
> Duration: 三至四分钟 (three to four minutes)
> Outline:
> a) 我熬夜原因 (经常加班，回家后喜欢看电视，看微信，等等)
> b) 曾想改掉这个习惯，用的方法有早起，去健身房，少看电视和手机，但没成功
> c) 熬夜不健康，会使我们皮肤干燥，肠胃不好，免疫力降低等
> d) 决心改掉：早睡早起，坚持一项喜欢的体育活动，规定每天看手机，看电视的时间等

This part has introduced and discussed the listening process in L2 and cognitive activities and load undertaken by the test-takers. The specific features of the Chinese spoken language—e.g. speech rate, topic-prominence structure and discourse characteristics—create more challenges and difficulties for CFL learners during a listening test. Research has also revealed that vocabulary and strategic competence are important to the overall performance in the assessment of listening. Thus, a construct definition for assessing LCC is proposed based on the 'default listening construct' with subcomponents of competencies in the Chinese phonological system, lexis, syntax, discourse and pragmatics, assisted by strategic competence for understanding, retaining and inferring the information conveyed by the input. Four types of test items and tasks are also introduced to provide teachers, with techniques for developing CBA listening tests. They should be selected according to the construct defined. Suggestions for selecting the input materials are given to ensure that the assessment of LCC can be as authentic, valid and reliable as possible.

6.3 Assessing speaking competence in L2 Chinese (SCC)

The competence in speaking fulfils the task of communication in a spoken language. To assess speaking in an L2 is challenging because, firstly, it involves phonological control, listening comprehension and the ability to produce functional and purposeful utterances and dynamics in interactive discourse. Secondly, it is challenging because of the co-constructed discourse and the impact of the test-takers' characteristics and interlocutor effects on their performance (Fulcher, 2003; Lu, 2005; O'Sullivan, 2012). Thirdly, the different conditions provided by face-to-face, telephone or online interaction and the automated test could produce inaccurate interpretations of the performance on speaking tests (O'Sullivan and Green, 2011).

Therefore, it is vital to understand the process of an L2 speaking test and the elements and factors involved in the process (see Figure 6.2). Compared to the process of summative CBA described in Chapter 3, there are several differences

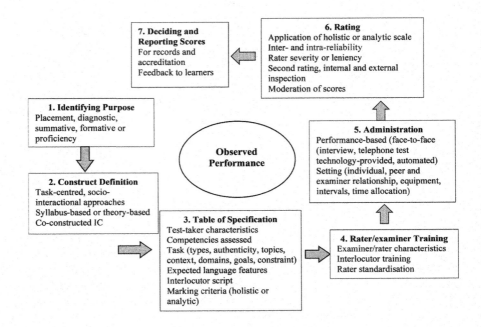

Figure 6.2 The Process and Elements Involved in an L2 Speaking Test

between the two processes for developing an achievement test consisting of sections on reading, grammar and writing and a speaking test consisting of only tasks to elicit performance of speaking ability. Firstly, *Observed Performance* is at the centre of the process and the focus of all the different stages for developing a speaking test. This is also the difference between a speaking and writing test and the tests of listening and reading, whereby better evidence is provided for the learners' competence (Green, 2014). Secondly, as it is the performance at the centre of assessment, task-centred and socio-international approaches for defining the construct would be most relevant if the learning objectives or levels of proficiency are the concern for a speaking test. In addition, as interactive tasks are often used, international competence (IC) is critical to the performance and needs to be specified for an assessment. Thirdly, more consideration should be taken for test-taker characteristics (e.g. ages, genders, personalities, cognitive styles, affective schemata, experiential backgrounds and familiarity with the culture of the target language, etc.) as they significantly influence their performance on a speaking test, especially when they are doing an interactive task. At the same time, the rater/examiner characteristics must be given attention, too, as their cultural and educational background and experience as an examiner can also significantly impact their performance as an interlocutor and rater. Accordingly, a test or interlocutor script is necessary to standardise the performance of the interviewer/

interlocutor during a face-to-face setting. Moreover, examiner/rater training should be held before the administration of an oral exam because the judgement of the performance, usually in the form of a score or grade, is decided at the examination. Though not in the figure, post-test validation studies should also be conducted if the speaking test is a high-stakes summative assessment and will be administered in future.

Defining the construct for assessing speaking competence in L2 Chinese (SCC)

Recent research suggests that there have been mainly two approaches to define the construct for assessing oral proficiency in L2, psycholinguistic individualist and sociolinguistic interactional (Roever and Kasper, 2018). The former shares the basic principles with the trait-based approaches discussed in Chapter 1 and regards fluency, pronunciation, lexical resources and grammatical range as the categories of salient features of spoken language. This approach proposes that the competence in productive spoken language consists of the following (Hulstijn, 2011c):

1   The *core components* of linguistic cognition (knowledge and speed) in the phonetic-phonological, morphological, morphosyntactic and lexical domains
2   The *periphery components* of metalinguistic knowledge, knowledge of various types of discourse and strategic competencies

A series of empirical studies have supported such a construct definition for assessing speaking competence, revealing that two distinctive features in L2 learners' speech account for 75% of the variance of their performance on speaking tests, the declarative knowledge of phonology, grammar and vocabulary, and the speed for processing linguistic information (Hulstijn et al., 2009; De Jong et al., 2012. See details in Chapter 2.5). Wu and Ortega (2013) find this construct definition, though a rather narrow definition for describing a full profile of oral communicative competence, is sufficient for discriminating L2 learners for different proficiency levels. Therefore, most of the high-profile ESL and CFL speaking tests such as IELTS, TOEFL, the ACTFL Chinese Oral Proficiency Interview (OPI, hereafter) and HSK speaking exams have assessed a combination of fluency, pronunciation, lexical resources, grammatical range and topic development in the test-taker's performance on speaking tests.

However, Roever and Kasper (2018: 332) point out that the psycholinguistic-individualist approach pays 'little attention to situational and social context of language use' and employs tasks only for obtaining a ratable amount of speech rather than the evidence for the overall competence, in which IC is indispensable. The sociolinguistic-interactional approach, on the other hand, emphasises learners' purposeful choices of linguistic resources and the effects on other parties in the spoken discourse and assesses the appropriateness, conventionality and effectiveness of their utterances. Nonetheless, there are challenges to testing learners' IC due to two factors, interlocutor effect and

150 *Assessing Pinyin and spoken language competence in L2 Chinese*

co-constructed interactive discourse, which make it difficult to differentiate what, in the test-takers' performance, contributes to IC and what their language deficiency is failing them task completion (Roever and Kasper, 2018). In the following example, an episode from an oral interview to assess SCC can demonstrate this.

Example 6.15: (E = examiner, L = learner; (:) in the transcription represents a short pause.)

  Turn 1/E: 中国人喜欢六，八。还有别的吗？ (The Chinese like numbers six and eight. Any others?)
  Turn 2/L: 有，他们也喜欢七和九。 (Yes, they also like numbers seven and nine.)
  Turn 3/E: 它们都象征什么？ (What do they symbolise?)
  Turn 4/L: 什么？象 (:) 什么？ (What? *Xiàng* what?)
  Turn 5/E: 它们有什么意思？ (What do they mean?)
  Turn 6/L: 谢谢。七有 (:) 往上去，走 不对 嗯 成 (:) 成功 (:) 成功的意思。 九是 (:) 是很长时间的意思 (Thank you. Seven means (:) go up, walk, no, er success (:), successful (:) it means successful. Nine (:) means a very long time.)

Until Turn 4 of the discourse, the CFL learner who is learning Stage 4 as standardised by the ICCLE benchmark has done well in the discourse with an interlocutor examiner. The performance started to be 'problematic' when the learner could not understand the word 象征 in Turn 5 used by the examiner, which is beyond the learning objectives. After applying the meaning-negotiation strategy, the learner continued in the discourse and started to search his vocabulary to express the symbolic meanings of 七 and 九 in Turn 6, with pauses, hesitation and inaccurate words. The self-monitoring and compensation strategies were also applied. However, will the apparent lack of vocabulary be interpreted as evidence of a lack of competence? Will the applied negotiation, self-monitoring and compensation strategies be taken as IC for the co-constructed discourse? Roever and Kasper (2018) argue that episodes such as Example 6.15 highlight the interlocutor effects in OPIs that either facilitate or limit the learners' performance which may underestimates their competence because of expressed difficulty in understanding.

Therefore, the construct definition for assessing SCC must acknowledge the CFL learners' IC, which includes the routines in conversations that both native speakers and L2 speakers carry out for effective communication. According to recent studies (Schegloff, 2006; Roever and Kasper, 2018; Batenburg et al., 2018), those routines are as follows:

- Opening exchanges or new topics by asking for or providing information, and using preliminaries before making a request
- Distributing turns by asking and answering questions or responding to other speakers' turns

Assessing Pinyin and spoken language competence in L2 Chinese 151

- Repairing problems in communication by checking own and others' understanding, clarifying meanings, correcting own or others' mistakes and applying compensation strategies
- Organising longer stretches of speech by maintaining topics through extending and elaborating ideas

In summary, defining the construct for assessing SCC should apply both primarily psycholinguistic-individualist and the sociolinguistic-interactional perspectives, integrating the core linguistic components and the periphery components of metalinguistic knowledge. Moreover, Bygate (1987) points out that speech is a 'real-time' phenomenon formulated and articulated with considerable speed and fast planning so that the 'automaticity' of speech production in an L2 is expected in the learners' performance in both interactive and monologue discourses, which relies on linguistic accuracy and fluency of speech.

Research on the assessment of SCC has investigated mostly the relationship between pronunciation, vocabulary (breadth and depth), grammar (accuracy and complexity) and fluency (speech rate, hesitations, pauses, and false), and the scores awarded for overall performance on oral proficiency tests (e.g. Yuan, 2010; Jin and Mak, 2012). It has been suggested that there is a positive correlation between the CFL learners' SCC and their fluency and accuracy in spoken Chinese, though the correlation between the overall proficiency levels and grammatical complexity is inclusive. As expected, those studies have adjusted the measures to assess the accuracy, fluency and complexity of L2 speech in Chinese. Those adjustments are as follows:

1 The fundamental analysis unit for Chinese pronunciation is defined as a syllable comprising an initial, a final, and a tone.
2 Systematic segmentation specifications are employed for measuring word tokens and types.
3 Instead of using the T-unit, the Terminal Topic-Comment Unit is created to analyse grammatical accuracy and complexity.
4 Instead of using the number of words to measure fluency, the number of syllables is employed.

A substantial amount of research has also been done on CFL learners' interlanguage pragmatics by comparing their performance before and after studying abroad on applying speech acts for requesting and making and responding to a compliment (Taguchi et al., 2013; Li, 2012; Jin, 2012, 2015). They have suggested that the learners, in general, produce or respond with more appropriate targeted speech acts after a period of studying abroad. However, little research has been conducted on the relationship between the CFL learners' IC performance and their overall oral proficiency. Worth mentioning is the study by Tsai and Chu (2017) which shows that native speakers, heritage learners and CFL learners use different amounts of discourse markers in their oral production. Native speakers use the most, and heritage learners use more than the CFL learners, showing that the learners perform much less topic development, topic shifting, lexical retrieval, conceptual sequence and turn holding.

Thus, based on the reviewed approaches for defining the construct for the assessment of L2 speaking and the studies on SCC, the following components of the construct for assessing SCC are identified (see Table 6.3).

Table 6.3 Construct Definition for Assessing SCC

Construct for assessing SCC	Subcomponents of competence
Linguistic Competence	*Accuracy*: Pinyin and tones, intonation, grammar and vocabulary
	Discourse/textual competence: appropriate behaviours in interactive (opening and closing, adjacency pairs, turn-taking) and monologue (cohesion and rhetorical organisation) discourse
	Pragmatic and sociolinguistic competence: appropriate and accurate use of language functions, register, formality and tone to establish identity and situational sensitivity with topical and cultural knowledge
Speed for Processing Information	*Real-time automaticity:* fast planning and prompt speech production
	Fluency: fewer hesitations, repetitions, false starters, self-correction, re-selecting vocabulary and restructured sentences
Interactional Competence	*Initiating* topics by asking for or providing information, and using preliminaries
	Distributing turns by initiating and responding
	Repairing problems in communication by checking, clarifying and confirming, correcting mistakes, and applying compensation strategies
	Sustaining in the discourse by extending and elaborating topics
Communication Strategies	*Applying achievement strategies:* paraphrase, word coinage, cooperative strategies, and avoidance strategies on form or function

Tasks for assessing SCC

Two types of tasks for assessing L2 spoken competence have been researched extensively and debated: *direct* and *indirect* tasks. The former is perceived as a real-world and authentic task that elicits performance for reality. The latter is not a real-world task, though it may indicate the potential for performance in reality. Wang (2011) examined the speaking tests of the New HSK exams and concludes that direct tasks such as OPI, role play, simulation and discussion for assessing L2 Chinese speech elicit performance of communicative competence and provide the test-takers with opportunities to meet the demand of the task based on their linguistic knowledge. They also offer examiners opportunities to intervene in the interaction when the learners deviate from the expected performance. However, the disadvantages are that it is difficult to be sure that they elicit the expected performance based on the construct for assessment. To Wang (ibid.), this is because (1) the CFL learners' oral production is often constructed with personal choices of the language resources available in the vocabulary and the range and complexity of the grammatical structures, resulting in a situation that a task originally designed for a specific proficiency level actually elicits the performance of higher or lower levels; (2) a learner's performance is affected by other parties in an interactive task who cannot fulfil the task demands, which resembles the situation presented by Example 6.15; (3) with a large population of test-takers, the practicality of direct tasks is not ideal due to cost and time, the recruitment of oral examiners and the vigorous training programmes for them to improve inter- and intra-rater reliability, which has been introduced and discussed in Chapter 3.5.

Indirect tasks (e.g. reading aloud, mimicry/repeating sentences, making sentences with words heard, answering questions heard, retelling messages or stories) have been considered cost-effective, saving time and being easy to administer for both CPT and CBA speaking tests. In comparison to direct tasks, the rater reliability can be more controlled as scoring is usually done without face-to-face interaction, and recently more online speaking tests have been provided to make assessments more accessible, cost effective and comparatively easier to administer and rate. Therefore, in recent years, some CPTs have provided speaking tests with more indirect tasks to elicit performance on the discrete-point construct of competence in spoken Chinese. The issue is that indirect tasks do not provide information for what the language learners can do in real-world. Instead, 'an inference is made from on more artificial tasks' (Davies et al., 1999: 81).

Authenticity is a critical issue for the validity of the assessment of L2 speaking, according to Bachman and Palmer (1996). They recommend that both 'real-world' authenticity and interactional authenticity be employed to endorse practicality and construct validity. McNamara (1996) distinguishes tasks of the strong or weak version of authenticity for assessing the actual or potential competence for target language use. Assessment of SCC has applied both direct and indirect tasks by summative CBA and CPT speaking tests. Table 6.4 provides a list of the tasks presently employed by the CPTs, which presents a mixed picture of practice by the standardised testing of SCC.

The first observation is that most of the CPT speaking tests provide tasks with prerecorded audio or video of the examiner interlocutor delivered through the computer or online. Such task modes do not elicit the interaction through face-to-face or telephone modes. Test-takers do not have opportunities to manage and influence the discourse, which is certainly not co-constructed (Green, 2014; Galaczi and Taylor, 2018). As a result, it is unlikely they assess IC and some of the pragmatic and sociolinguistic competencies in spoken discourse, which is the most common mode of human interaction. Some computer-delivered or online speaking tests maintain that the interaction is similar to the co-constructed nature of face-to-face interaction, offering opportunities to examiners and learners to talk in time. However, studies have suggested that raters agree that the performance is different from that in the real world and the marking criteria for IC based on authenticity are difficult to apply for such tests (Davis et al., 2018). In other cases, research has suggested that examiners in online tests behave differently from those in the face-to-face mode so that the discourse features produced also differ, which

Table 6.4 Types and Modes of Tasks Used by the Speaking Tests of Chinese Proficiency Tests

CPT and Mode	Proficiency Level and Types of Tasks
HSKK Computer-delivered prompts	**Primary Level (CEFR A)** Listening and repeating Listening and responding Answering questions heard	**Intermediate Level (CEFR B)** Listening and repeating Describing pictures Answering questions heard	**Advanced Level (CEFR C)** Listening and retelling Reading aloud Answering questions heard
TOCFL Computer-delivered prompts	**Band A (CEFR A)** Answering questions heard Describing an experience and video clip	**Band B (CEFR B)** Describing experiences and a picture Stating opinions	**Band C (CEFR C)** Stating opinions Role playing Responding to viewpoints Summarising articles and expounding viewpoints
ACTFL OPI Face-to-face/telephone/ computer-delivered interaction	**Face-to-face OPI:** four stages to decide levels of test-takers' oral proficiency including warmup, level checks, probes and wind down **Computer OPI:** same stages plus a background survey to decide the topics and a self-assessment to determine the test for a broad level of the ACTFL standards
AAPIL Computer-delivered interaction	**Novice:** talking and answering questions on familiar topics **Intermediate:** talking, describing, discussing and asking questions on familiar topics **Advanced:** talking at length and expressing oneself on familiar topics and new concrete social, academic and general topics
AP Chinese Test Computer-delivered prompts	**The diagnostic test for five levels:** Interpersonal task: responding to thematically linked questions Presentational task: presenting a given aspect of Chinese culture
SCT Computer/telephone Automated	Reading aloud words and sentences, repeating sentences, answering short questions, recognising tones in words and sentences, building sentences and retelling a passage

undoubtedly will impact the learners' discourse (Nakatsuhara et al., 2017). Thus, teachers and test developers that consider computer-delivered tests to assess SCC for practicality and accessibility should be aware of the problem and ensure that the instrument-related reliability of their speaking tests is not affected.

The other observation is that tasks used by CPTs are mostly indirect, especially the tasks employed by HSKK and SCT, some of which are typically automated speaking tasks that measure the features of L2 learners' talk through the Automated Speech Recognition (ASR) systems which are designed with a 'decoder', the search algorithm, and three 'knowledge sources', namely the lexicon, language model and acoustic models. This approach for assessing speaking is drawn from a psycholinguistic construct known as 'facility in L2' and 'mechanical' language skills (Bernstein et al., 2010: 356), the two building blocks of the core spoken language ability independent of social skills, intelligence, academic aptitude or charisma. Although automated tests are intended to reduce the rater and interlocutor variability mentioned earlier, doubts and challenges have been expressed to its capacity for assessing IC and competence on authentic tasks (Galaczi and Taylor, 2018) and the reliability of automated scoring (Xi, 2012).

A comprehensive study by Beijing University and Pearson (2014) on SCT developed by Beijing University and Pearson was conducted to verify the construct validity and reliability of automated scoring. The test uses a speech recogniser to measure the grammatical correctness of learners' responses and the occurrences of expected vocabulary, the latency of the speech features of the responses, rate of speaking, position and length of pauses and phonemes produced by 1,822 native speakers and 3,554 CFL learners of seven first languages. The results suggest that the test succeeds in discriminating the performance of different abilities in L2 spoken Chinese with satisfactory internal reliability and concurrent validity with those of HSKK and the OPIs provided by the U.S. government Interagency Language Roundtable speaking scale. The study also shows that the SCT automated scoring strongly correlates positively with that of expert human rating.

Interests in the indirect task with the psycholinguistic approach by assessment of SCC can also be observed by the studies of the Elicited Imitation Test (EIT). EIT, a task that requires test-takers to repeat sentences heard, is found to be a valid test method to predict L2 learners' overall oral proficiency in English and other languages (e.g. Ortega et al., 2002; Erlam, 2006). For assessing SCC, Zhou and Wu (2009) followed the test specification established by Ortega et al. and composed 30 sentences of 7 to 19 characters with a wide range of vocabulary and grammatical structures to investigate the relationship between performance on the EIT test and tasks requesting describing motion events, willingness to communicate and overall L2 Chinese proficiency (Wu, 2011; Zhou, 2012). They found a positive relationship between the two performances. Wu and Ortega (2013) take the study further by examining the relationship between the performance of heritage and CFL learners on EIT and a picture-prompted narrative task. They found that the higher the EIT score the students received, the better they performed on the narrative task.

The extensive application of indirect tasks by the CPTs could have been due to the findings of those studies. It may also be the case that those discrete-point constructs can assess the overall competence of speaking competence. However, further studies are necessary to draw any conclusion about the advantages and disadvantages of automated tests and indirect tasks for assessing SCC. At present, it is recommended that a variety of tasks be used to compensate for the disadvantage of one type of task with the advantage of another to realise the assessment purposes (Brown, 2004; Green, 2014). Interestingly, CFL classroom teachers have used more direct tasks to assess their learners' SCC, as suggested by the small survey I conducted in 2018 and 2019 (see Chapter 4.4). The participants reported that the top three tasks used for assessing lower-level learners' SCC are describing pictures, repeating sentences and role play, and those for higher-level learners are discussion, timed individual speech and interviews. This revelation is encouraging as CBA speaking tests have a greater impact on CFL learners. However, this means that the teachers must be trained to reduce interlocutor effect, and the standardisation of raters must be organised to improve reliability for valid assessment of SCC.

Examiner/rater training and rating scales for assessing SCC

Classroom teachers not only develop the tests for assessing SCC but also are the interlocutors, examiners and raters when speaking tests are administered to their students. For summative CBA oral exams, most institutes would require a second examiner and expect that they have both the acquired knowledge and competence for assessment (KCA, see Chapter 4.3). Training or standardisation of oral examiners/raters for both CBA and testing organisations, according to McNamara (1996), can ensure that the examiners' backgrounds, experiences and individual perceptions influence less their understanding of test constructs, use of tasks, interlocutor behaviour and application of marking criteria. The training sessions are important and can improve the inter- and intra-rater reliability for speaking tests. Brown (2012) discusses rater training extensively, and her recommendations are mostly related to the specific demands of the summative CBA. The following are based on Brown's discussion and adapted for the CFL context, which will benefit pre- and in-service CFL classroom teachers or raters for CPTs. In Chapter 3.5, rater training sessions are also introduced for general practice in the process of summative CBA. The following are specifically for examiner/rater training for assessing speaking.

1   *Start with a discussion of the purpose, construct, tasks, criteria and expected performance*
    Classroom teachers are different in their education, professional and personal backgrounds and KCA, which affect their understanding of the criteria selected, the implementation of the tasks and the interpretation of the observed performance. The native and non-native speaker examiners/raters could have differences regarding the expected performance from the same task. Therefore, a training session should start with discussing the purpose, construct, tasks, criteria and expected performance of a speaking test. For example, when assessing the learner's performance on the task in Example 6.15, some

Assessing Pinyin and spoken language competence in L2 Chinese 157

teachers may emphasise the importance of accurate and exact vocabulary used and fluent execution of the pronunciation and grammar called for by the task. They might neglect the learner's IC and communicative strategies employed, which are equally important for assessing, judging the performance as unsatisfactory because the learner does not know the word 象征 and the hesitation pauses produced. Therefore, it is always worthwhile to discuss the expected behaviour elicited by a task based on the construct for assessment and how exactly the marking scale can be used to evaluate the observation of behaviour. Only when they can visualise the performance of the competencies intended by a specific task can their rating meet the standards and reflect the learners' learning achievement or proficiency.

2   *Standardise interlocutor performance to reduce interlocutor effect*
The interlocutor effect can be a result of the examiners' different styles of speaking, e.g. teacherly or casual style (Brown, 2003), or the discourse preferences of native- or non-native oral examiners (Lu, 2005). Brown (2004) also finds that interlocutor examiners could ask test-takers the same questions with different wording, accommodate their speech to that of the learner (e.g. faster or slower, simple or complex structures, easy or difficult vocabulary), and probe or extend topics to different extents. Davies et al. (1999) add that the interlocutor effect can also be that they allocate a different number of turns and degrees of empathy given to different candidates. Therefore, the condition and spoken input to the test-takers will vary, and their performance will be different. They also adhere to the interlocutor script to different extents. As the teachers will be the interlocutor first in an oral exam, the training session, as Figure 6.2 shows, should be before the administration of a test to standardise interlocutor performance. Organising examiners to watch videos or listen to audio samples of examiners conducting interactive tasks is the most employed practice, followed by discussion. Another practice is to provide an *interlocutor script* to guide what and how the examiner should speak when conducting an interactive task. The moments in the video when the examiner departs from the script should be found, and the consequences can be recognised and discussed too. The following Dos and Don'ts as used by the British Council's VOTE: Oral Testing video (1983) will be also helpful.

- Maintain eye contact with the test-taker.
- Speak clearly and loud enough.
- Don't correct the test-takers' mistakes.
- Don't speak so quickly that it is difficult for the test-taker to understand.
- Don't speak too much.
- Don't be condescending (e.g. saying the test is hard for the test-taker).

The other source leading to interlocutor variability with negative impact is when examiners adjust their speech to suit the test-takers', whose

158 *Assessing Pinyin and spoken language competence in L2 Chinese*

performances are judged as below or above the expected performance. According to Lazaraton (1996: 19), those adjustments include the following:

a) Repeating, reformulating and rephrasing questions
b) Supplying alternative or easier vocabulary
c) Completing turns or sentences for the learners
d) Giving evaluative responses such as 'good'

Consequently, the input provided will be easier, potentially changing the construct for assessment and eliciting an unintended performance. Training sessions should address these interlocutor behaviours and help examiners to use the script provided. Otherwise, this type of interlocutor variability threatens the judgement of test-takers' performance and fairness of a test (Ross, 1992; Lazaraton, 1996).

3   Use rating scales as an integral part of training to improve inter- and intra-rater reliability.

Two types of rating scales for assessing L2 speaking have been widely used by proficiency and CBA oral tests: *holistic and analytic rating scales*. Both are usually drawn from the targeted competence descriptors or standards. However, the holistic scales provide only one global score or grade for test-taker performance. In contrast, the analytic scales provide several scores for different components of language competence (see Table 6.5 and 6.6). The total of the sub-scores is taken as the overall judgement of a test-taker's performance.

Table 6.5 Holistic Rating Scale for Performance on a Paired Role Play

Score	Performance Description
5	Impressive accuracy of Pinyin, grammar, vocabulary and fluency. Takes turns and speaks with appropriate speech acts. Uses necessary communicative strategies to lead in the interaction and contribute significantly to task completion.
4	Accurate Pinyin, vocabulary and grammar with occasional errors. Fluent in general. Takes most turns actively and appropriately. Tries to communicate and collaborate with the partner to complete the task, though not successful in all cases due to lack of language abilities and IC.
3	Sometimes difficult to understand and be understood because of language problems. Hesitates and pauses often hesitate to search for words and sentence structures. Passive in the interaction but tries to cooperate with the partner to complete the task.
2	Difficult to understand and be understood most of the time, causing communication breakdowns. Low accuracy and fluency. Fails to take turns frequently and is unable to repair in the interaction. The task was either not completed or completed by the partner.
1	Not able to understand the partner. The partner cannot understand either. Produces very little meaningful output in the interaction. The task is not completed.

Assessing Pinyin and spoken language competence in L2 Chinese 159

When using a *holistic rating scale*, the examiners/raters consult the performance descriptions at different bands and decide which of them best matches the observed performance. Holistic scales are often designed and written according to the defined constructs and expected performance by a proficiency-test developer or the teachers on a language programme for CBA speaking tests. They should certainly be tailored for the different tasks (direct, indirect, semi-direct, etc.) to reflect the specific expected responses as task characteristics demand different sets of competencies. The holistic rating scale in Table 6.5, for example, is written for an interactive task requiring learners to demonstrate competence for taking turns in sequences of spoken discourse and specific components of IC and communicative strategies. It can be applied to assess the performance observed for the task in Example 6.16 (see p. 169).

Furthermore, examiners/raters need to know the advantages and disadvantages of the holistic and analytic rating scales to create or select their marking schemes to suit the tasks they have designed to assess learning achievements. Green (2014: 150) points out that when holistic scales are applied, there is 'a natural tendency to make a holistic judgement of learners' abilities in spoken language or a straightforward experience to the examiners/raters depending on their instinct which could be often accurate'. Nevertheless, though instinct may play a role, it is the examiners who are trained and experienced that provide reliable holistic scoring (Batenburg et al., 2018). Without training, inter- and intra-rater scoring reliability could be still at risk, even if it is an experienced teacher, as holistic scales consist of general descriptions that do not express the nuances of the expected performance on a specific task. The study by Li et al. (2019) finds that, when using a holistic scale to rate performance on L2 Chinese requests, refusals and compliments, though the examiners could agree on the scores awarded, their feedback to the learners was different and less informative as the impressionistic interpretation of the performance does not provide the specifics as constructively as expected.

Analytic rating scales, on the other hand, require not only several scores on different criteria for performance but also provide quantitative distinctions to reflect strong to weak performance (see Table 6.6). Different weightings are also allocated for each criterion, depending on the defined constructs for assessment as requested by tasks. The analytic scale in Table 6.6 is written to assess the performance on a monologue task, which differentiates the performance on five criteria. As the task

Table 6.6 Analytic Rating Scale for Performance on Monologue or Presentation Task

Criterion & Weighting	Score	Performance Description
PC 20%	5	Almost native speaker's Pinyin and tones.
	4	Accurate sounds with some inaccurate tones. It is not difficult to understand.
	3	Frequent tone errors. Difficult to understand in general.
	2	Constant mispronunciation and tone errors. Difficult to understand.
	1	Unintelligible sounds and incorrect tones most of the time.

(*Continued*)

160 *Assessing Pinyin and spoken language competence in L2 Chinese*

Table 6.6 (Continued)

Criterion & Weighting	Score	Performance Description
Vocabulary 20%	5	Accurate vocabulary in breadth and depth is appropriately used for the topic.
	4	Accurate vocabulary in adequate breadth and depth is sometimes used inappropriately.
	3	Limited vocabulary to express the ideas. Some are not used accurately and appropriately.
	2	Inaccurate and very limited vocabulary to express the ideas even in a simple way.
	1	Very few available words to express the ideas.
Grammar 10%	5	Very easy to understand with very few mistakes for both the basic and unique structures (BSs and USs).
	4	Accurate grammar with few mistakes for BSs; more errors for USs, though still easy to understand.
	3	Not easy to understand due to some misused BSs and most of the used USs.
	2	Difficult to understand for grammar mistakes in all aspects.
	1	Incomprehensible as no correct formulation of grammar structure produced.
Discourse Competence 20%	5	Coherent and well-organised speech with effective use of a wide range of cohesive devices (CDs) and unique Chinese textual features (UCTFs).
	4	Coherent and organised speech with appropriate use of CDs and some UCTFs.
	3	Generally coherent but not organised speech with some misused CDs and very few uses of UCTFs.
	2	Mostly incoherent speech with CDs most used incorrectly and no use of UCTFs.
	1	Incoherent and confusing speech with no correct use of CDs and UCTFs.
Fluency 20%	5	Speech naturally flows with one or two hesitations.
	4	Speech is overall fluent with a few hesitations and pauses to search for words.
	3	Speech is hesitant and frequently pauses to search for words or structures.
	2	Speech is overall slow and intermittent to organise thoughts and language.
	1	Speech frequently stops and is uncompleted.
Pragmatic Competence 10%	5	All appropriate register, tone and language functions are precisely applied. Cultural and topical references (CTR) are presented with desired idiomatic expressions and figures of speech (IEFS).
	4	Most appropriate register, tone and language functions are adequately applied. CTR are mostly presented with necessary IEFS.
	3	Some appropriate register, tone and language functions are adequately applied. Basic CTRs are presented with no IEFS.
	2	Minimum appropriate register, tone and language functions are applied. Little CTR and no IEFS are presented.
	1	Nearly no appropriate register, tone and language functions are applied. No CTR and IEFS is presented.

Assessing Pinyin and spoken language competence in L2 Chinese 161

is not interactive, the scale prioritises PC, Vocabulary, Fluency and Discourse competence as they are weighed more than Grammar and Pragmatic competence. The advantages of analytic scales are as follows (Green, 2014: 150):

a) Highlight the intended construct being assessed and encourage the examiners to focus on them
b) Improve reliability by differentiating performance across criteria expressed by a score profile
c) Enable examiners to observe performance with a mindset for multifaceted factors so that the strengths and weaknesses of the learners' language development are revealed
d) Provide informative feedback for both teaching and learning

Analytic rating scales are very useful as training instruments to help examiners/raters to understand and recognise the variety of features of the expected competence. The disadvantage is that such scales demand examiners to undertake more complex cognitive processes and workloads. It is, therefore, questioned if raters can differentiate several criteria quickly and accurately and arrive at a reliable and fair assessment of the learner's performance. For example, when an examiner rates a learner's oral production as shown by Example 6.16 with the analytic scale in Table 6.6, the rater will be very much challenged when listening to the learner, analysing the speech and deciding a score for each of the criteria. The challenges are as follows:

1 Quantitatively, it is hardly possible for the rater to be sure of the number of pauses, fillers or hesitations and mistakes made for Pinyin, grammar and vocabulary.
2 Qualitatively, time constraint does not allow a full analysis of the types of errors and inappropriateness produced on discourse, pragmatics, IC or communicative strategies.

Example 6.16:

嗯：如果你不认识我：我妈妈是中国人：嗯：跟：：一位英国人结婚了：嗯 所以 嗯 肯定 我爸爸： 想：： 学汉语 所以他： 会说汉语 嗯 因为： 见面的时候 他们都住在中国 嗯 我妈妈： 做了我爸爸的翻译 嗯 (laughing) 我爸爸嗯： 最好：： 嗯 学汉语的方法是： 做很多的中国朋友 嗯 ...

Notes of transcription:

a) Underlined: errors of grammar or vocabulary
b) : represents a pause shorter than two seconds; :: represent pauses of more than two seconds
c) 嗯: a filler
d) Italics: incorrectly pronounced or tonal mistakes

Therefore, recommendations have been given: (1) that analytical scales be written with no more than four or five criteria to reduce the cognitive workload for examiners/raters of speaking tests (Green, 2014); (2) that the rater use an analytic scale and the interlocutor examiner use a holistic scale (Galaczi and Khabbazbashi, 2016).

Rater severity and leniency are the main causes of unsatisfactory rater reliability, which can be resolved by using the mean score given to a group of learners or the multifaceted Rasch techniques (Fulcher, 2003). In CBA contexts, 'double rating' is another method to eliminate leniency and severity (McNamara and Adams, 1991), which is also known as 'second marking', as described by the process of summative CBA in Chapter 3. However, to prevent problems with rater reliability, rater training and standardisation is the first solution. The training can follow the following steps recommended by Fulcher (2003: 145):

1. Going through the criteria in the rating scale with the trainees to see if there are different interpretations of the expected test-takers' performance, followed by discussion and resolutions.
2. Asking the trainees to rate a set of the learners' oral production samples typical of each band in the rating scale used (e.g. five bands in Table 6.5 and Table 6.6).
3. Providing standardised scores for the samples marked by the trainees for them to discuss the differences, and individual feedback should also be provided.
4. Organising trainees to rate another set of samples to see if the scores given are converging to the standardised scores. This process can be repeated if the correlation is not satisfactory.
5. Concluding the training with a summary of the different interpretations of the rating scale and the harsh and lenient scoring produced. Confirming that the resolutions and censorship reached should be applied.

To conclude, this chapter starts with the discussion of assessing PC, which emphasises that competence for the tonal features of spoken Chinese is a critical component of PC as they decide intelligibility and the conveyance and enhancement of meanings. Furthermore, assessment of PC consists of testing the abilities for using digital or online dictionaries, transcribing Pinyin of the unknown words that the CFL learners hear during interaction so they can find the meanings. PC also plays an important part in assessing LCC and SCC, though competencies in listening comprehension and speaking involve much more complicated cognitive activities and real-time processing of information. They also consist of knowledge of vocabulary, grammar, discourse, pragmatics, IC, etc. in the receptive or productive mode. In addition, the characteristics of the Chinese spoken language as the input for the assessment of LCC can decide the item difficulty of a listening test. The tasks, on the other hand, must be designed to request the test-takers to apply top-down or bottom-up strategies for locating specific information and

Assessing Pinyin and spoken language competence in L2 Chinese 163

overall understanding. Research on assessing SCC has emphasised linguistic components and focused on the relationship between the CFL learners' levels of oral proficiency and the accuracy and fluency of learners' speech. IC and communicative strategies have been the much-expected competencies for SCC in the interactive discourse. The high-profile CPTs have employed more indirect tasks for speaking tests than the CBA of CFL programmes so that training and standardising the examiners/raters is vital to the validity and reliability of the assessment of SCC, which can help teachers to understand the construct, task, expected performance and holistic or analytic scales. This chapter has offered suggestions for the practice of developing PC tests and the assessment of LCC and SCC and application of holistic and analytic scales.

Further readings

1 Zhang, H. (2018) for a review of the research of Chinese sound acquisition as an L2. It is important to understand that assessment of PC needs to focus on suprasegmental features and lexical tones rather than on segmental features, vowels and consonants.
2 Chapters 1 and 5 in Buck, G. (2001). Chapter 1 discusses the processes of listening comprehension as an interaction between the L2 listeners' inferencing and hypothesising supported by their language competence and world knowledge, and the characteristics of the input for listening tests. Chapter 5 introduces the relevant aspects of creating tasks for a listening test.
3 Hughes (2003), Chapter 10, testing oral ability, for the procedure of developing speaking tests. Pay attention to the specified content and categorisation of the skills for assessing interactive discourse.

Reader activities

1 Examine the Pinyin tests on the following which you and your colleagues have designed or used for beginner learners who have studied your CFL course for one, two and three months:

   a) Are those tests designed to assess performance on both phonetics and tones? Is it the case that the tests for earlier learning stages are more focused on phonetics and those for later stages more on tones?
   b) Are the sandhi of T3, 不 and 一 and the tone pairs such as T1-T1, T4-T4, T2-T2, T1-T3, T2-T3, T2-T1 and T2-T2 also included in the tests?
   c) Do the tasks in the tests integrate characters or other language competencies?

2 You are designing a listening test for students at the advanced level (e.g. HSK Level 5 or 6, ACTFL Advanced High levels or TOCFL Band C) on your programme. The test is a summative assessment based on the taught

learning objectives. You need to refer to Figure 3.3 in Chapter 3. Complete the following table to assure the following:

- The constructs are closely related to the learning objectives to assess learning achievement.
- The listening processes reflect the constructs of competence.
- The tasks facilitate the performance expected.
- The marking criteria focus on learning achievement.

Competence Assessed	Input Text	Question/Task Types	Marking Criteria

3   Review the tasks you or your language programme have been using for assessing the speaking competencies of beginner, intermediate and advanced learners and decide on the following:

- The task types used for the beginner, intermediate and advanced learners
- The approaches for defining the constructs that the tasks are intended to assess
- The expected performance that the tasks are designed for
- The suitability of the rating scales applied for assessing the performance

4   Reflect on the following with a colleague or classmate on a postgraduate course:

- Do you think that your beliefs about language education, your teaching experiences and your educational and cultural background have influenced your scoring performance on speaking tests? What are they? And how have they influenced you?
- Do you usually give lower or higher scores to a speaking performance than your colleagues? What are the criteria in the rating scale that you feel are more important than others?
- How have you made sure that your scoring is consistent when you are an oral examiner for a group of pupils or students?

7 Assessing written language and orthographic competence in L2 Chinese

Assessing written language competence in L2 Chinese has been debated extensively since Chinese has become one of the major modern languages to teach/learn since the economic rise of China. As the script consists of logograms constructed with strokes, radicals, and sub-character components, those who read and write in Chinese undertake different cognitive processes from those who read and write phonographic writings. In the first part of Chapter 5, the special features of the Chinese script are introduced to explain the challenges for the assessment of vocabulary competence (VC). This chapter will focus on the characteristics and functions of the structures, components, radicals and strokes which contribute to the constructs for assessing orthographic competence (OC) in L2 Chinese. Since VC and OC are inherently involved in assessing reading comprehension and writing, the second and third sections of this chapter will discuss the constructs for assessing literacy in L2 Chinese and the techniques for assessments. Following the structure of Chapter 5 and 6, the sub-sections in this chapter will first identify and define the constructs for assessing OC and competencies in reading and writing in consultation with related research and studies. The conventional and recently developed techniques for assessing those competencies will be introduced with examples developed by CPTs and summative and formative CBA. Recommendations to improve validity and reliability are also given for assessments of receptive and productive abilities of written Chinese.

7.1 Assessing orthographic competence in L2 Chinese

Studies on teaching writing the Chinese script, as summarised by Zhang and Ke (2020), have focused on two issues: the best time to teach and how to teach the script. The two issues are important to assessing OC because if the time is delayed till learners have learnt Pinyin or teaching Pinyin and the script concurrently as some have recommended (e.g. Packard, 1990; Jiang, 2007), the assessment of OC needs to be adjusted to the learning objectives. If handwriting is not a priority of instruction for CFL beginner learners (Allen, 2009) or reading is taught more than writing (多认少写) (Jiang, 2007), the assessment of CFL learners' OC should also accommodate and emphasise VC and reading comprehension. If teaching practice focuses on 'converted writing' from Pinyin to characters on the keyboard

DOI: 10.4324/9781315167923-8

or digital screens (Xu, 2020), assessments should be computer-assisted rather than by pencil and paper.

Nevertheless, as Perfetti (2012) points out, learning and reading in languages generally depend on writing the written form regardless of the specific features of the orthography. In general, language-literacy education still starts with handwriting in the digital age. Children in schools learn their alphabet through handwriting and are judged on their literacy through paper-pencil assessments. Most first-year pupils of primary schools in China have been learning to write the characters on paper or by 'writing in the air' (a class exercise during which the teacher shows the stroke order of a character on the blackboard/whiteboard and the pupils follow the movement with their arms). Although they will type on computers and digital devices later for their education, assessments of their literacy levels are usually conducted by handwriting. Thus, it is questionable if the L2 learners of Chinese should do differently and learn the script by reading more, writing less, handwriting less and doing converted writing more. As research has suggested, delaying character instruction and emphasising reading could impede learning progress and the development of VC and OC in L2 Chinese (e.g. Everson, 2011a; Li and Ye, 2013). Furthermore, the studies mentioned in Chapter 2.5 should not be overlooked. They have suggested that there is a strong association between handwriting and word recognition, reading, and overall language development in Chinese.

Hence, as proposed by the CFL Model (see Chapter 2.5), OC in L2 Chinese discussed in this chapter refers to the competence for writing by hand on paper or the screens of electronic and digital devices rather than 'converted writing' on the keyboard. Composition with converted writing, however, is part of assessing the CFL learners' competence in productive written language and will be discussed in the third section of this chapter. Some CFL teachers and academics may disagree with such an approach due to concerns with the efficiency of classroom instruction in limited time (e.g. two to three hours on average per week for minor or optional CFL courses in UK universities, which has been generally considered less than necessary for learning Chinese). Others are worried that the learners, especially those at lower levels, will be frustrated and demotivated if the same amount of time is allocated to teaching writing the script as to reading, listening and speaking. Those views are concerning because research has shown that converted writing/ tying does not contribute to learning the meanings and forms of characters, especially the meaning in depth (Guan et al., 2015; Zhang and Min, 2019).

Identifying the constructs for assessing orthographic competence

Li et al. (2005) propose that two interacting mechanisms contribute to the role of logograph writing. One is *orthographic awareness*, which facilitates the development of coherent, effective links amongst visual symbols, phonology and semantics. The other is the established *motor activity* resulting in the pairing of hand-movement patterns with language stimuli. The awareness includes knowledge of the constituent elements of characters such as strokes and radicals and the components organised in a structure (Scrimgeour, 2011). The motor activity can help to establish long-term motor memory of Chinese characters, facilitating the consolidation process of lexical representations in the cognitive system and making mental organisations of written Chinese (Li et al., 2005; Zhang and Min, 2020). Furthermore, according to Guan et al. (2011: 510), a writing-related visual system is also crucial to writing characters. The coupling of visual and motor systems 'may help establish the spatial configuration of strokes and radicals, which along with a temporal sequence of motor movements associated with stroke composition, completely defines the shape of the character'.

In addition, to identify the constructs for assessing OC, we also need to specify what 'orthography' entails to OC in Chinese. The Cambridge English Dictionary defines 'orthography' as 'the accepted way of spelling and writing words'. In Chinese, 'orthography' means正字法 (rules for writing characters), which prescribes that people must write standardised characters in both the simplified and traditional versions. Variant characters or characters created individually and incorrectly written are not acknowledged and accepted (Shi, 2000). For the context of L2 Chinese education, Shi proposes three criteria for assessing CFL learners' OC:

1 Characters must be written with the correct types and number of strokes and the sub-character components (including radicals) constructing them.
2 Characters must be written with the correct structural relationship of the strokes and sub-character components.
3 A whole-character glyph must be used.

For example, when writing 药, learners need to write the radical 艹 (the semantic component meaning 'plant') on top of 约 (the phonetic component). Though the right part of 约, 勺 ('spoon'), is only one stroke different from 匀 ('even', 'evenly'), they should not be confused in writing. Further, none of the strokes in a character can be missing, and the logographic structure (top-bottom structure with a left-right structure for the phonetic component) should be completed in entirety and accurately.

Research has shown that as mastery of Chinese handwriting progresses from stroke, to radical and to the whole character (Wu et al., 1999), assessment of OC has also been based on criteria for local level on stroke and radical, and global level on shape and configuration of characters. Degrees of conformity at the two levels are judged for basic stroke-form correctness, radical correctness, conformity to the conventional shape and proper configuration (Taft et al., 1999; Wang and Xu, 1993; Guan et al., 2015). Specifically, the appropriate size and compactness of each stroke and radical, the conformity to a squared configuration and the accuracy of the component relationship are examined for the quality of CFL learners' OC.

Therefore, writing correctly all the elements in a character in a specific structure is required to meet the standards for orthography in addition to the learners' orthographic awareness and knowledge of the Chinese script. Firstly, strokes are the smallest elements in the construction of a character. The eight basic strokes

168 *Written language and orthographic competence in L2 Chinese*

are the vertical and horizontal line, dot, left-falling and right-falling line, rising line, hook and left curve (横, 竖, 点, 撇, 捺, 提, 勾 and 弯). The frequency of the first six strokes being used is 77.82 % amongst the other 31 strokes. There are also variant forms of strokes, e.g. a longer or shorter vertical line. Simple strokes such as those mentioned also combine to form complex strokes. For instance, there are three strokes in 勺, a shorter downward-left stroke on the left, a dot inside and a stroke called 横折钩 ㄱ, which is formed by a horizontal line, a left-falling line and a hook. Writing strokes in appropriate sizes and with required compactness is therefore critical to the correctness and intelligibility of a character. For instance, there are three left-falling strokes in 秋 (see Image 7.1). They are of different lengths and connected with the relevant strokes for a radical or the whole character.

Secondly, the construction of a character is configured in a square, which is divided further into another four squares as shown by Image 7.1 to regulate the different components in terms of positions. The four primary structures have been regarded as left-right, top-bottom, fully enclosed and half-enclosed, amongst which the first two construct 86.04 % of the Chinese characters (Shi, 2000). As Image 7.1 shows, 秋 (autumn) is in the left-right structure. On the left, it is 禾, a radical meaning 'grain' and denoting crops or harvest. 火, meaning 'fire', is on the right. Both components are of the same size in the square. Characters in the same structure may vary in size. Image 7.2 shows that 晴 (clear or sunny) is also in the left-right structure with two components. However, the radical on the left, 日 ('the sun' or 'day'), is smaller than 禾 in 秋. On the right, 青 has a top-bottom

Image 7.1 Structure and Components of 秋

Image 7.2 Structure and Components of 晴

structure and takes up more space in the square. Such variations include, for instance, equal left-right, small left-big right, etc. (Liu et al., Vol. 1, 2003).

Writing those seemingly slightly different strokes or components in a character is important for the quality of orthography produced by learners. Or they may change a character into another or make it a pseudo- or non-character. For example, if 我 ('I') is written without the left-falling stroke at the top on the left, it is 找, meaning 'to look for'. Pseudo - characters are formed by adding, deleting, or moving a stroke from one location to another within a character—e.g. if 药 is written with 艹 only on 勺, it is a pseudo-character because, although it is incorrectly written, it can still be recognised as 药. If 匀 is written instead of 勺 in 药, it is a non-character as it neither exists as a character nor is recognised as 药. To significantly reduce those three typical errors made by the CFL learners, Shi (2000) recommends that at the beginning and intermediate stage of learning, teaching should focus on developing learners' competence for recognising the differences between strokes and sub-character components and practising writing them as much as necessary.

Thirdly, stroke order has been considered an instrumental element for improving OC as it can assist learners to learn, memorise and write aesthetical, symmetrical and balanced characters (Sun, 2006). Studies have shown that when learners are taught to write in stroke order with repeated practice, it can stabilise the motor programmes in memory. Such memory can last for long periods, provide clearer mental representations and help learners write characters more efficiently and accurately (Flores d'Arcais, 1994; Guan et al., 2015). As a result, beginner CFL learners should be taught stroke orders and required to practise on square paper (see Image 7.3) and practise as many times as necessary for accuracy and memorisation. The basic stroke orders that have been widely recognised and taught, according to Liu et al. (Vol. 1, 2003: 44), are as follows:

1 Horizontal before vertical (e.g. 十)
2 Downward left before downward right (e.g. 人)
3 From left to right (e.g. 妈)
4 From top to bottom (e.g. 只)
5 From outside to inside (e.g. 月)
6 Outside before inside before closing (e.g. 国)
7 Middle before two sides (e.g. 小)

In summary, the constructs for assessing OC in L2 Chinese are presented in Table 7.1.

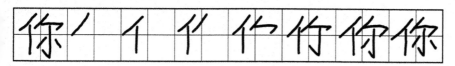

Image 7.3 Stroke Order of 你

170 *Written language and orthographic competence in L2 Chinese*

Table 7.1 Construct Definition for Assessing OC

Constructs for assessing OC	Subcomponents of competence
Orthographic awareness	1 Knowledge of the functions of strokes, radicals and components for the construction of characters 2 Awareness of the simple and complex strokes, variations of strokes and character constructions 3 Knowledge of orthography in Chinese (正字法), the standards for assessing OC at micro level (variant, created and incorrectly written characters are not acknowledged) and micro level (appropriated sizes and compactness of each stroke and radical and conformity to a squared configuration and accuracy of the component relationship)
Motor and visual competence	1 Can visually differentiate the sizes and correctness of strokes, radicals, components and characters configured in different constructions 2 Can visually differentiate characters not accepted in Chinese orthography and assess the extents of conformity at macro and micro level 3 Can write correctly strokes in required variations in appropriate sizes and connections 4 Can write radicals and character components in required sizes, shapes and constructions 5 Can write characters in conventional stroke order 6 Can write characters in squared specific constructions with components in required sizes and compactness

Tasks and techniques for assessing OC

Assessment of OC has been a priority for formative and summative CBA of the CFL programmes rather than for the Chinese proficiency tests. Especially, OC tests are usually designed and administered to beginner learners as PC tests have been. Some programmes provide a more extensive assessment of most of the competencies summarised in Table 7.1. Some, on the other hand, only concentrate on writing the whole character through dictation exercise, which emphasises the results of the visual and motor skills contributing to OC. The following examples demonstrate the techniques that examine both the learners' orthographic awareness and motor and visual competencies in writing the Chinese script.

Example 7.1: Draw a line between the radical and the component according to the meanings given. Then, you should write the characters on the lines.

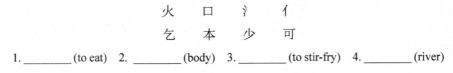

1. _____ (to eat)   2. _____ (body)   3. _____ (to stir-fry)   4. _____ (river)

Example 7.1 tests if the learners have the orthographic awareness about not only the functions of radicals to the semantic meanings of characters but also

Written language and orthographic competence in L2 Chinese 171

the constructions of those characters. The questions also assess if they know the propositions of the components and can express the differences in handwriting. For instance, although 口 and 火 are two independent characters, they are the semantic radicals for 吃 and 炒 and should be written as the smaller components. Example 7.2, on the other hand, examines learners' knowledge and visual competence for recognising variant characters and characters created individually and incorrectly written. Furthermore, it examines their ability to judge if the characters are written with the correct strokes and components in appropriate sizes and compactness in the correct structural relationships. For example, 谢 should be written with compactness between the three components, 昨 has a smaller left part and the second left-falling stroke in 听 is too long and not in the appropriate size. Example 7.3 looks at whether the beginner learners can identify simple and combined strokes and the various forms of the same stroke.

Example 7.2: Circle the incorrect characters in the pairs of handwritten characters based on the meanings given.

1. cry 哭 哭	2. bed 床 床	3. electricity 电 电
4. fruit 果 菓	5. thank 谢 谢	6. tea 苶 茶
7. rest 休 体	8. yesterday 昨 昨	9. listen 听 听

Example 7.2 Correctly and Incorrectly Written Chinese Characters

Example 7.3: Give your answers on the lines to the following questions about the characters.

1   How many strokes are there in the characters?
2   What are the same strokes in each character if there is any?
3   Write down the same strokes in each character which may vary.

国　1 _____ 2 _____ 3 _____
笔　1 _____ 2 _____ 3 _____
九　1 _____ 2 _____ 3 _____
弟　1 _____ 2 _____ 3 _____
账　1 _____ 2 _____ 3 _____

Examples 7.4, 7.5 and 7.6 prioritise assessment of the motor competence for writing characters. Example 7.4 requires the learners to write the characters consisting of different components in a squared structure so that their performance is shown for OC (边, 泳, 童, 国, 唱, 拿, 间 and 病), with the correct strokes in prescribed sizes and compactness in the appropriate structural relationship.

Example 7.5 is usually a typical exercise or homework for those who learn handwriting characters. Such questions in FA can effectively demonstrate the learner's competence for writing symmetrical and balanced characters and reveal whether they have clearer mental representations of characters associated with long-term memory. Nonetheless, Example 7.6 is the ultimate test item for assessing OC by judging conformity in writing at local (stroke and radical) and global (shape and configuration) levels. In addition, such questions can also reveal the learners' PC and indicate if they have the grammatical knowledge to form the sentences (他们叫什么名字? 我的汉语老师很忙。这是北京大学。).

Example 7.4: The following groups of strokes, radicals or characters make up eight characters you have learnt. Form them into the characters in the squares.

1 辶 力   2. 氵 永   3. 立 里   4. 口 玉   5. 口 日 日   6. 人 一 口 手
7. 门 日   8. 广 丙

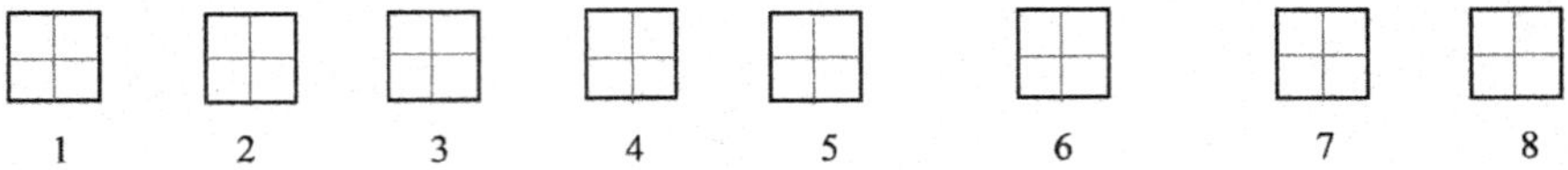

Image 7.4 Stroke Order of 你

Example 7.5: Write the following characters in stroke order on the squared paper provided.

你   爸   知   是   做

Example 7.6: Write the characters on the lines according to the Pinyin provided.

1 Tāmen jiào shénme míngzì?
2 Wǒ de hànyǔ lǎoshī hěn máng 。
3 Zhè shì běijīng dàxué 。

1 _____
2 _____
3 _____

In addition, dictation and cloze tests are integrative methods that assess OC. Dictation exercises of words, phrases, sentences or short passages certainly depend more on the learners' OC than the cloze tests. Not being able to write the characters will impede further assessment of VC, GC or DC. The more characters the learners can write, the more their responses can reveal their other competencies required. Cloze tests, on the other hand, also involve understanding the provided text so that decisions are made to provide the missing words. Therefore, it is less challenging to the learner's ability in OC than dictation. However, cloze test items to assess

OC in L2 Chinese need to be provided carefully so that the expected response is not in the text provided. In Example 7.7, for instance, the expected response for (3) is 教室 (classroom). However, as 教 has been presented in 教学楼, the test-takers may copy, which could affect the reliability of the question as the expected responses are newly learned characters.

Example 7.7: Fill in the blanks with one- or two-character words to complete the following text.

我们学校的办公楼和 (1) _____ 馆楼都不大，但教学楼很大，一共有六 (2) _____，有五十多个 (3) _____。教学楼里还有一 (4) _____ 咖啡厅和小超市，所以同学们都 (5) _____ 在教学楼里学习。

Marking schemes for OC test items such as Example 7 has been another issue that affects the reliability of tests for assessing OC. Firstly, there have not been widely accepted marking criteria. Secondly, most teachers on the CFL programmes have judged their learners' performance according to their intuitive impression rather than a marking rubric based on the constructs for assessing OC. Thus, practical and user-friendly marking schemes must be created to apply for test items that assess OC. Since the test items for Examples 7.2, 7.3 and 7.5 provide the characters that the learners need to write, the marking schemes focus on orthographic knowledge or visual competence of OC. Examples 7.1, 7.4, 7.6 and 7.7, on the other hand, assess mainly the motor competencies, and a marking scheme for OC can be as follows (adapted based on Guan et al., 2015; Shi, 2000) if one score is allocated to a character accurately written by the test-takers. Undoubtedly, such rubrics should also be applied for composition in handwriting as one of the marking criteria.

1. At micro level:
   a) The total mark is deducted if a variant or created character is provided.
   b) Half a mark is deducted if a character is incorrectly written.

2. At macro level:
   a) 0.2 score is deducted for a stroke written with inappropriate size or recognisable distortion (e.g. 9 in Example 7.2).
   b) 0.2 score is deducted for a stroke variation incorrectly written (e.g. 3 in Example 7.2).
   c) 0.5 score is deducted for a radical or character written without required compactness (e.g. 5 in Example 7.2).
   d) 0.5 score is deducted for a character written without conformity to a squared configuration and the required variation of construction (e.g. equal left-right, small left-big right, etc.).
   e) 0.5 score is deducted if a character is written with an incorrect component relationship (e.g. 7 in Example 7.2).

This part has discussed what is required of the CFL learners' OC, orthographic awareness and motor and visual competence and the measures for assessment of the competence. The techniques are unique and must rely on the teachers' creativity to design tasks that reflect the subcomponents of OC. As there has not been a standard marking scheme, the construct definition for assessing OC and the marking schemes employed by studies on writing the script will be most useful to refer to when setting up OC assessments.

7.2 Assessing reading comprehension in L2 Chinese

Similarly to the assessment of listening comprehension, reading comprehension is the other language ability that does not manifest itself directly for observation (Hughes, 2003). As competence in reading involves language competencies in grammar, vocabulary, discourse and pragmatics, the assessors must ensure that test items are designed to assess reading rather than other language competencies. Therefore, to define the construct for assessing reading in L2 Chinese, it is important that we understand the reading comprehension process in Chinese, especially how the CFL learners complete reading tasks. This part will first discuss the process of reading in Chinese and the cognitive activities engaged, followed by a presentation of the construct for assessment. Measures and techniques will be introduced to examine the CFL learners' competence in understanding written information.

Reading processes in L2 Chinese

Some have hypothesised that reading in Chinese is a strictly visual form-to-meaning process because of the specific characteristics of the Chinese script (e.g. Chen et al., 1988), suggesting that phonology may not be involved when a word or text is decoded. On the contrary, studies have shown that reading in Chinese is essentially consistent with the identification-with-phonology hypothesis for reading in alphabetic languages. This is because 'in Chinese, the elementary unit is also a spoken syllable that happens to be a morpheme, often a word' (Perfetti et al., 2005: 45; Shen and Ke, 2007). The difference, though, is that phonological activation for reading in alphabetic languages occurs at the pre-lexical level which leads to word identification, while for reading in Chinese, phonological activation occurs at the lexical level, where both graphic (character) and phonological information (syllable) is activated at the same time. For example, when reading 渔, a one-syllable word, the reader would recognise a radical on the left that means 'water' and a phonetic component meaning 'fish' on the right. Then, the reader can recognise that 渔 possibly means 'catching fish in water'. If the next character is 夫 ('a male', 'husband', etc.), it refers to 'fishman'; if it is followed by 业 ('trade', 'profession', 'business', etc.), it refers to the job or industry of fishing.

Word recognition is certainly essential to reading in Chinese and CFL learners' reading comprehension. Yet, does this mean the processes of reading Chinese, the competencies and strategies are very different from those for reading in other languages? Shen (2019) reviewed research on reading in L2 Chinese and summarised that in general, reading in Chinese and alphabetic languages both rely on the development of phonological and morphological awareness and share the bottom-up, top-down and interactive processes. Contextual information and the learners' prior language experience are also critical to reading comprehension. However, she argues that the unique linguistic features of the Chinese script restrain reading in L2 Chinese, which results in some differences in cognitive and non-cognitive processing and delays the development of morphological awareness essential to reading comprehension.

Firstly, reading Chinese requires a word-segmentation processing stage which is absent in alphabetic languages. As introduced in Chapter 5, Chinese texts consist of sentences with no space between words of one, two, three, four or even more characters so that readers must group relevant characters into lexical units to make sense of a text. For instance, when reading 星期六 我们去看电影 吧? The reader must correctly separate the characters into six units, 星期六, 我们, 去, 看, 电影, 吧, to apply their other linguistic knowledge to understand the sentence. Secondly, the many homophones and multi-meaning free morphemes in Chinese (e.g. 的 and 得, 厉害 and 利害, etc.) encountered by readers challenge further the readers' ability to use contextual cues for lexical access and process sentences (Shen, 2019). Thirdly, the degree of semantic transparency is another factor that affects access to word meanings (e.g. 欢乐 and 快活, 懂 and 明白) and can cause misunderstanding a sentence or part of a text (Li and Li, 2008). Fourthly, synonyms and near synonyms such as 感动 and 感激, 安静 and 宁静, and 故乡 and 家乡 affect the accuracy of reading comprehension, and according to Zhang and Jiang's study (2015), the ability to differentiate the meanings of synonymous could predict the reading competence of the intermediate and advanced CFL learners. Finally, the learners' linguistic backgrounds, the character- or non-character background in the CFL context, also assist or restrain lexical access to reading in Chinese (Jiang and Fang, 2012). It has been well known that, when deciding on word meanings for reading comprehension, Japanese-speaking learners usually outperform those whose first languages are English, German, France, Spanish, etc.

Some may argue that reading in other languages also involves word decisions about homophones and multi-meaning free morphemes (e.g. 'source' and 'sauce', 'heel' and 'heal', 'brake' and 'break', etc.), degrees of semantic transparency (e.g. 'pigsty', 'strawberry' and 'hotdog') and differentiation of synonyms and near synonyms ('debate' and 'discuss', 'hungry' and 'peckish'). However, apart from the difficulties to recognise the characters that are learnt or unlearnt, CFL learners also undergo different reading processes while taking different strategies. Shen's study (2008) suggests that during the bottom-up process the CFL learners need to apply word-decision strategies such as matching target constituent characters to existing mental lexicon, combining semantic information of constituent characters and decoding the meaning of individual characters to derive word meaning. In the top-down process, strategies such as using contextual information and background knowledge are applied for word recognition. Thus, the interaction of the bottom-up and top-down approaches are both applied when the meanings of words are being decided during reading in Chinese.

A substantial amount of research for reading in English as a foreign language has been conducted about the components of skills associated with the bottom-up and top-down processes. As Hubley (2012) summarises, in the bottom-up process, readers decode the smallest linguistic units such as morphemes and words to larger grammatical structures at the sentence level. Therefore, the micro skills are assessed (Brown, 2004), which are the competence for discriminating the distinctive meanings of the graphemic and orthographic features and recognising and interpreting keywords, word orders, grammatical categories and patterns and their roles amongst clauses and discoursal functions. To complete the bottom-up process, readers also need to retain chunks of language in their short-term memory and comprehend writing with an adequate rate of speed. During the top-down process, the readers use their background or prior knowledge and experiences to 'guess' the written information. Therefore, the macro skills demanded and assessed are competence for recognising the rhetorical forms and communicative functions of written discourse, distinguishing literal and implied meaning by using background knowledge, identifying new and given information, contextual cultural references, etc. Furthermore, reading strategies, such as detecting purposes for reading, guessing meanings of unknown lexis, skimming, scanning, etc., are important for the top-down process (Hughes, 2003: 139).

However, most studies regarding the CFL learners' reading have been on word recognition (e.g. Taft et al., 1999; Ke, 1998; Shen, 2008; Shen and Ke, 2007), and a few have investigated the CFL learners' cognitive activities and strategies for reading beyond a lexical access level. Those studies have shown that (1) learners of different proficiency levels from non-character backgrounds undertake a much wider range of bottom-up or top-down strategies (Chang, 2011); (2) learners from character backgrounds, although having the advantage of applying the bottom-up subskills, are not in overall more competent than those from the non-character background (Li and Wang, 2017); (3) the learners of lower proficiency levels may outperform those at higher levels on top-down subskills such as understanding gist and implied information or recognising relevant meanings and inferring word meanings (Chen, 1999: 273), which suggests that Chinese readers 'rely heavily on a more diffused, context-dependent approach as opposed to a more focused, word-dependent strategy'.

Therefore, it seems that the CFL learners are sensitive to the cognitive demands imposed by the orthographic and linguistic structures of the Chinese language and adapt their processing strategies to comprehend the written information. In other words, to understand the written texts, CFL readers alternate bottom-up and top-down approaches and are engaged simultaneously with finding meanings in the larger stretch of text while attending to word recognition. The interaction of bottom-up and top-down strategies suggests that learners bring their background knowledge to the topics and the schemata about text types and genres to meet the task demand (Hubley, 2012). Such a reading process by CFL learners proposes that the construct definition for assessing the CFL learners' competence for reading comprehension must integrate the specific features of the Chinese written language, the characteristics of reading processes and the abilities demanded by the communicative purposes.

Defining the construct for assessing reading in L2 Chinese

The language-specific frameworks for Chinese language education, ICCLE and EBCL (see discussion in Chapter 2), define the constructs for competence in receptive written language and express them with Can-Do Statements. For example, the descriptions of overall reading competence by ICCLE (Hanban, 2014: 7) for Stage 2 (equivalent to CEFR A2) is to 'recognise basic characters, words, sentences and short textual materials, understand program requirements and gather relevant information from short textual materials'. This competence description has followed the principles of CEFR (CoE, 2018) and EBCL (2012b). Thus, based on the discussion about the reading processes in L2 Chinese and studies on the CFL learners' reading strategies, the constructs for assessing reading in L2 Chinese are defined as follows (see Table 7.2). When developing reading comprehension tests for learners of different proficiency levels on CFL courses, we should select the constructs in consideration of the purposes for assessments, the competencies assessed and the levels of proficiency.

The abilities applied for reading activities depend on the types of reading undertaken (Urquhart and Weir, 1998). When the reading tasks are reader driven, e.g. reading for specific information, the main competencies called for are those for top-down reading processes. When the reading purpose is to obtain certain specific information, the abilities needed are those mainly for bottom-up reading processing. Learners apply the abilities alternatively for bottom-up and top-down reading approaches, as discussed earlier. However, applying both approaches is not only for word recognition by the CFL learners but also for achieving different purposes for reading, e.g. reading for gist or specific details or references. Thus, the construct definition in Table 7.2, though defined as consisting of three components, is an interactive and cooperative operation during the process amongst the different components to understand texts at the local and global levels to complete the tasks. Furthermore, amongst the constructs defined, the use of domain knowledge is categorised as one of the subcomponents based on the interactionist approach to construct definition discussed in Chapter 1. For the reading tests by CBA, the graded themes, topics and domains as defined by the language frameworks and benchmarks are important for the specifications of tests. If the content of the input contains unfamiliar topics and themes, the validity of the assessment will be at a risk. Therefore, how to successfully implement the constructs for assessing reading will depend on the selected input, measures and techniques for designing the reading tasks for different purposes of assessment.

178 *Written language and orthographic competence in L2 Chinese*

Table 7.2 Constructs for Assessing L2 Chinese Reading Competence

Constructs of competence for reading	Subcomponents of constructs
Competence for bottom-up processing in reading	1 Have the required mental lexicon/graded vocabulary for the targeted proficiency or summative level 2 Can segment words in sentences into meaningful units 3 Know the meanings and use of known characters and words 4 Can interpret the meanings of unknown characters through applying orthographic awareness about radicals, semantic and phonetic components 5 Can decide the exact contextual meanings and grammatical functions of homophones, multi-meaning free morphemes, synonyms and near synonyms 6 Can understand word orders and variations and basic and unique sentence structures 7 Can distinguish different devices for cohesion and coherence, the specific features of topic chain, ellipsis, substitution, temporal sequence, foreground and background in Chinese texts 8 Can retain explicit meanings in short-term memory and at the required rate of speed to understand larger stretches of text
Competence for top-down processing in reading	1 Can decide the purposes for reading 2 Can apply background and domain knowledge to guess the meanings of unknown words or idioms 3 Can recognise and understand communicative functions, rhetorical forms, styles, register and references in different types of texts 4 Can understand through reasoning the logical connections between events or ideas presented 5 Can differentiate main and supporting ideas, new and given information and literal and implied meanings 6 Can apply culturally specific references to understand and interpret the context 7 Can use reading strategies such as scanning and skimming
Competence for interactive approach in reading comprehension	1 Can compensate for weakness in bottom-up or top-down processing of reading with the alternative approach 2 Can simultaneously engage with the understanding of long stretch of text at the global level and local level on the orthographic, lexical and grammatical details of texts

Designing tasks to assess reading in L2 Chinese

To ensure the validity and reliability of the assessment of reading, four elements are essential for designing a reading comprehension test: *learner characteristics*, *construct(s) for assessment*, *texts selected*, and the *tasks employed* to generate the expected responses. They are also the main contents in a table of specifications for writing a reading comprehension test. In Figure 7.1, the relationship between those four elements is presented and their specifics are also listed. Firstly, as the figure shows, successful implementation of the four elements of a reading test will

Written language and orthographic competence in L2 Chinese 179

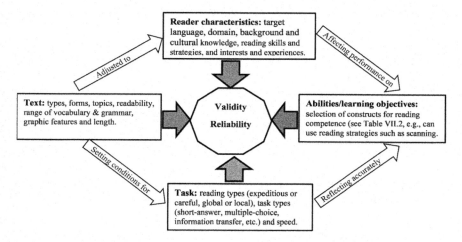

Figure 7.1 The Relationship Between the Elements Important for Assessing Reading Abilities

contribute to the validity and reliability as indicated by the shaded arrows. Secondly, learner characteristics affect their performance of competencies, which is elicited by the tasks that should reflect accurately the construct(s) for assessment, syllabus or theory based. Thirdly, tasks for different types of reading and of different types with different demands of speed are conditioned by the texts selected. The conditions for the tasks vary with the types, topics, lengths and readability in terms of linguistic features, etc. The selection of the texts, however, depends on the learners' characteristics, including what they have learnt in the target language, domains, reading skills, background knowledge, etc.

There have been some concerns or misconceptions about the four elements when writing a test to assess reading in L2 Chinese. Some CFL teachers and CPT developers have been worried that it is unfair to test the reading competence of the learners from both non-character and character backgrounds with the same test. Therefore, the condition provided for the tasks is changed by adding Pinyin to the text or the unknown vocabulary. In a way, consideration of the learner's characteristics has greatly changed the construct for assessment and the difficulty level of the test. Such practice has seemed welcome due to the perception that Pinyin and characters coexist as the script of the written language (DeFrancis, 2006) and reading and writing can be taught later (Allen, 2009) or even through a 'penless' method (Xu and Jen, 2005). That some high-profile CPs have used both Pinyin and characters in their reading tests for lower levels of proficiency (e.g. HSK Level 1 and 2) has seemed to support such practice.

Teachers of CFL programmes have also been challenged by two things. It is nearly impossible to select or write a text for a reading test for learners who have achieved Stage 1 or Stage 2 (CEFR equivalent are A1 and A2) because they learn only 150 or 300 characters. With such amounts of learnt vocabulary and a limited range of grammatical structures and discourse devices, it is a struggle to produce coherent texts for assessment. The solution has been to provide both Pinyin and the meanings of any unknown characters in the text. Nonetheless, reading new vocabulary is part of the real-world task. No one starts reading in any language after they have learnt all the vocabulary, which has called for an important competence through the top-down strategies to guess the meanings of unknown vocabulary and decide the contextual meanings. In reality, the learners can accomplish such tasks for reading comprehension. The question is whether the test writer can utilise the learner's previous knowledge for understanding a text with some new vocabulary. Example 7.8 can demonstrate such a case where the learners of Stage 1 have not learnt '男' (*nán*, male) and are asked to guess and decide the contextual meaning of the character.

Example 7.8:
   Test-takers read: 他姐姐的男朋友不是中国人，他很高，在我们学校学汉语。
   Question: Answer the following questions in English.

1 Who is very tall?
2 What is this person learning?

The other challenge to teachers who are writing reading tests for learners at higher proficiency levels is they are often not sure if unknown vocabulary should be in the texts. If they can, how many can be included? According to Hubley (2012), dealing with unfamiliar words is a norm in L2 reading. However, the amount should be restricted to 5%–10% of the total word count of a selected text for assessment, which should also be applied to reading in Chinese. The test writers should also consider the other textual features such as reading types because they also provide the conditions for tasks. If the question demands understanding at the global level for expeditious reading, knowing all the vocabulary is not necessary. On the contrary, if understanding at the local level for careful reading is required, the vocabulary for the specifics is essential. To demonstrate, Example 7.9 is selected from Boya Chinese, Intermediate II (Li et al., 2006: 120) and two questions, one short-answer question and a multiple-choice task, are written.

Example 7.9:

   Test-takers read: 轻的泪，是人的泪，而动物的泪，却是有重量的泪。那是一种发自生命深处的泪，是一种比金属还要重的泪。也许人的泪中还含有虚伪，还有个人恩怨，而动物的泪里却只有真诚，也只有动物的泪，才更是震撼人们灵魂的泪。第一次看到动物的泪，我几乎是被那一滴泪惊呆了。

Questions

1 Why does the writer say that animal tears have weight?
2 Choose the correct answer.

The writer feels that _____.
   a) As animal tears have weight, they show more sadness than human tears.
   b) Human tears may not be as sincere and moving as animal tears.
   c) As animal tears are heavier than metals, they are from the bottom of the heart.
   d) Human tears are more shocking than animal tears at the first sight.

The text has 78 characters if the repeated characters such as 的, 是, 泪, 人, 一, etc. are excluded. The words beyond the learning objectives for Stage 5 are 虚伪, 恩怨, 真诚, 震撼 and 灵魂, though there are characters that the students have learnt, e.g. 真, 诚, 震 and 灵. Thus, the text contains approximately 7% unknown vocabulary. The two questions are written in English to assess the learners' abilities for, firstly, deciding the purpose for reading, which in this case is expeditious reading for the main ideas. To answer the first question, they must understand the first two sentences rather than a particular word or expression. Moreover, the first part of the second sentence, 那是一种发自生命深处的, does not contain a new word for the learners. The stem of the multiple-choice question asks for the overall feeling of the author, for which the learners need to differentiate the main and supporting ideas in the passage and understand the implied meanings. During this process, they can find the correct answer, b, without having to know the exact meanings of those unknown words. This type of reading and the questions designed both assess other reading competencies rather than knowing the contextual meanings of unknown vocabulary.

The third debate that the CFL teachers have been undertaking is whether questions should be written in Chinese or CFL learners' first languages as learners are usually required to provide answers in the language in which the questions are asked. As has been observed, the learners would often copy the original sentences or phrases to provide answers in Chinese, which is feasible even if they do not know the vocabulary as the logographic features offer them the clues. This might be especially the case if questions require the understanding of specific details in a text when the ability for scanning is called for. For example, if the following questions are also based on the text for Example 7.9, the teachers can find the 'possible answers' copied without alternation from the original text even if the learners do not know the meanings of 虚伪, 恩怨 and 震撼人们灵魂.

1 动物的泪比什么还要重？
  Possible answer: 是一种比金属还要重的泪。
2 人的泪也许含有什么？
  Possible answer: 也许人的泪中还含有虚伪，还有个人恩怨。
3 只有动物的泪才能做到什么？
  Possible answer: 才更是震撼人们灵魂的泪

On the other hand, if the first question in Example 7.9, 'Why does the writer say that animal tears have weight?' is in Chinese (为什么作者说动物的泪有重量?), some students might not fully understand the question and purpose of the question will not be fulfilled, which is a scenario that should be avoided. Or it will take the test-taker much more time to understand and explore the first two sentences to answer the question correctly as there is no discourse marker 因为 that signals the location of the answer. Therefore, the assessment of reading competence in L2 Chinese involves more dimensions than that in other languages. The test writers for a standardised proficiency test or CBA must be very clear about the abilities assessed, the text selected to provide the condition for the task and the manners in which the task is executed.

As many have observed, the CPTs such as HSK and TCOFL have favoured multiple-choice questions (MCQ) for assessing reading. The CBA of the CFL language programmes, on the other hand, have employed more task types such as short answer, true or false and MCQs. The concern has been whether MCQ is a more efficient technique to elicit the performance of reading abilities. Test developers such as HSK or TOCFL have the resources to pretest multiple choices, analyse them for difficulty and discrimination efficiency and train and retrain the item writers, while it is not a technique for classroom teachers to write with confidence for the validity and reliability of their reading tests. Alderson (2000) warns that MCQ may not assess reading ability but other cognitive skills. They may also trick learners into choosing information that is new or they are unfamiliar with. Further, it is difficult to ensure that the plausible but incorrect options will appeal to the weaker reader but not the stronger ones. Thus, as the MCQ in Example 7.9 shows, the test writer must make sure that the four options are structurally similar but different in content. Hughes (2003) recommends that MCQs must have four options to prevent successful guessing work. He also warns that although MCQs allow testing receptive skills without involving productive skills and ensure the reliability of marking, they could severely restrict what can be tested because the distracters are not always effective.

Therefore, alternative types of questions are recommended—for example, short-answer questions, gap filling, information transfer, ordering and recalling tasks and summary writing, etc. *Short-answer questions* are highly recommended in comparison to MCQs for their authenticity, validity and flexibility to assess abilities for bottom-up and top-down processing of written texts (Alderson, 2000; Hughes, 2003; Brown, 2004). They are also much easier to design and write. For assessing L2 reading in Chinese, short-answer questions can serve multiple purposes whether written in Chinese or the learners' first language (see Example 7.10). Marking depends on the completeness of the answer, and a penalty for responses copied directly from the text should be installed. As writing is involved, the fewer unknown characters are needed in the answer, the fairer it will be for the test-takers.

Example 7.10: 请根据短文回答以下问题。

1. 动物的泪比什么还要重? (Scanning for specific information at the local level)
2. 人的泪与动物的泪有什么不同? (Skimming a stretch of text to get overall meanings)
3. 人的泪还是动物的泪有更真的感情? (Understanding the meanings of unknown words)

The *true-or-false questions* are also easier to write, though, with a 50% probability of choosing the correct answer, this type of task for assessing reading is more appropriate for formative assessment or consolidation exercises in the classroom or as homework. For CBA by CFL programmes, a variety of techniques should be used for formative or summative purposes so that the information on learners' reading competence can be collected more objectively. Table 7.3 summarises the advantages and potential problems of five different types of tasks for assessment of reading based on the recommendation made by Hughes (2003), Alderson (2000), Brown (2004) and Urquhart and Weir (1998). As test reliability can be improved by using more types of tasks, those tasks can compensate for the disadvantages of the main technique employed.

Table 7.3 Recommended Tasks and Their Advantages and Potential Problems

Task Type	Example or Description of Task	Advantages	Potential Problems
Gap filling	Fill in the gaps with words or short phrases based on the passage you read. 作者____看到动物的泪时，被____了。她/他觉得动物的泪比人的泪____，更真诚，没有____和____。	Different from the cloze test, the gaps are selectively deleted to assess specific constructs of abilities, e.g. scanning, reading for the main idea, grammar, vocabulary, etc.	An indirect method which lacks authenticity. Washback might not be positive for learners. When responses include characters not in the text, it may become a test for OC. Alternative answers are commonplace; marking is not clear-cut.
Information transfer (from text to pictures, tables, graphs or charts)	Indicate where the different furniture is in the drawing based on what you have read about Li Nan's room.	An authentic and direct method for testing reading that minimises writing the script. Positive washback.	Provided that learners are familiar with the subject matter, unfamiliarity with tabular and graphic presentation of information could involve non-reading cognitive activities.

(continued)

Table 7.3 (Continued)

Task Type	Example or Description of Task	Advantages	Potential Problems
Ordering (sentences or paragraphs)	Arrange the following sentences in a logical order. 1 因为北京人对传统很重视 2 春节是中国最重要的传统节日 3 他们吃团圆饭, 守夜 4 在北京过春节更有意思 5 还吃很多传统食品 6 比如烤鸭，火锅和各种小吃	Effective for assessing knowledge of written discourse, the ability for functions of discourse devices and cohesion. Ordering paragraphs assesses knowledge of topical chain, textual structures and coherence.	Marking is difficult due to alternative ordering or partially correct ordering. Marks can be awarded for only the correct order, which causes further problems for mark allocation and fairness of tests. Suitable for formative assessment.
Recalling any idea units or specific details	Students are asked to recall any ideas or certain aspects of information in a text which is taken away after timed reading. Answers can be in either Chinese or learners' first languages.	An integrated approach for assessing reading in writing skills. A technique reflects real-world tasks when necessary to recall information read.	Questioned for testing memory. Marking is difficult, so scores only awarded for accurately recalled units of information are proposed. A difficult task if recalling is in Chinese.
Summary writing	Students are asked to write a summary of the whole or part of a text. Time and word limit is given. Answers can be in either Chinese or learners' first languages.	An integrated approach involves comprehension of the main and supporting ideas and reading for gist and details. Writing competence is required of the test-takers.	Marking is difficult. Understanding the gist of a text may be subjective. A holistic rating scale is recommended. Summary writing skills may affect reliability. A difficult task if the summary is written in Chinese.

Reading competence is a paramount skill for literacy in any language. To the CFL learners, reading Chinese script is challenging but an obligatory language competence for the most common communication they will encounter in a Chinese-speaking community. This section has discussed the reading processes in L2 Chinese, the strategies required for comprehension of written information and the specific concerns with the practice for assessing the reading abilities CFL learners who are from different linguistic backgrounds. The proposed principle is that the learning objectives and the construct of assessment should not be sacrificed for the challenging features of the written language. Solutions for solving those concerns have also been discussed, and recommendations to compensate for the disadvantages and potential problems of a few techniques are provided. Readers are also advised to consult Hubley's (2012) summary of the subskills tested and the typical ways to test them. The next part will discuss the assessment of another competence of literacy in L2 Chinese, the competence in the written language in productive mode.

7.3 Assessing productive written language in L2 Chinese

Writing in L2 Chinese has been neglected as research focus has been on orthographic competence (OC) (Guan et al., 2013a). As OC is one of the constructs of competence for testing writing in L2 Chinese, the discussion in this part will focus on the abilities that build up the L2 competence for writing in Chinese. By 'writing' in this section, the author means the ability to describe and inform clearly and logically with well-developed text organisation that achieves the intended purpose. The questions asked by the assessors, in this case, are 'How well have the CFL learners written the script?' 'How have they used grammatical structures and vocabulary?' 'Have they expressed what they intend to the reader?' 'Have they connected the sentences cohesively and a stretch of text coherently?' 'Have they arranged the paragraphs in an appropriate text structure?' 'Have they achieved their purposes to describe or inform?' In other words, writing in L2 Chinese is not much different in nature from writing in other L2 languages except that CFL learners' written samples are in characters. Based on such a notion, this part will describe the writing process in L2 Chinese and the measures for writing quality and define the constructs for assessing writing in Chinese. The main issues, practices and techniques for assessment are discussed, and recommendations for better practice will be provided.

The writing process and measures for writing quality

To define the constructs for assessing the CFL learners' competence for writing in Chinese, we should first know the writing process and the essential language abilities and cognitive skills for the language activity. Flower and Hayes (1981) proposed that writing is fundamentally a cognitive performance consisting of mainly three stages: planning, translating and reviewing. Planning is the stage where ideas and information for writing on a specific topic are resourced and organised for the purpose. The next step is to translate the ideas and information into words and sentences and put them on paper in the script of a language. Then, reviewing includes evaluation of the draft text, recognising, deleting unsatisfactory parts or adding further ideas. Studies conducted on L1 writers have evidenced that the writing process is cyclical by nature toward the completion of a written text. Flower and Hayes (ibid.) also found that writers at different proficiency levels are engaged differently in the process. The more proficient writers are more independent and initiative, planning more thoroughly and reviewing and revising for content, organisation and suitability to the readers. The less proficient, on the other hand, are more concerned with grammar, vocabulary or spelling. Berninger and Swanson (1994) studied further the writing process in the alphabetic languages and distinguished two separate components of the translation stage: text generation (finding the language to express ideas) and transcription (representing the language as written symbols). Transcription is recognised in two forms, handwriting (HW hereafter) and spelling, due to the differences that they induce to the writing process.

The three studies worth attention on the writing process by L1 writers of Chinese are by Liu (2013), Yan et al. (2012) and Guan et al. (2013b). Liu's examination of the writing processes of a narrative by L1 Chinese and L2 English writers is a baseline and a comparative study through analysing data collected from questionnaires, journals and semi-structured interviews. The results show that the processes undertaken by the

L1 Chinese and L2 English writers share the same stages—task examining, planning, formulation, evaluation and reviewing—which are both cyclical in a constant interplay of thinking, writing and revising. The difference lies in what the L1 and L2 writers did in the formulation process (translating and writing down ideas) and reviewing processes. The L1 writers, the native speakers of Chinese on a university English course, paid much more attention to coherence, punctuation and appropriateness of wording through repeated use of keywords or sentences for logical order, rhetorical devices and discourse markers. In contrast, the L2 English writers, the same students on the English course, worked significantly more on the topic sentences for the paragraphs, attempting to assign one topic sentence for each paragraph to achieve coherence and then working on the sentence structures and appropriate wording. When reviewing their draft texts, the L1 writers focused on punctuation, coherence, content and wording while the L2 writers on grammar and vocabulary. Although the study did not address issues related to OC of the L1 Chinese writers, it is a useful reference because it provided evidence that L1 and L2 writers pay attention to different elements during the writing process due to the linguistic differences between the Chinese and English languages.

On the other hand, Yan et al. (2012) applied Berninger and Swanson's distinctions of the two modes of transcription to explore the underlying dimensions engaged in the writing process by young L1 writers at different developmental stages and the relationship between writing quality and HW of the script. They found that the five qualitative measures of writing—depth of content, sentence organisation, paragraph organisation, topic sentence and intelligibility—are highly correlated with the overall writing quality of the writing samples produced by the Cantonese-speaking children aged between six and nine. More importantly, the study defines the OC for composition as HW fluency, the ability to write the script as well and as quickly as the writers can. The confirmatory factor analysis revealed that HW fluency on a timed writing task was highly predictive of overall writing quality, suggesting that automaticity for handwriting the logographic script can unload cognitive demand in the writing process, providing more cognitive space for higher-level compositional activities for depth of ideas, organisation and intelligibility.

Guan et al. (2013b) also included HW fluency as an integral aspect of competence for writing compositions in their longitudinal research because the motor and visual automaticity is part of OC (see Table 7.1) and can help writers to complete tasks more swiftly with more accuracy. They allow the executive attention and language competence to generate well-structured and well-written text. The study also proposed a five-factor model for writing quality in Chinese and applied confirmatory factor analysis to see if it can be generalised to writing samples in Chinese produced by pupils aged between ten and thirteen at the lower developmental stage and those at a higher stage. The five factors contributing to writing quality are:

1 Macro-organisation: topic sentence, logical ordering of ideas and number of key elements (main idea, body and conclusion)
2 Complexity: mean length of T-unit and clause density
3 Productivity: total number of characters and different characters
4 Spelling and punctuation: number of alternative characters of a similar pronunciation or homophone as the target character, number of alternative

characters of a similar orthographic form of the target character and number of punctuation errors
5   HW fluency: speed for copying strokes and characters in 60 seconds

The results revealed that the constructs for writing quality are multi-trait and consist of both qualitative and quantitative measures. Furthermore, HW fluency is positively correlated with not only the overall quality of writing but also the other four factors: complexity, productivity, spelling and punctuation and macro-organisation. Interestingly, though, the longitudinal study revealed that the associations became weaker when overall language development advanced, suggesting that OC may not contribute as much to the writing performance of writers at a higher-level development stage compared to those at a lower-level stage.

A further issue for assessing writing in L2 Chinese related to the transcription process is the role of keyboarding or converted writing (CW hereafter) from Pinyin to characters. As discussed in the first part of this chapter and Chapter 2.5, HW and CW of the Chinese script require different language and cognitive activities. CW has been considered an easier method to transfer the Chinese language from spoken to written form than HW, which demands not only orthographic awareness but also motor and visual competence. On the other hand, CW demands retrieving the Pinyin (without the tone) for a targeted character, VC to recognise the character amongst a considerable number of homophones or the characters with the same spelling of Pinyin and locating the wanted keys accurately and as quickly as possible. Thus, questions have been raised about whether HW and CW may have different effects on language learners' performance for productive written language, especially in the case of CFL. To date, only a few studies have investigated this issue.

A meta-analytic review of the impact of HW in English, Dutch, Turkish, Korean, Chinese, etc. suggests that there is a positive and statistically significant association between handwriting fluency and measures for assessing writing quality except for complexity (Feng et al., 2017). The analysis also shows that the performance of handwriting and keyboarding are significantly related only to speed, which emphasised the importance of handwriting for writing competence. The two studies focus on the impact of HW and CW on CFL learner's performance in L2 Chinese writing, however, found that elementary and pre-intermediate CFL learners performed better when they used Word processor (Zhu et al., 2016), and the raters rated the CW samples higher than they did the HW versions for intelligibility and presentation regardless of the raters' empathy for CW or HW (Zhang and Min, 2019). The studies admit that the 'more professional' presentation and better intelligibility of the CW versions are superior to the handwritten versions, which could alleviate the cognitive workload for high-order thinking for generating ideas, choosing vocabulary and organising sentence and paragraph structures.

Furthermore, the reality is that, though it is a developing country, by June 2021, China's internet presentation had reached 71.6%. This suggests that most of the Chinese people nowadays are skilled users of the internet, computers or digital devices and are accustomed to typewriting in written communication. It may be a better mode of writing for writers to present their linguistic competence with confidence. Nonetheless, the beneficial effect of HW is undeniable for writing quality in any language (e.g. Graham et al., 2000). Many have advocated that HW should be the main mode for writing when teaching beginners and learners at lower levels. When they have built a solid foundation in Chinese, CW can be implemented in teaching and assessment (e.g. Zhang and Min, 2019; Yan et al., 2012; Feng et al., 2017) because the operation of CW needs language proficiency to be carried out for. Writing tasks (Wong et al., 2011). Therefore, both HW and CW are the construct of competence in productive written Chinese, with the former for assessing beginners or lower-level learners and the latter for higher-level learners.

Three other measures for assessing the quality of written production by CFL learners are T-unit, error and discourse analyses. The T-unit analysis measures the complexity of written texts by examining the length of T-units and the rate of error-free T-units that reflect the quality and the stages of interlanguage development. Studies of cross-sectional and longitudinal data have suggested that lack of error rather than length of T-unit is a more effective quantitative measure to discriminate the proficiency levels of university CFL learners (Jiang, 2013). The complexity of advanced learners' written production is usually improved but at the cost of accuracy (Zhao, 2017). Those results have corresponded to the assumption that T-unit or syntactic complexity might not be reliable measures for assessing writing quality 'because grammar and syntax are sometimes more ambiguous and difficult to categorise in Chinese as compared to English' (Yan et al., 2012: 2). The measures obtained through discourse analysis of how CFL learners develop topics by applying unique Chinese grammatical structures, topic chaining and the use of zero pronouns has found that, in comparison to native Chinese, English-speaking CFL learners tend to overproduce nouns and pronouns and underuse zero pronouns (Jin, 1994; Xiao, 2011). Both heritage and non-heritage learners also tend to write structurally loose SVO structures and repetitive short sentences and excessive nouns and pronouns without sufficient topic chains. The written discourse, as a result, lacks cohesion and depth of content, with fragmented chunks which often confuses readers (Xiao, bidi.).

A great amount of error analysis has been conducted and published in China. In the UK, the first comprehensive error-analysis study with substantial data was conducted by Xiang and Ji (2017). They examined the handwritten samples of argument-based essays produced by university students learning to achieve CEFR C1 proficiency. The analysis showed that at the discourse level, the errors were incomplete discourse structures (48%), disorganised paragraphing (24%) and lack of main elements (e.g. introduction, topic sentence and conclusion: 28%). In terms of syntactic structures, the most common errors are problematic complex structures (35%) and incorrect comparative, emphasis and negative structures (32%). Most observed lexical errors are those for using near synonymies (e.g. 明确 and 明显; 55%) and functional words (e.g. 上, 里, 再, 又; 26%). This study has provided detailed descriptions of the written texts produced by advanced CFL learners in UK higher education, suggesting that the accuracy of grammatical structures and appropriate use of lexical items are equally important as text organisation and discourse to quality of writing.

Defining the construct for assessing writing in L2 Chinese

The influential language frameworks and benchmarks (e.g. CEFR, EBCL) have applied the task-centred approach to defining the construct for assessing writing abilities that are presented as Can-Do Statements (CDSs). Those CDSs are various behavioural acts for completing a task rather than based on theories about L2 writing or the writing processes. In addition to the overall description of written language competence, there are also specific CDSs attuned to the competencies demanded by writing different types of texts (e.g. creative, transactional, evaluative and interactive writing) (CoE, 2018; EBCL, 2012a). The communicative strategies as production strategies are defined as separate from the CDSs, which consist of planning, compensating, monitoring and repairing. In contrast, the ACTFL and ICCLE guidelines have adopted the trait-based approach for their construct definition for assessing writing (ACTFL, 2012a, 2012b; Hanban, 2008), specifying the competencies in terms of characterised abilities for the written discourse or desired performance for producing written texts.

The approach adopted by the construct definition presented in Table 7.4 for assessing the competence to produce written texts in L2 Chinese is different from those of the language frameworks or guidelines. It is driven and based on the characteristics of the writing process that consists of planning, translating (in two sub-processes of text generation and transcription) and reviewing as the behavioural traits called for by completing a writing task. It also reflects the impacts of HW (indicative of overall interlanguage development) and CW (representing the lifestyle of current CFL learners and satisfactory intelligibility). Moreover, the measures that have been used to assess the quality of writing (e.g. depth of content, sentence and paragraph organisation, accuracy, complexity, fluency, productivity, intelligibility, etc.) are integrated into the construct for assessing the CFL learners' competence for writing.

Noticeably, apart from the components of competence for the translating process, those for the planning and reviewing processes are mostly strategic competencies contributing to the quality of writing. The rationale is that interactiveness is an important characteristic of language assessment, especially for testing writing that involves not only the learners' language competence but also strategic and topical knowledge and affective schemata (how test-takers respond emotionally to test tasks). Such a construct definition aims to associate assessment with teaching practice as some CFL teachers have been teaching only the language knowledge needed for writing, although composing behaviour is cognitive and requires many sub-processes within the three phases of planning, translating and reviewing (Flower and Hayes, 1981). Therefore, instruction for writing should also follow the process and engages learners in cycles of the three stages. The CBA for writing needs to mirror the cognitive activities of the writing process and positively impact learning.

Table 7.4 Constructs for Assessing L2 Chinese Writing Competence

Constructs of competence for writing	Components of constructs
Competence for planning in the writing process	1 Can understand the demand and purpose of the writing task and set up goals for the readers 2 Can gather the information or ideas demanded by tasks on the specific domains or subjects 3 Can organise the information or ideas in appropriate types of writing and text structures 4 Can decide on the materials and language resources used for the task in terms of relevance and content 5 Can retrieve information and ideas to expound on the topics for breadth and depth 6 Can arrange the shreds of ideas or information in different paragraphs based on a logical order with the key elements of a coherent text
Competence for translating in the writing process	7 Can present the ideas or information accurately with appropriate lexical expressions and the unique Chinese grammatical structures 8 Can apply both the discourse devices and the unique topic-chaining and necessary zero-pronoun features to achieve cohesion and coherence amongst sentences in a paragraph 9 Can use punctuations to denote different logical relationships between sentences and ensure smooth flow of meanings 10 Can organise paragraphs to develop ideas and present information coherently with key elements such as introduction, topic sentence or conclusion 11 Can adopt appropriate text types, e.g. descriptive, narrative, expository and argumentative, with different tones, styles and registers for different readers and themes 12 Can communicate in different types of writing, e.g. creative, reports, essays, emails, messages, forms, online conversation/discussion 13 Can transcribe ideas and information through handwriting or converted writing with fluency and accuracy for satisfactory intelligibility
Competence for reviewing in the writing process	14 Can evaluate and diagnose whenever necessary the mistakes and problems in content, style and language of the written text 15 Can reorganise, delete or add paragraphs or sentences to improve relevance, cohesion, coherence and flow of ideas 16 Can revise wording and sentence structures to express meanings clearly 17 Can resolve problems in terms of text types, tones and register to improve the content and suit the readers 18 Can effectively proofread the script and punctuation

To implement a construct definition for assessing writing, Weigle (2012: 219) recommends that the specific constructs selected for assessment be determined by learning contexts, learning objectives, proficiency levels or types of texts. For example, when assessing writing competence for business purposes, the text types may be memos, analyses of diagrams or minutes of a meeting, etc. The constructs of the competence are different from those for testing writing for medicine, for which the text types might be a referral to a consultant in the hospital or a review report. For assessing overall competence or proficiency in writing, the constructs selected also vary. For instance, the constructs selected to test lower-level learners are mostly those for the translating process in terms of accuracy of vocabulary, grammar, handwriting, etc. For assessing the writing abilities of the higher-level learners, the constructs are usually those for text organisation, styles and register, development of ideas and arguments, etc. (Weigle, 2002; Brown, 2004). The summative and formative CBAs usually select the constructs in view of the learning objectives, though it has been advocated that assessment of HW in writing is necessary for beginners and lower-level learners, whereas CW should be taken as a mode of writing when assessing higher-level learners.

Designing tasks for assessing L2 Chinese writing

Assessing speaking and writing has been considered the performance assessment which involves using direct and authentic tests. In other words, the tasks to elicit the performance of writing competence should be authentic tasks resembling real-world performance. The context, agenda, constraint and outcome of such tasks should be as close as to those in real life so that the performance can more accurately predict the test-takers' abilities to use a language for communication and study or work in the circumstances when it is called for. In comparison, non-performance tests or indirect tasks involve few of the cognitive processing and strategies essential to performance in reality and can hardly be used to generalise a learner's actual competence (Weir, 2005b). However, although direct/performance tests are appealing for face validity, there are a few problems with developing such authentic tasks to test writing. Firstly, it is not always practical to administer tasks 'representative of the population of tasks that we should expect the students to be able to perform' to elicit valid samples of writing and provide a valid and reliable assessment of the performance (Hughes, 2003: 83). As a result, studies have been conducted to explore the concurrent validity of types of tasks for assessing L2 Chinese writing with classroom teachers' assessment or the learners' overall proficiency. The correlations was examined between learner performance on three types of tasks, topic-based, picture-based and multiple-choice questions, with the classroom teachers' assessment of the learners' writing competence (Zhao and Xie, 2006). It was found that the indirect tasks, multiple choices, did not predict the learners' writing competence, whereas the picture-based task had the strongest correlation with the teacher's rating. To explore further if the performance on picture-based tasks correlates with learners' overall proficiency and their teachers' assessment, Li and Zhao (2012) compared two forms of picture-based tasks: a sequence of pictures and a picture provided with an introduction and a conclusion which required learners to complete the story by filling the missing parts. They found that the sequence of pictures had a much higher correlation with teacher ratings and the test-takers' proficiency levels. Zhu et al. (2013) conducted a G-theory study of the three writing tasks of the writing paper of HSK Level 5: arranging words/phrases provided to make a sentence, writing based on keywords provided and picture-based writing. The results also suggested that the sentence-making items contributed the least if used to generalise the learners' writing competence. It is the picture-based writing task that contributed most. Thus, it seems that practical tasks with some characteristics of authenticity such as describing pictures may succeed in assessing CFL learners' competence in producing written texts in Chinese.

Summative and formative CBA in the CFL context, however, have used more sentence making or word-order test items and topic-based tasks than picture-based tasks. As discussed in Chapter 5.2, making sentences with provided characters involves many more elements of testing grammar than writing. The construct implemented in such tasks is mainly those related to grammatical and lexical knowledge. On the other hand, the widely used topic-based tasks are flexible and can accommodate various learning objectives for assessing both higher- and lower-level writing. A common practice is to select one of the topics covered during the instruction period or to combine two topics into one as the topic for summative assessment. For example, in a summative writing assessment for learners who should have achieved ICCLE Stage 5 and learnt *The Practical Chinese New Reader* Vol. 4 (Liu et al., Vol. 4, 2003), the topics for the writing paper are possibly 做为独生子女的利与弊 (Advantages and Disadvantages of Being an Only Child) or 大学生不应该兼职打工 (University Students Should Not Work Part-time). The required character productivity should be at least over 400. Required productivity is usually specified for two reasons. Firstly, the number of graded vocabulary and lexical items increases with the levels of proficiency, and the more competent the learners are, the more vocabulary they can use for writing. Secondly, research has shown that the number and variety of characters and the number of characters used from the graded characters and lexical items are the two features of the learners' writing samples that human rating and automated rating agree on (Huang et al., 2014; Ren, 2004). This suggests that the variety and productivity of the logographic script could be a consistent indicator of the quality of writing in L2 Chinese.

Hughes (2003: 89) recommends the following for assessing writing, which should be applied for testing L2 Chinese writing, especially if the assessment uses topic-based tasks:

1   *Setting as many separate tasks as feasible to elicit a representative sample.* Performance on one topic-based task can produce a rather limited sample for the assessor to judge a learner's competence for writing. In particular, the CFL learners of different proficiency levels would usually prepare and memorise two or three essays based on the topics covered by an instruction period for the writing section in a summative assessment. To them, it is necessary because remembering the vocabulary involved in a topic will help greatly to write them. Can written samples learnt by heart represent the learners' competence? Probably, we cannot say so. Therefore, more than one task and tasks that are difficult to predicate should be set to collect more evidence for assessment. Another approach to achieve this aim is to accompany summative assessment with the formative of homework counted

towards the final overall performance on a CFL course. The homework should consist of several different types of tasks, too.

2 *Testing only writing ability and nothing else.* A valid writing test should not depend on the learners' imagination, creativity, range and depth of knowledge on certain subjects or reading ability. For a CBA, setting topics within those learnt or covered can prevent a writing test from testing other competencies. In addition, the instruction for writing tasks should be brief and easy to understand and will not cause unnecessary confusion. Writing tasks depending on reading comprehension of an article or short text is not recommended because they do not involve all the three writing processes and the translating process will involve borrowing the vocabulary and grammatical structures in the text provided. Test-takers would also copy from the text the characters they are not able to write. Therefore, charts, diagrams, tables and illustrations/pictures are highly recommended for assessing L2 writing.

3 *Restricting test-takers' writing with provided outlines or points.* Writing tasks should be well defined for students to know what is required of them so that they cannot avoid using and writing the grammatical structures or vocabulary expected. Outlines or points to cover included in the instruction are important for a topic-based task as they can help the learners to focus on the topic and the required content. The outlines or points, however, should be in phrases rather than in sentences, preferably in the student's first language, especially for students of lower proficiency levels (see Example 7.11). In addition, test-takers should not be given choices of tasks, which may make scoring difficult due to inconsistency of the content and construct validity.

Example 7.11: Write on the following topic. You must follow the outline and write at least 90 characters.

Topic: 我的一个朋友
Points to cover: (1) name; (2) nationality; (3) study course; (4) where she/he is now; (5) how you knew each other; (6) what you do together; (7) when you usually meet.

4 *Keeping tasks as authentic as possible for learners to relate themselves to the life, study or work, people and society in the countries where the target language is spoken.* In consideration of practicality and the importance of authenticity for performance tests, it is desirable to design real-world tasks for assessment. However, in consideration of the CBA and classroom condition, it is difficult to set tasks that replicate the way the Chinese communicate with each other in the written language, e.g. texting and emailing each other, posting blogs, responding and commenting on social media or writing on computers for work, study or other purposes. Therefore, a continuum of authenticity is necessary for learning through formal instruction and assessments (McNamara, 1996). Figure 7.2 proposes such a continuum for tasks that present the different degrees of authenticity for assessing writing competence in L2 Chinese.

Not Authentic	Semi-Authentic	Authentic
- Ordering words in a sentence - Filling gaps in sentences or paragraph - Arranging sentences in a logical order - Translating sentences or texts	- Picture-based writing - Keyword-based writing - Topic-based writing with outline or points - Writing imaginary biographies, narratives or reports with details provided in phrases in 1st language or Chinese	- Filling forms - Writing greeting or birthday cards and notes - Writing diary entries - Texting on phones to friends or on social media - Writing emails or letters for different purposes - Interpreting charts, diagrams, tables - Writing reports, essays or documents for academic and professional purposes
Characteristics - No planning process - Different reviewing process - Indirect/non-performance testing - Not approximate to real-life situations - Hardly indicative of writing ability - Timed	**Characteristics** - Little planning process - Semi-direct testing - Resembles some of the cognitive strategies applied for writing in day-to-day life - Indicative of the performance in real-life situations - Timed or untimed	**Characteristics** - Involves the three processes of writing - Direct/performance testing - Predicative of writing ability for real-life situations - Timed or untimed

Figure 7.2 A Proposed Continuum of Authenticity of Tasks for Assessing L2 Chinese Writing

The tasks listed in the figure are certainly not all those we can use for writing tests. Though only three categories of task authenticity are presented for the continuum, further degrees of approximation to the real-life situation can be recognised if necessary for testing writing for different purposes. More types of tasks can also be added to the categories. Certainly, direct and authentic tasks are most appropriate for the assessment of writing, sometimes only indirect or semi-direct tasks can be used. As a result, teachers must have the information regarding the construct validity of those tasks and their predictive validity of the CFL learners' overall proficiency.

Regarding timed writing tasks, Weir (2005b) and Weigle (2002) argue that the timed impromptu test for assessing writing employed by standardised tests and summative CBA has limitations in construct validity, authenticity, interactiveness and could impact on learning less positively. They suggest that a portfolio is an alternative to assesses writing with a collection of papers produced over a period with specified learning objectives to develop productive L2 written competence. This practice may still be new to some CFL teachers and programmes, though it is observed that the continuous assessment installed by some of the CFL programmes is similar to the approach recommended by Weir and Weigle (ibid.). The development of writing competence in an L2 is a cyclic process and requires continuous effort and work from the teacher and learners through formative assessment. In addition, the feedback from the teachers to the students provided with an analytic rating scale can effectively improve the quality of writing.

Rating written samples in L2 Chinese

After the construct for assessing competence in writing has been defined, the appropriate tasks have been selected and sufficient samples of writing are provided, scoring the written samples is the next concern for the validity and reliability of a writing test. Firstly, we need to know that rater standardisation is important as rater characteristics could affect the scores they give to the performance and the reliability of the test. It has been recommended that rater training or standardisation be provided pre-rating to improve inter-reliability effectively (Hughes, 2003; Brown, 2004; Green, 2013). As writing and speaking tests are both assessments of competencies in the productive mode, the procedure for standardising raters of writing tests can follow that for training raters of speaking tests (see Chapter 6.3).

Secondly, the other measure for improving reliability is to select or write an appropriate rating scale that stands for the criteria to assess the language and strategic competence in the productive written mode. In Chapter 6.3 the advantages and disadvantages of holistic and analytic scales are introduced, which mostly also apply to the scales for written samples, except that there is a time constraint for raters of speaking tests, and comparatively, raters of writing tests have more time to distinguish the features in the learners' scripts in correspondence to the performance descriptions in the rating scales. This is to say that the cognitive processes and workload undertaken by the raters of written samples are less complex and demanding. The holistic, analytic or primary trait scales for rating writing performance are introduced as follows and discussed with samples for demonstration.

The choice of holistic or analytic scales depends on the purposes of testing writing, according to Weigle (2002). A CFL course can develop its scales or select existing published rating scales by standardised tests or other authoritative benchmarks or guidelines. Hughes (2003) recommends that if an existing published scale is selected, it must consist of similar constructs to assess the learning objectives. It must also be modified to suit the CBA purpose. If the programme decides to construct its rating scale, it should be tested, modified, trailed and revised as many times as necessary. The scales introduced here should be treated with caution because they are developed by the author to demonstrate how to rate L2 Chinese written samples. This is because accessible and established rating scales for L2 Chinese writing tests are scarce at the present.

Holistic scales for writing tests could produce higher inter-rater reliability in comparison to analytic scales. They tend to highlight the writer's strengths so that they serve well for placement purposes (Weigle, 2002; ibid.; Hughes, 2003). For example, when assessing some post-beginner learners who have completed elsewhere ICCLE Stage 1 (equivalent to CEFR A1, Hanban, 2014) for a credit-bearing Stage 2 course, a topic-based writing task is assigned (see Example 7.11). A writing test should be administered in this case as the common concern is whether the learners can cope with the expected learning outcomes of the written language. A holistic rating (see Table 7.5) is constructed to evaluate the response to the task, which is based on the construct definition presented in Table 7.4. The format adopts the rating rubrics for the TOEFL Test of Written English (Educational Testing Services) that have been highly recommended by Hughes (2003) and Weigle (2002).

| Topic: | 我的一个朋友 |

王芳是我的朋友。她是中国人，她学习中国li
史。她在北京。王芳的ying语不好，她的中文好
她是我的朋友学ying语。我是她的朋友学中文。
我们认识一年，她的家也在北京。我们星qi二
下午见，她学习ying语，我学习中文，从三点dao
五点。我们吃饭，说hua，很高兴。

Example 7.11 Handwritten sample: 我的一个朋友

Table 7.5 Holistic Rating Scale for L2 Chinese Writing

Score	Characteristics of the Written Sample
6	• Well on the topic and task with depth and development of the topic • Well-organised with appropriate style, register for the targeted readers • Accurate basic and unique Chinese syntactic structures • Accurate and appropriate vocabulary with productivity and a variety of lexical items • Cohesive and coherent with characteristics of Chinese discourse (e.g. topic-prominent, appropriate use of pronouns, discourse markers and punctuations) • Fluent and accurate HW or excellent OC at lower levels without Pinyin and problems of character writing, e.g. size, shape and connection of radicals or components, or distorted constructions; accurate and well-presented CW
5	• On the topic and task with adequate development • Generally organised text structure with some inappropriateness in style and register causing slight misunderstanding • With few grammatical errors • Overall accurate and appropriate vocabulary with productivity and variety as required • Cohesive and coherent with characteristics of Chinese discourse but influenced by 1st or 2nd features • Overall accurate HW with one or two Pinyin and problems of character writing; CW with a few incorrectly selected characters
4	• Slightly off the topic and task and lacking effective development • Adequately organised text structure with some inappropriateness in style and register causing misunderstanding • With some grammatical errors • Some inaccurate and inappropriate use of vocabulary, lacking productivity and variety • Obvious influences of 1st or 2nd and problematic with topic chaining, pronouns, discourse markers and punctuations • HW with some Pinyin and problems with character writing; CW with some incorrectly selected characters

Score	Characteristics of the Written Sample
3	• Often off the topic and the task is not completed • Largely disorganised text without appropriate style and register • Consistent grammatical errors • Many inaccurate and inappropriate vocabularies and short of productivity and variety • Heavily influenced 1st or 2nd features and lacking characteristics of Chinese discourse • HW with more Pinyin and problems with character writing; CW with more incorrectly selected characters
2	• Off the topic and incomplete with the task • Disorganised text • Serious and frequent grammatical • Mostly inaccurate and inappropriate vocabulary and not meeting the required productivity • Not characteristic of Chinese text • HW with mostly Pinyin, incorrect or non-characters; CW with mostly incorrect characters
1	• Off the topic with a few incomplete sentences • Disorganised text • Not in grammatical structures • With only a few recognisable characters or words well under the required productivity • No textual features • HW of a few characters; nearly all Pinyin; CW with no complete sentence
0	• Only a few characters or phrases are written, or the topic was copied, or no response • Some words in 1st or 2nd language or Pinyin

Based on the holistic scale, the written sample for Example 7.11 has completed the task and responded to all the points required. It is considerably easy to understand with details provided about the friend. However, the awarded score is 4 because of the following:

1. Slightly off the topic (e.g. 她的家也在北京)
2. Some obvious grammatical errors (e.g. 她是我的朋友学英语，我们认识一年, 从三点到五点, etc.)
3. Incorrect use of near synonymy of 聊天, 说话
4. Lacking features of Chinese discourse and misuse of pronunciation (e.g. use of full stop for most sentences and 她的家)
5. No HW fluency and accuracy (e.g. disproportionate characters: 芳, 是, 的, 她, 习, 点, etc.; incorrectly written characters: 史, 朋, 星, 饭; and Pinyin for 历, 英, 话)

Analytic scales for rating L2 scripts, on the other hand, are often for diagnostic purposes and provide teachers and learners with informative and explicit feedback about the strengths and weaknesses in writing (Weigle, 2002; Brown, 2004; Hughes, 2003; Brookhart, 2013). Using an analytic scale for formative assessment

198 *Written language and orthographic competence in L2 Chinese*

improves the development of writing competence as self-assessment will be based on the standards and competence descriptions. The learners will have explicit information about their strengths or weaknesses in writing on text organisation, grammar, vocabulary, transcription of the ideas and meanings planned, etc. Classroom teachers can also adjust the weightings of the criteria to suit different proficiency levels. For example, the analytic scale for lower-level proficiency can emphasise HW, grammar or vocabulary, whereas for higher levels it can prioritise text organisation and development on topics (Weigle, 2002). In addition, such rating scales can also vary with the genres of writing demanded by tasks because argumentative or narrative essays require different text organisation, register and style.

Table 7.6 is an analytic scale for assessing L2 Chinese writing. It has six criteria with different weightings and five levels of performance for each criterion. General categories of performance with ranges of scores are also noted for the different performances to provide clarity to the raters. The weightings are also varied with the modes of writing. When CW is required for the task, the weightings will be lower than in the mode of HW for reduced task demand in the process of transcribing the planned content, organisation, grammar, vocabulary and discourse into the script. Automatically, increased percentages will be added to the other criteria. A response to a chart-based task (see Example 7.12) designed for CFL learners at ICCLE Stage 4 level (equivalent to CEFR B2) about the overseas travels taken by the Chinese (see Figure 7.3) is marked based on the analytic scale. The task demands extensive writing because the learners must interpret the chart and discuss the reasons behind the figures.

Table 7.6 Analytic Rating Scale for L2 Chinese Writing

Criterion and Weighting	*Score Range*	*Grades and Characteristics of Written Sample*
Content/Task Completion 25% + 1% in WC	25–21	*Excellent:* knowledge of the topic, thorough development in depth and successful completion of the task
	20–16	*Good*: knowledge with adequate development lacking depth to fully complete the task
	15–11	*Average:* adequate knowledge and development lacking both depth and details to complete the task
	10–6	*Fair:* limited knowledge and development without effectively completing the task
	5–1	*Poor*: little knowledge without development failing the task
Text Organisation 15% + 1% in WC	15–13	*Excellent*: well-organised paragraphs with clearly stated ideas with appropriate style and register
	12–10	*Good:* organised text with some inappropriateness in style and register causing slight misunderstanding
	9–7	*Average*: somewhat disorganised text with ideas stated in an incomplete logical sequence of inappropriate style and register
	6–4	*Fair*: disorganised text with disconnected and confusing ideas and inappropriate style and register
	3–1	*Poor*: disorganised text failing to communicate

Criterion and Weighting	Score Range	Grades and Characteristics of Written Sample
Grammar **15% + 1% in WC**	15–13	*Excellent*: accurate unique Chinese structures in complex constructions when necessary
	12–10	*Good:* accurate basic and unique structures with some errors when in complex forms
	9–7	*Average*: accurate basic structures and frequent errors with unique structure
	6–4	*Fair*: inaccurate basic structures with a few problematic unique structures
	3–1	*Poor*: with no mastery of Chinese grammatical structures
Vocabulary **15% + 1% in WC**	15–13	*Excellent*: impressive, accurate and appropriate use of vocabulary productive in range and variety
	12–10	*Good*: accurate and appropriate use of vocabulary with required productivity and variety
	9–7	*Average*: some inaccurate and inappropriate use of vocabulary and lack of productivity and variety
	6–4	*Fair*: inaccurate and inappropriate use of vocabulary below required productivity and variety
	3–1	*Poor:* most vocabulary in other languages than in Chinese and well below the required productivity
Discourse **15% + 1% in WC**	15–13	*Excellent:* cohesive and coherent with characteristics of Chinese discourse (e.g. topic-prominent, appropriate use of pronouns, discourse markers and punctuations)
	12–10	*Good*: cohesive and coherent with characteristics of Chinese discourse but errors with discourse devices and punctuations
	9–7	*Average*: obvious influenced of 1st or 2nd and problematic with topic chaining, pronouns, discourse markers and punctuations
	6–4	*Fair*: heavily influenced by 1st or 2nd features and lacking characteristics of Chinese discourse
	3–1	*Poor*: not characteristic of Chinese text
Transcription **15% for HW** **10% for CW**	15–13	*Excellent*: fluent and accurate HW or OC at lower levels without Pinyin and problems of character writing in size, shape and connections of radicals or components, or distorted constructions; accurate and well-presented CW
	12–10	*Good*: accurate HW with one or two Pinyin and problems of character writing; CW with a few incorrectly selected characters
	9–7	*Average*: HW with some Pinyin and problems with character writing; CW with some incorrectly selected characters
	6–4	*Fair*: HW with more Pinyin and problems with character writing; CW with more incorrectly selected characters
	3–1	*Poor*: HW of mostly Pinyin and problems with character writing; CW with no complete sentence

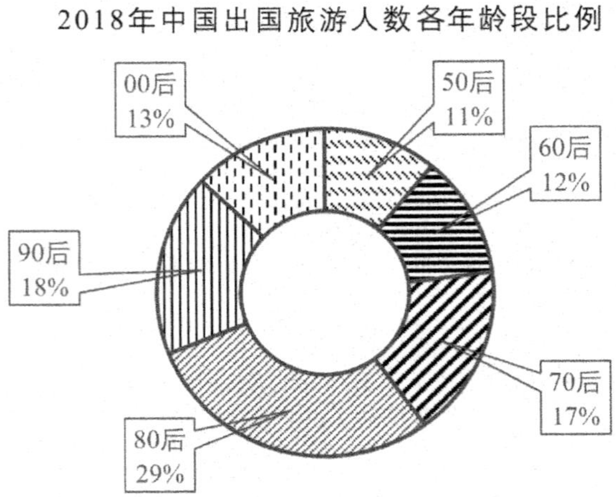

200 *Written language and orthographic competence in L2 Chinese*

2018年中国出国旅游人数各年龄段比例

Figure 7.3 Chart-Based Writing Task

Example 7.12: A chat-based writing task:

> Interpret the following chart about the overseas travels taken by different age groups in China in 2018. Please also discuss the reasons. You must write 300–350 characters and give a title to your essay.

A response to the task:

中国2018年出国旅游年令组比例和原因
       CW V

2018 年很多中国人旅游，有的在国内，有的在国<u>外</u>，在国内旅游的人
                 Dp
多，去国外的少，<u>可能因为</u>到国外旅游更贵。出国旅游的人中有不同的
      G
年令组，50后，60后，70后，80后，90后和00后。80后出国旅游的最多，
CW
占<u>人</u>数的29%，第二多的是90后，占18%，70后比90后少一点，占
 V   Dp   Dp
17%。60后和00后的人数差不多，50后人数最少，只占11%。我<u>想</u>80
                   V
后出国旅游的人最多，因为他们比90后和00后<u>比较</u>有钱，对外国的风景
              G
和文化也有兴趣。另外，他们30多岁，身体<u>健</u>康，不怕出国旅游累。 90
              V
后和70后也喜欢去外国旅游，但是90后没有那么多的钱，70后有孩子
和<u>爸爸妈妈</u>，他们不能<u>离开</u>家很<u>远</u>。50后和60后<u>出国少</u>，因为他们可能
 V   V G   G

不太喜欢外国的<u>地方</u>和菜，他们觉得出国也很累。00后还很小，虽然他们
　　　　　　　V
很喜欢出国看看，但是他们没有很多钱，不能经常出国旅游。

After examining the script on the six criteria constructed by the analytic scale, raters should underline and label the errors or problematic parts according to the different criteria in the analytic scale, e.g. V for Vocabulary; Dp for Punctuation for Discourse; G for Grammar, etc. Then, the rater will give a score for each of the criteria, in this case, 18 for Content, 9 for Organisation, 10 for Grammar, 9 for Vocabulary, 10 for Discourse, and 12 for transcription, making a total of 68 for the overall performance. To the rater, though the task is addressed and completed, the lack of details and elaboration shows that the L2 writer does not know the topic well, which has been covered during the instruction period. Although the first three sentences can be considered an introduction, the mistake of punctuation did not structure the text organisation explicitly. Moreover, a conclusion is missing, and the essay is only one paragraph. The productivity of characters has met the requirement, though a lack of vocabulary variety is evident for a CFL learner at the upper-intermediate proficiency level. Certainly, this is only one rater's assessment of the typed script and can be seen as lenient or harsh by some readers. If the test is one of the components of a summative assessment with a high stake, a second rater will mark it. The final score will be inspected by the internal and external examiners, and the final score will be decided after moderation (see Chapter 3 for the process of developing summative assessment).

Weigle (2002) and Brown (2004) also discussed the advantages of the *primary trait scoring* (PTS hereafter), which helps raters to know 'how well students can write within a narrowly defined range of discourse' set up by specific writing task (Weigle, ibid.: 110). PTS emphasises the task at hand and prioritises the degrees of success of task completion for a specific goal. For example, if a task requires an L2 learner to write a lab report, a PTS scale will focus on the clarity of the steps involved with the experiment and the result. Since planning the content is mostly done by the task demand, such rating scales usually focus on the test-takers' performance during the transcribing and reviewing process, specifically on assigning the primary rhetorical trait, describing the expected performance on the task at different levels in terms of organisation, supporting details, fluency, syntactic variety, etc. (Weigle, ibid.). Example 7.13 is a picture-based writing task as a formative assessment for the CFL learners studying for ICCLE Stage 2 (equivalent to CEFR A2). The PTS drawn up to assess the writers' performance is as follows (see Table 7.7).

Example 7.13: A picture-based writing task
　　Describe the events presented in the series of pictures. You must write no less than 150 words on the lines. If you do not know or cannot write some of the characters or words in Chinese, you can write them in English.

This part of the chapter has discussed the writing process for L2 Chinese and the measures applied for assessing the writing quality produced by the learners. The research has suggested that accuracy of vocabulary and syntactic structures are much more salient features of the learner-produced texts rather than complexity because communicating information and ideas in writing is mostly a cognitive activity, and the understanding of the readers is prioritised. As the method for

202 *Written language and orthographic competence in L2 Chinese*

Figure 7.4 Picture-Based Writing Task

Table 7.7 A PTS for Rating the Picture-Based Task

Criteria	5	4	3	2	1 or 0
Task Completion	All pictures are described in logical sequence and details.	All pictures are described in a logical sequence with little details.	Some pictures are described in a logical sequence. No details.	Most pictures are described in illogical sequence. No details.	No, or one or two pictures described.
Discourse	Cohesive text. Appropriate use of connectives, pronouns and punctuations.	Cohesive text. Some errors in connectives, pronouns and punctuations.	Mostly incohesive text. Frequent errors of pronouns, connectives and punctuations.	Confusing text. Many errors in connectives, pronouns and punctuations.	Not much text to read.
Grammar	Accurate sentence structures.	Accurate sentences with a few errors.	Some inaccurate sentence structures.	Many inaccurate sentence structures.	No structured sentences.
Vocabulary	All learned and needed characters are produced except 河, 树 and 处.	A few learned and needed characters are not produced.	Some learned and needed characters are not produced.	Many learned and needed characters are not produced.	Many Pinyin or English for learned characters.
HW	Well presented on the lines with few disproportionate characters.	Some are off the lines with some disproportionate characters.	A lot is off the lines with many disproportionate characters.	Most are off the lines with disproportionate characters.	Few characters are written correctly.

transcribing the planned ideas into texts is a vital issue regarding the transcribing stage in the writing process, the issues related to the handwritten and typewritten texts have been introduced, and it was concluded that though the coexistence of the two for assessment needs to be accepted when assessing L2 Chinese writing, CW fluency should be a construct for assessing higher-level CFL learners. The proposed construct definition for assessing L2 Chinese writing competence and recommended rating scales have reflected the discussion and conclusions with rated samples. A proposed continuum of task authenticity has also been presented to balance the validity and practicality of language tests as certain semi-direct tasks may successfully evaluate the competence for real-world performance. The standardisation of raters is essential for the reliability of writing tests, and familiarising with the holistic or analytic scale and primary trait scoring is a key element of training sessions for raters.

To conclude, this chapter has introduced the orthographic awareness and motor-visual competence required of the CFL learners' OC, the processes of reading and writing in L2 Chinese and the knowledge and abilities demanded to complete the test items and tasks of reading comprehension and writing tests. OC in Chinese as the basic literacy language ability is considerably different from that in other languages because the features of the script require the writers to construct characters in a square with different components in harmony, symmetry and equilibrium. Thus, the components of OC are radically different from other languages, and the measures and techniques for assessment of the competence are also different, which this chapter has defined, presented and recommended. The differences between the processes of reading and writing in Chinese from in other languages exist mainly in word recognition and transcription of generated texts. CFL learners also undergo top-down and bottom-up processes in reading and planning, translating and reviewing stages in writing. The construct definitions proposed have taken a process approach and identified specific subcomponents that the CFL learners must have to complete the reading and writing tasks. However, due to the characteristics of the Chinese script, there have been concerns with assessing character background and non-character background learners in reading and the two modes of transcribing in writing. The proposed principle is that the learning objectives and the construct of assessment should not be sacrificed for the challenging features of the written language, and both HW and CW are included as the modes for transcribing generated text into the written language, with the condition that assessments should integrate CW only when CFL learners have learnt the foundations of the Chinese language. Specific measures for assessing reading and writing abilities have been established in the proposed construct definitions, and the techniques and issues regarding rating have also been discussed to help teachers to improve the validity and reliability of their assessments.

Further readings

1 Chang et al. (2014) for the importance of teaching CFL beginner learners orthographic knowledge and writing the Chinese script.
2 Chang, C. (2011) to understand the reading process in L2 Chinese and the cognitive and metacognitive strategies applied by CFL learners.
3 Guan et al. (2013b) for the writing process in Chinese and measures for writing quality.

Reader activities

1 If you are teaching beginner learners or have done so, have you assessed OC as described in the first part of the chapter? Make a list including what you have done about the following:

- Assessing the accuracy of character writing
- Assessing whether the radicals and components are written proportionally or in a balanced way
- Assessing knowledge about the construction of Chinese characters, e.g. radicals, components or structure

2 Select a topic amongst those in the textbook you are teaching. Firstly, try to find a piece of writing on the internet or public domain that you can adapt for the reading comprehension part of the end-of-instruction summative assessment. If you cannot find a suitable piece, write the passage and design five questions by consulting the tasks/items introduced in the second part of the chapter. Then, share the passage you have adapted or written with a colleague or peer student for comments.

3 The portfolio approach for assessing and developing CFL learners' competence for writing has advantages over the timed prompts for proficiency and summative assessment of writing. It can benefit the students with positive washback. Complete the following table to draw up a portfolio assessment of the learners you are teaching.

Week of Teaching	Topic	Task	Rating scale	% of total Course Mark
3				
5				
7				
9				
11				

References

ACTFL (2012a) *Proficiency Guidelines*. Available at www.actfl.org/publications/guidelines-and-manuals/actfl-proficiency-guidelines-2012 (Accessed on 12th Oct. 2018).
ACTFL (2012b) *Performance Descriptors for Language Learners*. Available at www.actfl.org/publications/guidelines-and-manuals (Accessed on 12th Jan. 2019).
ACTFL (2016) *Assigning CEFR Ratings to ACTFL Assessment*. Available at www.actfl.org/sites/default/files/reports/Assigning_CEFR_Ratings_To_ACTFL_Assessments.pdf (Accessed on 2nd Aug. 2020).
ACTFL (2020) *Sample and Rationale for Rating: ACTFL Chinese Test at Novice Level*. Available at www.actfl.org/resources/actfl-proficiency-guidelines-2012/chinese/simplified-characters (Accessed on 2nd Aug. 2020).
ACTFL and NCSSL (2017) *ACTFL-NCSSFL Can-Do Statements*. Available at www.actfl.org/publications/guidelines-and-manuals/ncssfl-actfl-can-do-statements (Accessed on 10th Jan. 2018).
Adey, P. (2005) 'Issues arising from the long-term evaluation of cognitive acceleration programmes,' *Research in Science Education*, 35: 3–22.
Alderson, J. C. (2000) *Assessing Reading*. Cambridge, New York, Melbourne, Madrid, Cape Town, Singapore, Sao Paulo: Cambridge University Press.
Alderson, J. C. (2005) *Diagnosing Foreign Language Proficiency: The Interface between Learning and Assessment*. London, UK: Continuum.
Aljaafreh, A. and J. Lantolf. (1994) 'Negative feedback as regulation and second language learning in the zone of proximal development,' *The Modern Language Journal*, 78: 465–83.
Allen, J. R. (2009) 'Why learning to write Chinese is a waste of time: A modest proposal,' *Foreign Language Annals*, 41(2): 237–51.
American Federation of Teachers, National Council on Measurement in Education and National Education Association (1990) *Standards for Teacher Competence in Educational Assessment of Students*. Available at https://buros.org/standards-teacher-competence-educational-assessment-students (Accessed on 20th Jan. 2018).
AP Released Paper (2007) *Chinese Language and Culture Released Exam: Multiple Choice Questions*. Available at https://apcentral.collegeboard.org/pdf/2007-chinese-released-exam-final.pdf (Accessed on 16th Mar. 2018).
Bachman, L. (1990) *Fundamental Considerations in Language Testing*. Oxford: Oxford University Press.

Bachman, L. (2005) *Statistical Analyses for Language Assessment*. Cambridge: Cambridge University Press.
Bachman, L. and B. Damböck (2017) *Language Assessment for Classroom Teachers*. Oxford: Oxford University Press.
Bachman, L. and A. Palmer (1982) 'The construct validation of some components of communicative proficiency,' *TESOL Quarterly*, 16: 449–65.
Bachman, L. and A. Palmer (1996) *Language Testing in Practice*. Oxford: Oxford University Press.
Bachman, L. and A. Palmer (2010) *Language Assessment in Practice: Developing Language Assessments and Justifying Their Use in the Real World*. Oxford: Oxford University Press.
Batenburg, E. S. L. van, R. J. Oostdam, A. J. S. van Gelderen and N. H. de Jong (2018) 'Measuring L2 speakers' interactional ability using interactive speech tasks,' *Language Testing*, 35(1): 75–100.
Beijing University and Pearson (2014) *Automated Test of Spoken Chinese: Test Description and Validation Summary*. Available at www.versanttest.com/technology/SpokenChineseTestValidation.pdf (Accessed on 20th Jun. 2019).
Berninger, V. W. and H. L. Swanson (1994) 'Modifying hayes and flower's model of skilled writing,' in Butterfield, E. C. and J. S. Carlson (eds.) *Advances in Cognition and Educational Practice*. Greenwich, England: Jai Press Inc, 57–81.
Bernstein, J., A. Van Moere and J. Cheng (2010) 'Validating automated speaking tests,' *Language Testing* 27(3): 355–77.
Black, P. J. (1993) 'Formative and summative assessment by teachers,' *Studies in Science Education*, 21: 49–97.
Black, P. J., C. Harrison, C. Lee, B. B. Marshall and D. William (2004) 'Working inside the black box: Assessment for learning in the classroom,' *Phi Delta Kappan*, 86(1): 8–21.
Black, P. J. and D. William (1998a) 'Assessment and classroom learning,' *Assessment in Education: Principles, Policy and Practice*, 5: 7–74.
Black, P. J. and D. William (1998b) 'Inside the black box: Raising standards through classroom assessment,' *Phi Delta Kappan*, 80(2): 139–48.
Black, P. J. and D. William (2003) 'In praise of educational research: Formative assessment,' *British Educational Research Journal*, 29: 623–37.
Black, P. J. and D. William (2009) 'Developing the theory of formative assessment,' *Educational Assessment, Evaluation and Accountability*, 21(1): 5–31.
Borg, S. (2003) 'Teacher cognition in language teaching: A review of research on what language teachers think, know, believe and do,' *Language Teaching*, 36(2): 81–109.
Broadfoot, P. (2005) 'Dark Alleys and blind bends: Testing the language of learning,' *Language Testing*, 22: 123–41.
Brookhart, S. M. (2013) *How to Create and Use Rubrics for Formative Assessment and Grading*. Alexandria, USA: ASCD.
Brown, A. (2003) 'Interviewer variation and the co-construction of speaking proficiency,' *Language Testing*, 20: 1–25.
Brown, A. (2012) 'Interlocutor and rater training,' in Fulcher, G. and F. Davidson (eds.) *The Routledge Handbook of Language Testing*. Abington, UK: Routledge, 413–25.
Brown, H. D. (2004) *Language Assessment: Principles and Classroom Practices*. New York: Pearson Education.
Buck, G. (2001) *Assessing Listening*. Cambridge and New York: Cambridge University Press.
Burns, C. and D. Myhill (2004) 'Interactive or inactive? A consideration of the nature of interaction in whole class teaching,' *Cambridge Journal of Education*, 34(1): 35–49.

Butler, R. (1987) 'Task-involving and ego-involving properties of evaluation: Effects of different feedback conditions on motivational perceptions, interest, and performance,' *Journal of Educational Psychology*, 79(4): 474.

Bygate, M. (1987) *Speaking*. Oxford: Oxford University Press.

Cai, W. (2015) 'Investigating the roles of vocabulary knowledge and word recognition speed in Chinese language listening,' *Chinese as a Second Language Research*, 4(1): 47–65.

Cai, Y. and Y. Wang (2013) 'An empirical study on the use of Chinese listening strategies by preparatory students studying in China,' *Journal of Yunnan Normal University*, 11(1): 29–37.

Cai, Z. Y. and W. Cao (2002) '泰国学生汉语语音偏误分析 (Error analysis of the Thai CFL learners' phonological production),' in Wang, Q. J. (ed.) 汉语作为第二语言的学习者语言系统研究 *(Studies on the CFL learner language)*. Beijing: Commerce Press.

Cameron, J. and W. D. Pierce (1994) 'Reinforcement, reward, and intrinsic motivation: A meta-analysis,' *Review of Educational Research*, 64(3): 363–423.

Canal, M. and M. Swain (1980) 'Theoretical bases for communicative language approaches second language teaching and testing,' *Applied Linguistics*, 1(1): 1–47.

Cao, F., B. M. Ricklesb, Z. Vu, D. Zhu, L. Ho, L. N. Chan, J. Harris, J. Stafura, Y. Xu and C. A. Perfetti (2013) 'Early stage visual-orthographic processes predict long-term retention of word form and meaning: A visual encoding training study', *Journal of Neurolinguistics*, 26: 440–61.

Carless, D. (2006) 'Learning-oriented assessment: Principles and practice,' *Assessment & Evaluation in Higher Education*, 31(4): 395–8.

Carless, D. (2012) *From Testing to Productive Student Learning: Implementing Formative Assessment in Confucian-Heritage Settings*. New York and London: Routledge.

Carter, C. R. (1997) 'Assessment: Shifting the responsibility,' *Journal of Advanced Academics*, 9(2): 68–75.

Chalhoub-Deville, M. (2003) 'Second language interaction: Current perspectives and future trends,' *Language Testing*, 20: 369–83.

Chang, C. (2011) 'See how they read: An investigation into the cognitive and metacognitive strategies of nonnative readers Chinese,' in Everson, M. E. and H. H. Shen (eds.) *Research among Learners of Chinese as a Foreign Language*. Honolulu: University of Hawaii, National Foreign Language Resource Center, 93–116.

Chang, L. P. (2017) 'The development of the test of Chinese as a foreign language (TOFCL),' in Zhang, D. B. and C. H. Lin (eds.) *Chinese as a Second Language Assessment*. Singapore: Springer, 21–42.

Chang, L. Y., X. Yi, C. A. Perfetti, J. Zhang and H. C. Chen (2014) 'Supporting orthographic learning at the beginning stage of learning to read Chinese as a second language,' *International Journal of Disability, Development and Education*, 61(3): 288–305.

Chapelle, C. A. (1998) 'Construct definition and validity inquiry in SLA,' in Bachman, L. F. and A. D. Cohen (eds.) *Interfaces between Second Language Acquisition and Language Testing Research*. Cambridge: Cambridge University Press, 32–70.

Chapelle, C. A. (2012) 'Conceptions of validity,' in Fulcher, G. and F. Davidson (eds.) *The Routledge Handbook of Language Testing*. Abingdon and New York: Routledge, 21–33.

Chen, H. C. (1999) 'How do readers of Chinese process words during reading for comprehension?', in Wang, J. and H. C. Chen (eds.) *Reading Chinese Script: A Cognitive Analysis*. Mahwah, Jersey: Lawrence Erlbaum Associates, Inc., 257–78.

Chen, M. J., Y. F. Yung and T. W. Ng (1988) 'The effect of context on the perception of Chinese characters', in I. M. Liu, H.-C. Chen and M. J. Chen (Eds.) *Cognitive Aspects of the Chinese Language*. Hong Kong: Asian Research Service, 27–39.

Chen, N. F., D. W. Rong, T. B. Ma and H. Zhou (2016) 'Large-scale characterization of non-native Mandarin Chinese spoken by speakers of European origin: Analysis on iCALL,' *Speech Communication*, 84: 46–56.

Cheng, L. Y. and J. Fox (2017) *Assessment in the Language Classroom: Teachers Supporting Student Learning*. London: Palgrave.

Chinesetest.cn (2019) *Test Items in the Writing Papers and Examples of New HSK Level 3, 4 and 5*. Available at www.chinesetest.cn/godownload.do (Accessed on 6th Mar. 2019).

Chu, C. Z. (2006) 'A reflection on traditional approaches to Chinese character teaching-learning,' in Yao et al. (eds.) *Studies on Chinese Instructional Materials and Pedagogy*. Beijing: Beijing Languages University Press, 240–57.

Clarke, S. (1998) *Targeting Assessment in the Primary Classroom: Strategies for Planning, Assessment, Pupil Feedback and Target Setting*. Banbury, UK: Hodder Education.

Clarke, S. (2001) *Unlocking Formative Assessment*. London: Hodder and Stoughton.

CoE (2001a) *Common European Framework of References for Language: Learning, Teaching and Assessment*. Available at www.coe.int/en/web/common-european-framework-reference-languages/language-policy-in-the-council-of-europe. (Accessed on 10th Sept. 2019).

CoE (2001b) *Structured Overview of All CEFR Scales*. Available at www.coe.int/en/web/portfolio/overview-of-cefr-related-scales. (Accessed on 7th May 2020).

CoE (2018) *CEFR: Learning, Teaching, Assessment, Companion Volume with New Descriptors*. Available at https://rm.coe.int/cefr-companion-volume-with-new-descriptors-2018/1680787989 (Accessed on 7th May 2019).

Confucius Institute (2018) 'Confucius institute data analysis 2018,' 孔子学院院刊 *(Confucius Institute Magazine), Dec. 2018 Issue*. Available at www.jiaohanyu.com/article/697 (Accessed on 2nd Jan. 2019).

Coniam, D. (2009) 'Investigating the quality of teacher-produced tests for EFL students and the impact of training in test development principles on improving test quality,' *System*, 37(2): 226–42.

Corder, P. (1981) *Error Analysis and Interlanguage*. Cambridge: University of Cambridge Press.

Davies, A. (2008) 'Textbook trends in teaching language testing,' *Language Testing*, 25(3): 327–47.

Davies, A., A. Brown, C. Elder, K, Hill, T. Lumley and T. McNamara (1999) *Dictionary of Language Testing*. Studies in Language Testing, No. 7. Cambridge: CLES/Cambridge University Press.

Davis, L., V. Timpe-Laughlin, L. Gu and G. Ockey (2018) 'Face-to-face speaking assessment in the digital age: Interactive speaking tasks online,' in McE, J., J. Davis, M. Norris, M. E. Malone, T. H. McKay and Y. A. Son (eds.) *Useful Assessment and Evaluation in Language Education*. Washington, DC, USA: Georgetown University Press, 115–30.

Davison, C. and C. Leung (2009) 'Current issues in English language teacher-based assessment,' *TESOL Quarterly*, 43: 393–415.

DeFrancis, J. (2006) 'The prospects for Chinese writing reform,' *Sino-Platonic Papers, No. 171*. Available at www.sino-platonic.org/complete/spp171_chinese_writing_reform.pdf.

De Jong, N. J., M. P. Steinel, A. F. Florijn, R. Schoonen and J. H. Hulstijn (2012) 'Facets of speaking proficiency,' *Studies in Second Language Acquisition*, 34: 5–34.

Devitt, A. and W. M. Liu (2017) 'Bootstrapping learning in a Chinese beginners' classroom,' in Lu, Y. (ed.) *Teaching and Learning Chinese in Higher Education: Theoretical and Practical Issues*. Abingdon: Routledge, 157–76.

Donato, R. (2004) 'Aspects of collaboration in pedagogical discourse,' *Annual Review of Applied Linguistics*, 24: 284–302.
Douglas, D. (2000) *Assessing Language for Specific Purposes: Theory and Practice*. Cambridge: Cambridge University Press.
EBCL (2012a) *EBCL A1-A2+ Can-Do Statements*. Available at http://ebcl.eu.com/wp-content/uploads/2013/02/EBCL-A1-A2+-Can-do-Statements-Oct-2012.pdf (Accessed on 1st Sept. 2018).
EBCL (2012b) *EBCL Supporting Documents for Can-Do Statements*. Available at http://ebcl.eu.com/wp-Dcontent/uploads/2013/02/EBCL-Supporting-Documents-for-CDS-Oct-2012.pdf (Accessed on 1st Sept. 2018).
EBCL (2013) *Final Report (for the Public)*. Available at http://eacea.ec.europa.eu/llp/projects/.
Eggins, S. and D. Slade (1997) *Analysing Casual Conversation*. Sheffield, UK: Equinox Publishing Ltd.
Ellis, R. (2008). *The Study of Second Language Acquisition* (2nd ed.). Oxford, England: Oxford University Press.
Flores d'Arcais, G. B. (1994). 'Order of strokes writing as a cue for retrieval in reading Chinese characters,' *European Journal of Cognitive Psychology*, 6: 337–55. doi:10.1080/09541449408406519.
Erlam, R. (2006). 'Elicited imitation as a measure of L2 implicit knowledge: An empirical validation study,' *Applied Linguistics*, 27: 464–91.
Everson, M. E. (2011a) 'Best practices in teaching logographic and Non-Roman writing systems to L2 learners,' *Annual Review of Applied Linguistics*, 31(1): 249–74.
Everson, M. E. (2011b) 'The importance of standards,' in Everson, M. E. and Y. Xiao (eds.) *Teaching Chinese as a Foreign Language: Theories and Applications*. Boston, MA: Cheng & Tsui, 3–18.
Feng, L. X., A. Lindner, X. R. Ji and R. M. Joshi (2017) 'The roles of handwriting and keyboarding in writing: A meta-analytic review,' *Read and Write, Jan. 2019*. doi:10.1007/s11145-017-9749-x.
Flower, L. and J. R. Hayes (1981) 'A cognitive process theory of writing,' *College Composition and Communication*, 32: 365–87.
Fulcher, G. (2003) *Testing Second Language Speaking*. London and New York: Routledge.
Fulcher, G. (2010) *Practical Language Testing*. London, UK: Hodder Education.
Fulcher, G. and F. Davidson (2007) *Language Testing and Assessment*. London and New York: Routledge.
Galaczi, E. and N. Khabbazbashi (2016) 'Putting tests to the test: Six questions all teachers should ask,' *50th IATFL Annual Conference*, Birmingham, UK.
Galaczi, E. and L. Taylor (2018) 'Interactional competence: Conceptualisations, operationalisations, and outstanding questions,' *Language Assessment Quarterly*, 15(3): 219–36. doi:10.1080/15434303.2018.1453816.
Gardner, J. (2006) 'Assessment and learning: An introduction', in Gardner, J. (ed.) *Assessment and Learning*. London: Sage Publications, 1–8.
Genesee, F. and J. Upshur (1996) *Classroom Evaluation in Second Language Education*. Cambridge: Cambridge University Press.
Givon, T. (2001) *Syntax: An Introduction, Volume I*. Amsterdam and Philadelphia: John Benjamins Publishing Company.
Graham, S., K. R, Harris and B. Fink (2000) 'Is handwriting causally related to learning to write? Treatment of handwriting problems in beginning writers,' *Journal of Educational Psychology*, 92, 620–35. doi:10.1037/0022-0663.92.4.620.

Green, A. (2013) *Exploring Language Assessment and Testing: Language in Action*. Abingdon, UK: Routledge.

Guan, C. Q., Y. D. Liu, H. L. Chan, F. F. Ye and C. A. Perfetti (2011) 'Writing strengthens orthography and alphabetic-coding strengthens phonology in learning to read Chinese,' *Journal of Educational Psychology*, 103(3): 509–22.

Guan, C. Q., W. J. Meng and C. Perfetti (2015) 'Writing quality predicts Chinese learning,' *Read Writ*, 28: 915, 763–95.

Guan, C. Q., F. Ye, W. J. Meng and C. K. Leong (2013a) 'Are poor Chinese text comprehenders also poor in written composition?,' *Annual of Dyslexia*, 63: 217–38. https://doi.org/10.1007/s11881-013-0081.

Guan, C. Q., F. F. Ye, R. K. Wagner and W. J. Meng (2013b) 'Developmental and individual differences in Chinese writing,' *Read Writ*, 26(6): 1031–56. doi:10.1007/s11145-012-9405-4.

Guan, C. Q., F. F. Ye, R. K. Wagner, W. J. Meng and C. K. Leong (2014) 'Text comprehension mediates morphological awareness, syntactic processing, and working memory in predicting Chinese written composition performance,' *Journal of Educational Psychology*, 106(3): 779–98. doi:10.1037/a0035984.

Guder, A. (2014) 'Reading competence and graphemic competence: Impacts of the Chinese writing system on designing competence descriptors for the "European Benchmarks for the Chinese Language" (EBCL) project,' *CHUN-Chinesisch-Unterricht*, 29: 5–29.

Han, J. H. (2017) *Post-Lingual Chinese Language Learning: Hanzi Pedagogy*. London: Palgrave Macmillan.

Hanban (2007) *Chinese Language Proficiency Scales for Speakers of Other Languages*. Available at www.seiservices.com/APEC/WikiFiles/10.2.pdf (Accessed on 16th April 2018).

Hanban (2008) *International Curriculum for Chinese Language Education* (1st ed.). Available at www.hanban.org/article/2014-05/14/content_536059.htm (Accessed on 16th April 2018).

Hanban (2009) *Graded Chinese Syllabus, Characters and Words for the Application of Teaching Chinese to the Speakers of Other Languages*. Beijing: Beijing Language and Culture University Press.

Hanban (2014) *International Curriculum for Chinese Language Education* (Revised ed.). Available at www.hanban.org/article/2014-05/14/content_536059.htm. Accessed on 16th April 2018).

Harding, L. (2014) 'Communicative language testing: Current issues and future research', *Language Assessment Quarterly*, 11(2): 186–97.

Harlen, W. (2005) 'Teachers' summative practices and assessment for learning-tensions and synergies,' *The Curriculum Journal*, 16(2): 207–23.

Harlen, W. and M. James (1997) 'Assessment and learning: Differences and relationships between formative and summative assessment,' *Assessment in Education: Principles, Policy & Practice*, 4(3): 365–79.

Harley, B., J. Cummins, M. Swain and P. Allen (1990) 'The nature of language proficiency,' in Harley, B., J. Cummins, M. Swain and P. Allen (eds.) *The Development of Second Language Proficiency*. Cambridge, UK: Cambridge University Press, 7–38.

Harsch, C. (2014) 'General language proficiency revisited: Current and future issues,' *Language Assessment Quarterly*, 11(2): 152–69.

Harsch, C., H. A. Pant and O. Köller (2010) *Calibrating Standards-Based Assessment Tasks for English as a Frst Foreign Language: Standard-Setting Procedures in Germany*. Münster, Germany: Waxmann.

References

Harsch, G. and J. Hartig (2015) 'What are we aligning tests to when we report test alignment to the CEFR?,' *Language Assessment Quarterly*, 12: 333–62.

Hasselgreen, A., C. Carlsen and H. Helness (2004) *European Survey of Language and Assessment Needs. Part One: General Findings*. Available at www.ealta.eu.org/documents/resources/survey-report-pt1.pdf (Accessed on 16th June 2018).

Hayes, E. (1987) 'The relationship between "word length" and memorability among nonnative readers of Chinese Mandarin,' *Journal of the Chinese Language Teachers Association*, 25(3): 31–41.

He, A. W. and R. Young (1998) 'Language proficiency interviews: A discourse approach,' in Young, R. and A. W. He (eds.) *Talking and Testing*. Philadelphia and Amsterdam: John Benjamins, 1–24.

Heritage, M. (2008) *Learning Progressions: Supporting Instruction and Formative Assessment*. Washington, DC: Chief Council of State School Officers.

Hill, K. (2017) 'Understanding classroom-based assessment practices: A precondition for teacher assessment literacy,' *Language Testing and Assessment*, 6(1): 1–17.

Hodgen, J. and M. Webb (2008) 'Questioning and dialogue,' in Swaffield, S. (ed.) *Unlocking Assessment: Understanding for Reflecting and Application*. Abington and New York: Routledge, 73–89.

HSK (2018) 新汉语水平考试/HSK 词汇（2012 年修订版）*(New Chinese Proficiency Test/HSK Vocabulary (revised in 2012)*. Available at www.chinesetest.cn/godownload.do (Accessed on 15th Sept. 2018).

HSK Level 3 Sample Paper (2018) Available at www.chinesetest.cn/userfiles/file/dagang/HSK3.pdf.

Hu, B. (2011) 'The challenge of Chinese: A preliminary study of UK learners' perceptions of difficulty,' *Language Learning Journal*, 38: 99–118.

Hu, R. F. (2017) '汉语词汇测试自动命题研究 (Automatic Generation of Chinese Vocabulary Test Questions,' *Journal of Chinese Information Processing*, 13(1): 41–9.

Huang, Z., J. Xie and E. Xun (2014) 'Feature extraction for automated scoring of essays of the HSK,' *Computer Engineering and Applications*, Mar.: 118–22.

Hubley, N. J. (2012) 'Assessing reading,' in Coombe, C., S. J. Stoynoff, P. Davidson and B. O'Sullivan (eds.) *The Cambridge Guide to Second Language Assessment*. Cambridge, New York: Cambridge University Press, 211–17.

Hughes, A. (2003) *Testing for Language Teachers* (2nd ed.). Cambridge: Cambridge University Press.

Hulstijn, J. H. (2007) 'The shaky ground beneath the CEFR: Quantitative and qualitative dimensions of language proficiency,' *The Modern Language Journal*, 91(4): 663–7.

Hulstijn, J. H. (2011a). 'Linking L2 proficiency to L2 acquisition: Opportunities and challenges of profiling research,' in Bartning, I., M. Martin and I. Vedder (eds.) *Communicative Proficiency and Linguistic Development: Intersections between SLA and Language Testing Research*. Eurosla Monographs Series, 1, Rome: European Second Language Association, 233–8.

Hulstijn, J. H. (2011b). 'Explanations of associations between L1 and L2 literacy skills,' in Schmid, M. S. and W. Lowie (eds.) *Modeling Bilingualism: From Structure to Chaos*. Amsterdam, the Netherlands: John Benjamins, 85–111.

Hulstijn, J. H. (2011c) 'Language proficiency in native and nonnative speakers: An agenda for research and suggestions for second-language assessment,' *Language Assessment Quarterly*, 8(3): 229–49.

Hulstijn, J. H., A. Van Gelderen and R. Schoonen (2009) 'Automatization in second-language acquisition: What does the coefficient of variation tell us?,' *Applied Psycholinguistics*, 30: 555–82.

Huo, L. (2012) 'The impact of visual pedagogy on students' learning of Hanyu: A case study of a Western Sydney public school,' (MA thesis). Western Sydney University, Sydney.

Hymes, D. H. (1972). 'On communicative competence,' in Pride, J. B., J. Holmes (eds.) *Sociolinguistics: Selected readings*. Harmondsworth: Penguin, 269–93.

Jackson, N. E., M. E. Everson and C. Ke (2003) 'Beginning readers' awareness of the orthographic structure of semantic-phonetic compounds: Lessons from a study of learners of Chinese as a foreign language,' in C. McBride-Chang and H. Chen (eds.) *Reading Development in Chinese Children*. Westport: Praeger Publishers, 141–56.

Jiang, W. Y. (2009) *Acquisition of Word Order in Chinese as a Foreign Language*. Berlin: De Gruyter.

Jiang, W. Y. (2013) 'Measurements of development in L2 written production: The case of L2 Chinese,' *Applied Linguistics*, 34(1): 1–24.

Jiang, W. Y. (2017) 'Acquisition of word order in Chinese as a foreign language,' in Keacskes, I. and C. F. Sun (eds.) *Key Issues in Chinese as a Second Language Research*. New York and London: Routledge, 162–87.

Jiang, X. (2007) '"认写分流、多认少写" 汉字教学方法的实验研究 ("Reading and writing taught separately, read more and write less"),' *Word Chinese Language Teaching*, 80(2): 90–7.

Jiang, X. and Y. Fang (2012) 'The effects of context and word morphology on interpreting unknown words by learners of Chinese as a second language,' *Acta Psychologica Sinica*, 44: 76–86.

Jin, H. G. (1994) 'Topic-prominence and subject-prominence in L2 acquisition: Evidence of English-to-Chinese typological transfer,' *Language Learning*, 44(1): 101–22.

Jin, L. (2012) 'When in China, do as the Chinese do? Learning compliment responding in a study abroad program,' *Chinese as a Second Language Research*, 1(2): 211–40.

Jin, L. (2015) 'Developing Chinese complimenting in a study abroad program,' *Chinese Journal of Applied Linguistics*, 38(3): 277–300.

Jin, T. and B. Mak (2012) 'Distinguishing features in scoring L2 Chinese speaking performance: How do they work?,' *Language Testing*, 30(1): 23–47.

Jin, Y. and J. Wang (2012) 'A study on Chinese listening ability structure of foreign students at the beginning level,' *Language Teaching and Linguistic Studies*, 3: 35–41.

Johnson, D. W. and R. T. Johnson (1990) 'Cooperative learning and achievement,' in Sharan, S. (ed.) *Cooperative Learning: Theory and Research*. New York: Praeger, 23–37.

Johnson, J. S. and S. L. Gad (2009) 'The influence of rater language background on writing performance assessment,' *Language Testing*, 26(4): 485–505.

Jones, N. and N. Saville (2016) '*Learning Oriented Assessment*: A systemic approach,' in *Studies in Language Testing* (Vol. 45). Cambridge: Cambridge University Press.

Jones, W. (2012) 'Assessing students' grammatical ability', in Coombe, C., P. Davidson, B. O'Sullivan and S. Stoynoff (eds.) *The Cambridge Guide to Second Language Assessment*. New York: Cambridge University Press, 247–56.

Kasper, G. (2001) 'Four perspectives on L2 pragmatic development,' *Applied Linguistics*, 22(4): 502–30.

Ke, C. (1998) 'Effects of strategies on the learning of Chinese characters among foreign language students,' *Journal of the Chinese Language Teachers Association*, 33(2): 9–112.

Ke, C. (2006) 'A model of formative task-based language assessment for Chinese as a foreign language,' *Language Assessment Quarterly*, 3(2): 207–27.

Ke, C. (2012) 'Research in second language acquisition of Chinese: Where we are, where we are going,' *Journal of the Chinese Language Teachers Association*, 47(3): 43–113.

Kim, H. J. (2015) 'A qualitative analysis of rater behavior on an L2 speaking assessment,' *Language Assessment Quarterly*, 12(3): 239–61.

Kremmel, B. and L. Harding (2020) 'Towards a comprehensive, empirical model of language assessment literacy across stakeholder groups: Developing the language assessment literacy survey,' *Language Assessment Quarterly*, 17(1), 100–20. doi:10.1080/15434303.2019.1674855.

Kvasova, O. and T. Kavytska (2014) 'The assessment competence of university foreign language teachers: A ukrainian perspective,' *CercleS*, 4(1): 159–77.

Lado, R. (1961) *Language Testing: The Construction and Use of Foreign Language Tests*. New York, NY: McGraw-Hill.

Lazaraton, A. (1996) 'Interlocutor support in oral proficiency interviews: The case of CASE,' *Language Testing*, 13(2): 151–72.

Leung, C. (2004) 'Developing formative teacher assessment: Knowledge, practice and change,' *Language Assessment Quarterly*, 1: 19–41.

Leung, C. and B. Mohan (2004) 'Teacher formative assessment and talk in classroom contexts: Assessment as discourse and assessment of discourse,' *Language Testing*, 21(3): 335–59.

Leung, C. and A. Teasdale (1997) 'What do teachers mean by speaking and listening? A contextualised study of assessment in multilingual classrooms in the English National Curriculum,' in Huhta, V., L. Kohonen, L. Kurki-Suonio and S. Luoma (eds.) *Current Developments and Alternatives in Language Assessment: Proceedings of LTRC '96*. Jyväskyla, Finland: University of Jyväskyla, 291–324.

Li, C. N. and S. A. Thompson (1989) *Mandarin Chinese: A Functional Reference Grammar*. Berkeley, Los Angeles and London: University of California Press.

Li, J. and Y. Li (2008) 'On the transparency of lexical meaning,' *Studies in Language and Linguistics*, 28: 60–5.

Li, J. and J. Zhao (2012) 'Two picture-based tests of writing in Chinese as a second language: An experimental study,' *TCSOL Studies*, Sep.: 38–43.

Li, L. (2017) 'Can grammatical knowledge predict Chinese proficiency?,' in Zhang, D. and C. Lin (eds.) *Chinese as a Second Language Assessment*. Singapore: Springer, 141–58.

Li, N. H., J. Spinks, G. F. Eden, C. A. Perfetti and W. T. Siok (2005) 'Reading depends on writing, in Chinese,' *Proceedings of the National Academy of Sciences*, 102(24): 8781–5.

Li, P., H. Shu, and Y. Liu (2014) 'Neurocognitive approaches to the processing of Chinese,' in Huang, J., A. Li and A. Simpson (eds.) *Handbook of Chinese Linguistics*. Wiley Online Library, 511–33. Available at http://onlinelibrary.wiley.com/doi/10.1002/9781118584552.ch20/summary (Accessed on 8th Sept. 2018).

Li, R. and B. B. Ye (2013) '语文分进教学模式对汉字能力的影响—针对非汉语文化圈学习者的研究 (The influence of teaching speaking and writing separately on character competence: Study on learners from non-character background),' *Studies on the Chinese Language*, 4: 98–106.

Li, S. (2012) 'The effects of input-based practice on pragmatic development of requests in L2 Chinese,' *Language Learning*, 62(2): 403–38.

Li, S. (2014) 'The gap in the use of lexical cohesive devices in writing between native Chinese speakers and second language users,' *Journal of the Chinese Language Teachers Association*, 49(3): 25–47.

Li, S., N. Taguchi and F. Xiao (2019) 'Variations in rating scale functioning in assessing speech act production in L2 Chinese,' *Language Assessment Quarterly*, 16(3): 271–93. doi:10.1080/15434303.2019.1648473.

Li, S. and J. Wang (2017) 'Diagnostic assessment of L2 Chinese learners' reading comprehension ability,' in Zhang, D. B. and C. H. Lin (eds.) *Chinese as a Second Language Assessment*. Singapore: Springer, 183–202.

Li, X. Q., X. J. Qian and L. Huang (2006) *Boya Chinese, Intermediate II*. Beijing: Beijing University Press.

Ling, V. (2007) 'Studies on L2 acquisition of the Chinese script,' *Journal of the Chinese Language Teachers Association*, 42: 1–19.

Little, D. (2014) 'The common European framework of reference for languages: Perspectives on the making of supranational language education policy,' *The Modern Language Journal*, 91(4): 645–55.

Liu, M. H. (2013) 'Processes involved in Chinese and English writing: A study of Chinese university students,' *International Journal of Applied Linguistics & English Literature*, 2(6): 88–97.

Liu, X., K. Zhang, S. H. Liu, Y, Chen, S. D. Zuo and J. W. Shi (2003, 2008, 2012) *New Practical Chinese Reader* (Vol. 1 and 4). Beijing, China: Beijing Language and Culture University Press.

Liu, Y. (2017) 'Assessing Chinese in the USA: An overview of the major tests,' in Zhang, D. B. and C. H. Lin (eds.) *Chinese as a Second Language Assessment*. Singapore: Springer, 43–66.

Long, M. H. and J. M. Norris (2000) 'Task-based language teaching and assessment,' in M. Byram (ed.), *Encyclopaedia of Language Teaching*. London: Routledge, 597–603.

Lu, Y. (2005) 'A validation study of the ECCE NNS and NS examiners' conversational styles from a discourse analytic perspective,' in *Spaan Fellow Working Papers in Second or Foreign Language Assessment* (Vol. 3). Ann Arbor, MI: English Language Institute, University of Michigan, 73–100.

Lu, Y. (2014) 'A hybrid of inductive and deductive approach for teaching Chinese grammar: The analytic approach,' in Xing, M. J. and L. M. Li (eds.) *Developing Pedagogies for Teaching Chinese as a Foreign Language in Higher Education, Applied Chinese Language Studies V*. London: Cypress Book Company (UK) Limited, 1–11.

Lu, Y. (2017) 'Exploring the criterion-validity of HSK Level 3 and 4: Are assessment and CEFR standards related', in Y. Lu (ed.) *Teaching and Learning Chinese in Higher Education: Theoretical and Practical Issues*. Abingdon: Routledge, 13–34.

Lu, Y. and C. Ke (2018) 'L2 Chinese grammar development', in C. Ke (ed.) *The Routledge Handbook of Chinese Second Language Acquisition*. New York: Routledge, 175–221.

Lu, Y. and L. Y. Song (2017) 'European benchmarking Chinese language: Defining the competences in the written language,' in Lu, Y. (ed.) *Teaching and Learning Chinese in Higher Education: Theoretical and Practical Issues*. Abingdon: Routledge, 13–34.

Mackey, A. (2006) 'Feedback, noticing instructed second language learning,' *Applied Linguistics*, 27(3): 405–30.

Many, J. E., D. Dewberry, D. L. Taylor, and K. Coady (2009) "Profiles of three preservice ESOL teachers' development of instructional scaffolding,' *Reading Psychology*, 30(2): 148–74.

McNamara, T. F. (1996) *Measuring Second Language Performance*. London, UK: Longman.

McNamara, T. F. (1997) '"Interaction" in second language performance assessment: Whose performance?,' *Applied Linguistics*, 18: 446–66.
McNamara, T. F. and R. J. Adams (1991) 'Exploring rater behaviour with rasch techniques,' *Paper presented at the 13th Language Testing Research Colloquium, Educational Testing Service*, Princeton, NJ.
Messick, S. (1996) 'Validity and washback in language testing,' *Language Testing*, Nov. 1: 241–56.
Myers, J. (2019) *The Grammar of Chinese Characters: Productive Knowledge of Formal Patterns in an Orthographic System*. Routledge Studies of Eastern Asian Linguistics. London, UK: Routledge.
Nakatsuhara, I., C. Inoue, V. Berry and E. Galaczi (2017) 'Exploring the use of videoconferencing technology in the assessment of spoken language: A mixed-methods study,' *Language Assessment Quarterly*, 14(1): 1–18. doi:10.1080/15434303.2016.1263637.
Nassaji, H. and M. A. Swain (2000) 'Vygotskian perspective on corrective feedback in L2: The effect of random versus negotiated help on the learning of English articles,' *Language Awareness*, 9(1): 34–51.
Nation, P. (2013) *Learning Vocabulary in Another Language* (2nd ed.). Cambridge: Cambridge University Press.
Nation, P. (2018) *Test Your Students' Vocabulary Size*. Available at https://my.vocabularysize.com/
National Standards Collaborative Board (2015) Available at www.actfl.org/resources/world-readiness-standards-learning-languages/standards-summary (Accessed on 11th Jan. 2022).
Oller, J. W. Jr. (1979) *Language Tests at School: A Pragmatic Approach*. London: Longman.
Ortega, L., N. Iwashita, J. M. Norris and S. Rabie (2002) 'An investigation of elicited imitation tasks in crosslinguistic SLA research,' *Paper presented at the Second Language Research Forum*, Toronto.
O'Sullivan, B. (2012) 'Assessing speaking,' in C. Coombe, P. Davidson, B. O'Sullivan and S. Stoynoff (eds.) *The Cambridge Guide to Second Language Assessment*. New York: Cambridge University Press, 234–46.
O'Sullivan, B. and A. B. Green (2011) 'Test taker characteristics,' in L. Taylor (ed.) *Examining Speaking: Research and Practice in Assessing Second Language Speaking*. Cambridge, UK: Cambridge University Press and Cambridge ESOL.
O'Sullivan, B. and Y. Lu (2006) 'The impact on candidate language of examiner deviation from a set interlocutor frame in the IELTS speaking test' in IELTS research report,' *British Council and IDP: IELTS Australia*, 6: 91–115.
Packard, J. L. (1990) 'Effects of time lag in the introduction of characters into the Chinese language curriculum,' *The Modern Language Journal*, 74: 167–75.
Pan, W. G. (2006) 'Character-unit theory: Theoretical and philosophical reflection (字本位，理论的哲学思考,' *Language Teaching and Research*, 3: 36–45.
Perfetti, C. (2012) 'Thru but not wisht: Language, writing, and universal reading theory,' *Behavioral and Brain Sciences*, 35(5): 299–300.
Perfetti, C., Y. Liu and L. H. Tan (2005) 'The lexical constituency model: Some implications of research on Chinese for general theories of reading,' *Psychological Review*, 112(1): 43–59.
Phil, J. and L. Harding (2013) 'Defining the language assessment literacy gap: Evidence from a parliamentary inquiry,' *Language Testing*, 30(3): 381–402.
Poehner, M. E. and J. P. Lantolf (2005) 'Dynamic assessment in the language classroom,' *Language Teaching Research*, 9(3): 233–65.

Poehner, M. E. and J. P. Lantolf (2013) 'Bringing the ZPD into the Equation: Capturing L2 development during computerized dynamic assessment (C-DA),' *Language Teaching Research*, 17(3): 323–42.

Poehner, M. E. and X. Lu (2015) 'Computerized dynamic assessment (C-DA): Diagnosing L2 development according to learner responsiveness to mediation,' *Language Testing*, 32(3): 337–57. Available at Publicparts/documents/languages/lan_mp_511644_EBCLfinal.pdf (Accessed on 1st Aug. 2020).

Purpura, J. (2004) *Assessing Grammar*. Cambridge: Cambridge University Press.

Purpura, J. (2013) 'Assessment of grammar,' in Kunnan, A. J. (ed.) *Companion to Language Assessment*. Oxford, UK: Wiley-Blackwell, 100–24.

Purpura, J. (2016) 'Second and foreign language assessment,' *Modern Language Journal*, 100(Supplement): 190–208.

Read, J. (2000) *Assessing Vocabulary*. Cambridge: Cambridge University Press.

Rea-Dickins, P. (2004) 'Understanding teachers as agents of assessment,' *Language Testing*, 21: 249–58.

Ren, C. (2004) 'Objective scoring of essays of the HSK,' *Chinese Language Learning*, Dec.: 58–67.

Richards, J. C. and T. S. Rodgers (2001) *Approaches and Methods in Language Teaching* (2nd ed.). Cambridge: Cambridge University Press.

Roever, G. and G. Kasper (2018) 'Speaking in turns and sequences: Interactional competence as a target construct in testing speaking,' *Language Testing*, 35(3): 331–55.

Romagnoli, C. (2017) 'Chinese vocabulary acquisition and teaching: Basic concepts and research results,' in Keacskes, I. and C. F. Sun (eds.) *Key Issues in Chinese as a Second Language Research*. New York and London: Routledge, 125–42.

Ross, S. (1992) 'The discourse of accommodation in oral proficiency interviews,' *Studies in Second Language Acquisition*, 14: 159–75.

Rost, M. (2015) *Teaching and Researching Listening* (3rd ed.). Abington and New York: Routledge.

Sargent, W. K. and M. E. Everson (1992) 'The effects of frequency and density on character recognition speed and accuracy by elementary and advanced L2 readers of Chinese,' *Journal of Chinese Language Teachers Association*, 27(1/2): 29–54.

Schegloff, E. A. (2006) 'Interaction: The infrastructure for social institutions, the natural ecological niche for language, and the arena in which culture is enacted,' in Enfield, J. and S. C. Levinson (eds.) *Roots of Human Society*. Oxford: Berg, 70–96.

Schegloff, E. A. and H. Sacks (1973) 'Opening up closings,' *Semiotica*, 8(4): 289–327.

Schmidt, R. (1990) 'The role of consciousness in second language learning,' *Applied Linguistics,* 11: 127–58.

Schmitt, N. (2010) *Researching Vocabulary: A Vocabulary Research Manual*. London: Palgrave Macmillan.

Scrimgeour, A. (2011) 'Issues and approaches to literacy development in Chinese second language classroom,' in Tsung, L. and K. Cruickshank (eds.) *Teaching and Learning Chinese in Global Contexts: Multimodality and Literacy in the Media Age*. London and New York: Continuum International Publishing Group, 197–212.

Selinker, L. (1992) *Rediscovering Interlanguage*. Abingdon and New York: Routledge.

Seymour, P. H. K. (2006) 'Theoretical framework for beginning reading in different orthographies,' in R. J. Malateshal and P. G. Aaron (eds.) *Handbook of Orthography and Literacy*. London: Lawrence Erlbaum Associates, Inc., 441–62.

Shayer, M. and P. Adey (2002) *Learning Intelligence: Cognitive Acceleration across the Curriculum 5 to 15 Years*. Milton Keynes: Open University Press.

Shen, H. H. (2008) 'An analysis of word decision strategies among learners of Chinese,' *Foreign Language Annals*, 41: 501–24.
Shen, H. H. (2009) 'Size and strength: Written vocabulary acquisition among advanced CFL learners,' *Chinese Teaching in the World*, 23: 74–85.
Shen, H. H. (2010) 'Analysis of radical knowledge development among beginning CFL learners,' in Everson, M. E. and H. H. Shen (eds.) *Research among Learners of Chinese as a Foreign Language*. Honolulu: University of Hawai'i, National Foreign Language Resource Center, 45–65.
Shen, H. H. (2019) 'Chinese as a second language reading: Lexical access and text comprehension,' in Ke, C. (ed.) *The Routledge Handbook of Chinese Second Language Acquisition*. London and New York: Taylor and Francis Group, 134–50.
Shen, H. H. and C. Ke (2007) 'An investigation of radical awareness and word acquisition among non-native learners of Chinese,' *The Modern Language Journal*, 91: 97–111.
Shi, F. and B. Wen. (2009) 'Language transfer in English vowels produced by Chinese students and Chinese vowels produced by American students,' *Journal of Chinese Language Teachers Association*, 44(2): 17–32.
Shi, L. J. (2017) 'The impact of an online grammar self-assessment system on CFL learners and teachers,' in Y. Lu (ed.) *Teaching and Learning Chinese in Higher Education: Theoretical and Practical Issues*. Abingdon: Routledge, 177–98.
Shi, Z. Y. (2000) '外国留学生字形书写偏误分析 (Error analysis of Chinese characters written by foreign learners),' *Chinese Language Learning*, (2): 38–41.
Sinclair, J. and R. M. Coulthard (1975) *Toward an Analysis of Discourse*. Oxford: Oxford University Press.
Skehan, P. (1998) *A Cognitive Approach to Language Learning*. Oxford: Oxford University Press.
Spratt, M. (2005) 'Washback and the classroom: The implications for teaching and learning of studies of washback from exams,' *Language Teaching Research*, 9(1): 5–29.
Stiggins, R. J., M. M. Griswold and K. R. Wikelund (1989) 'Measuring thinking skills through classroom assessment,' *Journal of Educational Measurement*, 26: 233–46.
Sun, C. F. (2006) *Chinese: A Linguistic Introduction*. Cambridge and New York: Cambridge University Press.
Sutton, R. (1995) *Assessment for Learning*. New York: RS Publications.
Taft, M., Y. Liu and X. Zhu (1999) 'Morphemic processing in reading Chinese,' in Wang, J., A. Inhoff and H. C. Chen (eds.) *Reading Chinese Script: A Cognitive Analysis*. Hillsdale, NJ: Lawrence Erlbaum Associates, 91–113.
Taguchi, N., S. Li and F. Xiao (2013) 'Production of formulaic expressions in L2 Chinese: A developmental investigation in a study abroad context,' *Chinese as a Second Language Research*, 2(1): 23–58.
Tan, L., J. A. Spinks, G. F. Eden, C. A. Perfetti and W. T. Sio (2005) 'Reading depends on writing, in Chinese,' *Proceedings of the National Academy of Sciences*, 102(24): 8781–85. doi:10.1073/pnas.0503523102.
Tauroza, S. and D. Allison (1995) 'Expectation-driven understanding in information systems lecture comprehension,' in Flowerdew, J. (ed.) *Academic Listening; Research Perspective*. Cambridge: Cambridge University Press, 35–54.
Taylor, L. (2013) 'Communicating the theory, practice and principles of language testing to test stakeholders: Some reflections,' *Language Testing*, 30(3): 403–12.
Taylor, L. and E. Galaczi (2011) 'Scoring validity,' in Taylor, L. (ed.) *Examining Speaking: Research and Practice in Assessing Second Language Speaking*, Studies in Language Testing (Vol. 30). Cambridge, UK: UCLES/Cambridge University Press, 171–233.

Teasdale, A. and C. Leung (2000) 'Teacher assessment and psychometric theory: A case of paradigm crossing?,' *Language Testing*, 17(2): 163–84.

Teng, Y. J. (2017) 'Hanyu Shuiping Kaoshi (HSK): Past, present, and future,' in Zhang, D. B. and C. H. Lin (eds.) *Chinese as a Second Language Assessment*. Singapore: Springer, 21–42.

TOCFL Mock Test (2019) Available at www.sc-top.org.tw/mocktest.php (Accessed on 8th Jan. 2019).

Topping, K. J. (2005) 'Trends in peer learning,' *Educational Psychology*, 25(6): 631–45.

Torrance, H. and J. Pryor (1998) 'Investigating teacher assessment in infant classrooms: Methodological problems and emerging issues,' *Assessment in Education*, 2: 305–20.

Tsagari, D. and K. Vogt (2017) 'Assessment literacy of foreign language teachers around Europe: Research, challenges and future prospects,' *Language Testing and Assessment*, 6(1): 41–63.

Tsai, P. S. and W. H. Chu (2017) 'The use of discourse markers among Mandarin Chinese Teachers, and Chinese as a second language and Chinese as a foreign language learners,' *Applied Linguistics*, 38(5): 638–65.

Tsui, A. (1989) 'Beyond the adjacency pair,' *Language in Society*, 18(4): 545–64.

Urquhart, A. H. and C. J. Weir (1998) *Reading in a Second Language: Process, Product, and Practice*. London: Longman.

van Lier, Leo. (2004) *The Ecology and Semiotics of Language Learning: A Sociocultural Perspective*. Boston, MA: Kluwer Academic.

Vogt, K. and D. Tsagari (2014) 'Assessment literacy of foreign language teachers: Findings of a European study,' *Language Assessment Quarterly*, 11(4): 374–402.

Vygotsky, L. (1978) *Mind in Society*. Cambridge, MA: Harvard University Press.

Walsh, S. (2011) *Exploring Classroom Discourse: Language in Action*. Abington, UK: Routledge.

Walsh, S. (2012) 'Conceptualising classroom interactional competence', *Novitas Royal: (Research on Youth and Language)*, 6(1): 1–14.

Walsh, S. (2013) *Classroom Discourse and Teacher Development*. Edinburgh, UK: Edinburgh University Press.

Wang, D. (2017) 'Self- and peer assessment of oral presentation in advanced Chinese classroom: An exploratory study,' in Zhang, D. B. and C. H. Lin (eds.) *Chinese as a Second Language Assessment*. Singapore: Springer, 271–86.

Wang, J. M. (2011) 'The design of speaking tests,' in Zhang, W. X. and J. M. Wang (eds.) *Studies on Chinese Proficiency Test HSK (Revised)*. Beijing: Beijing Language and Culture University Press, 30–48.

Wang, N. (1997) '汉语字词的结构与意义 (The structure and significance of the Chinese characters and words),' in 汉语认知研究 (*Studies of Cognition of Chinese*). Jinan: Shangdong Education Press.

Wang, S. F. and Xu, G. R. (1993) *Practical Knowledge of Chinese Characters*. Beijing: Beijing Yanshan Press.

Wang, Y. J. and X. N. Shangguan. (2004) 'How Japanese learners of Chinese process the aspirated and unaspirated consonants in standard Chinese,' *Shijie Hanyu Jiaoxue (Chinese Teaching in the World)*, 18(3): 54–66.

Weigle, S. C. (2002) *Assessing Writing*. Cambridge Language Assessment Series, New York, Cambridge, Melbourne and Marid: Cambridge University Press.

Weigle, S. C. (2012) 'Assessing writing,' in C. Coombe, P. Davidson, B. O'Sullivan and S. Stoynoff (eds.), *The Cambridge Guide to Second Language Assessment*. New York, USA: Cambridge University Press, 218–24.

Weir, C. J. (2005a) 'Limitations of the common European Framework for developing comparable examinations and tests,' *Language Testing*, 22(3): 281–300.
Weir, C. J. (2005b) *Language Testing and Validation: An Evidence-Based Approach*. Basingstoke and New York: Palgrave Macmillan.
Wong, L. H., C. S. Chai and P. Gao (2011) 'The Chinese input challenges for Chinese as second language learners in computer-mediated writing: An exploratory study,' *The Turkish Online Journal of Educational Technology*, 10(3): 17–30.
Wu, J. and R. Wu (2010) 'Relating the GEPT reading comprehension tests to the CEFR,' in W. Martyniuk (ed.) *Aligning Tests with the CEFR: Reflections on Using the Council of Europe's Draft Manual*. Cambridge, UK: Cambridge University Press, 204–224.
Wu, S. L. (2011) 'Learning to express motion events in an L2: The case of Chinese directional complements,' *Language Learning*, 61: 414–54.
Wu, X., W. Li and R. C. Anderson (1999) 'Reading instruction in China.' *Journal of Curriculum Studies*, 31: 571.
Wu, Y. and Y. Chen (2006) 'A comparative study of learning strategies for listening between effective and less effective learnrs,' *Chinese Language Learning*, 2: 58–64.
Wu, Y. and L. Ortega (2013) 'Measuring global oral proficiency in SLA research: A new elicited imitation test of L2 Chinese,' *Foreign Language Annals, Vol. 46? 4* by American Council on the Teaching of Foreign Languages, 680–704.
Xi, X. M. (2012) 'Validity and automated scoring of performance tests,' in Fulcher, G. and F. Davison (eds.) *The Routledge Handbook of Language Testing*. Abington, UK: Routledge, 438–52.
Xiang, C. H. and Y. Ji (2017) 'An analysis of advanced L2 Chinese learners' common errors and their perceptions of errors in argument-based essays,' in Lu, Y. (ed.) *Teaching and Learning Chinese in Higher Education: Theoretical and Practical Issues*. Abingdon: Routledge, 201–28.
Xiao, Y. (2002) 'The effect of character density on learning Chinese as a foreign language,' *Journal of the Chinese Language Teachers Association*, 37(3): 71–84.
Xiao, Y. (2011) 'Discourse features and developmental in Chinese L2 writing,' in Everson, M. E. and H. H. Shen (eds.) *Research among Learners of Chinese as a Foreign Language*. Honolulu: University of Hawai'i, National Foreign Language Resource Center, 118–33.
Xie, Y. (2015) 'The acquisition of Mandarin basic vowels by American students: A comparison study of Monosyllabic and disyllabic words,' *Journal of Chinese Language Teachers Association*, 48(1): 91–108.
Xing, J. Z. (1993) 'Discourse functions of word order in Chinese: A quantitative analysis of diachronic texts,' (Doctoral dissertation). University of Michigan.
Xing, J. Z. (2006) *Teaching and Learning Chinese as a Foreign Language: A Pedagogical Grammar*. Hong Kong: Hong Kong University Press.
Xing, J. Z. (2015) 'A comparative study of semantic change in grammaticalization and lexicalization in Chinese and Germanic languages,' *Studies in Language*, 39(3): 593–633.
Xu, D. Z. (2020) 'The evolution of Chinese character competence and the development of Chinese L2 curriculum,' *The First Series of the EACT International Forum on Teaching Chinese as a Second Language*. Available at https://k.cnki.net/CInfo/Index/10419 (Accessed on 24th Mar. 2021).
Xu, P. and T. Jen (2005) '"Penless" Chinese language learning: A computer-assisted approach,' *Journal of the Chinese Language Teachers Association*, 40: 25–42.
Xu, T. Q. (2008) *Introduction to Character-Unit Theory*. Jinan: Shandong Education Press.

Yan, M. W., C. McBride-Chang, R. K. Wagner, J. Zhang, A. M. Y. Wong and H. Shu (2012) 'Writing quality in Chinese children: Speed and fluency matte,' *Read Writ*, 25(7): 1499–521. doi:10.1007/s11145-011-9330-y.

Yang, C. S. and M. Chan. (2010) 'The perception of mandarin Chinese tones and intonation by American learners,' *Journal of Chinese Language Teachers Association*, 45(1): 7–36.

Young, R. and G. B. Halleck (1998) '"Let them eat cake!" or how to avoid losing your head in cross-cultural conversations,' in Young, R. and A. W. He (eds.) *Talking and Testing: Discourse Approaches to the Assessment of Oral Proficiency*. Amsterdam and Philadelphia: Benjamins, 355–82.

Yuan, F. (2010) 'Measuring learner language L2 Chinese in fluency, accuracy and complexity,' *Journal of the Chinese Language Teachers Association*, 44(3): 109–30.

Zhang, D. (2012) 'Vocabulary and grammatical knowledge in L2 reading comprehension: A structural equation modelling study,' *The Modern Language Journal*, 96: 554–71.

Zhang, D. (2017) 'Developments in research on teaching Chinese as a second language,' in Zhang, D. B. and C. H. Lin (eds.) *Chinese as a Second Language Assessment*. Singapore: Springer, 67–90.

Zhang, D. and C. Lin (2017) 'Introduction,' in Zhang, D. and C. Lin (eds.) *Chinese as a Second Language Assessment*. Singapore: Springer: xi–xxi.

Zhang, D., X. Yang, C. Lin and Z. Gu (2017) 'Developing a word associates test to assess L2 Chinese learners' vocabulary depth,' in Zhang, D. and C. Lin (eds.) *Chinese as a Second Language Assessment*. Singapore: Springer, 115–40.

Zhang, H. (2013) 'The second language acquisition of mandarin Chinese tones by English, Japanese and Korean speakers,' (PhD dissertation). The University of North Carolina at Chapel Hill.

Zhang, H. (2016) 'Dissimilation in the second language acquisition of the Mandarin Chinese tones,' *Second Language Research*, 32(3): 427–51.

Zhang, H. (2018) 'Current trends in research of Chinese sound acquisition,' in Ke, C. (ed.) *The Routledge Handbook of Chinese Second Language Acquisition*. New York: Routledge, 217–33.

Zhang, P. P. (2005) 'On the nature of character-unit theory,' *Hanzi Culture*, 4.

Zhang, Q. and X. Jiang (2015) 'On the relationship between morphological awareness and reading in Chinese among intermediate and advanced learners of Chinese as a second language,' *TCSOL Studies*, 3: 11–17.

Zhang, Q. and G. Min (2019) 'Chinese writing composition among CFL learners: A comparison between handwriting and typewriting,' *Computers and Composition, Vol. 54*. Available at https://doi.org/10.1016/j.compcom.2019.102522 (Accessed on 3rd Dec. 2020).

Zhang, T. and C. Ke (2020) 'Research on L2 Chinese character acquisition,' in Ke, C. (ed.) *The Routledge Handbook of Chinese Second Language Acquisition*. London, UK: Routledge, 99–130.

Zhao, L. and X. Xie (2006) 'A study on different forms of test for assessing writing in Chinese as a second language,' in Xie, X. and J. Zhang (eds.) *Studies on Testing* (Vol. 3). Beijing: Economic Sciences Press, 117–33.

Zhao, S. (2017) 'The effect of instruction on L2 writing in Chinese: A T-unit analysis,' in Lu, Y. (ed.) *Teaching and Learning Chinese in Higher Education: Theoretical and Practical Issues*. Abingdon: Routledge, 229–49.

Zhou, Y. (2012) 'Willingness to communicate in learning Mandarin as a foreign and heritage language,' (Unpublished doctoral dissertation). The University of Hawaii at Manoa, Honolulu.

Zhou, Y. and S. L. Wu (2009) 'Development and pilot of a Mandarin L2 elicited imitation task,' (Unpublished manuscript). The University of Hawai'i at Manoa, Honolulu.

Zhu, Y., S. L. Feng and T. Xin (2013) 'Improving the dependability of the New HSK writing test score: A generalizability theory-based approach', *Journal of Psychological Science*, 36: 479–88.

Zhu, Y., S.-K. M. Shum, S.-K. B. Tse and J. J. Liu (2016) 'Word processor or pencil-and-paper? A comparison of students' writing in Chinese as a foreign language,' *Computer Assisted Language Learning*, 29(3): 596–617. https://doi.org/10.1080/09588221.2014.1000932.

Index

ability-in-individual-in-context 21
ACTFL (American Council on the Teaching of Foreign Languages) 2, 11, 25, 35–9; ACTFL-NCSSFL Can-Do Statements 38; APPL 37; CEFR ratings to ACTFL assessments 37–8; performance descriptors 36, 39; proficiency guidelines 36, 39; rationale for rating Chinese tests 35–6
AfL (assessment for learning) 54
Allen, J. R. 165, 179
alphabetic/alphabetical languages 48–9, 174–5, 185
analytic rating 158–61, 194, 199
assessment for learning 54; *see also* assessment, formative (FA); classroom-based assessment (CBA); norm-referenced test; proficiency test
assessment purposes 60; achievement 64, 73; diagnostic 36, 61; formative (FA) 1, 17, 55, 59, 61–3, 84–9, 106, 124, 126; placement 61, 74; summative (SA) 56, 61, 82, 84, 86, 100–2, 192, 201
Assessment Reform Group (ARF) 55, 84–6
automated speaking test 147, 155–6

Bachman, L. 18–19, 45–51, 56, 61–2, 65–6, 71, 74, 76, 84, 102–3, 153
basic sentence structures 120–1
Bernstein, J. A. 155
Black, P. J. 54, 84–7, 89, 92, 94, 97, 99
bottom-up processing/processes 6, 45, 139, 175–8, 182–203
Broadfoot, P. 55
Brown, A. 22, 157
Brown, H. D. 18, 60–1, 73–4, 77, 138, 145, 156, 176, 182, 195, 197
Buck, G. 141–3, 146

Canal, M. 10, 18
Cantonese learners of Mandarin Chinese 58
Carless, D. 87–90, 98, 101
CEFR (Common European Framework of References for Language: Learning, Teaching and Assessment) 2, 25–35; CEFR Learning, Teaching, Assessment, Companion Volume with New Descriptors 27–8; Global Scales 26; Self-Assessment Grid 26, 28, 38; Structure of the CEFR Descriptive Scheme 27
CFL CBA (classroom-based assessment for Chinese as a foreign language) 56–62; context 56–60; consequences 62; purpose 60–2
CFL Model (A CFL Model for Construct Definition for Assessing Learners' L2 Competence in Chinese) 46–51, 108, 131, 166; core competencies 47; peripheral competencies 46–7, 51; strategic competencies 49–51; two factors 51
Chalhoub-Deville, M. 21
Chang, L. Y. 48
Chapelle, C. A. 10, 14, 21
character background learner 58, 78, 178
Cheng, L. Y. 66, 71, 77, 99
Chinese characters 109; components 109, 116; construction/structure 116, 167–8, 171; density 58–9, 113; stroke order 166, 169; strokes 49–50, 166–9; radicals 48–50, 109; simplified 23, 58–9, 113; traditional 31, 59; types of characters 109
Chinese proficiency test (CPT) 8, 11, 15–16, 33, 57, 60, 75, 77, 112–13, 134, 153–5, 154

Index 223

classroom-based assessment (CBA) 1, 54–6; advantages 55–6; see *also* assessment for learning
cloze test (CT) 10, 13, 18, 118, 135, 144, 172
co-constructed discourse 81, 147, 150
CoE (Council of Europe) 26, 29
collocation 111–12, 117, 168
communicative competence model 18–19
communicative language ability (CLA) 14, 18–19, 50; components 18
compounding 109–10; derivation-like process 110; inflection-like processes 110–11
compounds character 50, 109, 111
computer-assisted 'penless' approach 8, 179
concurrent coexistence scripts 8, 33, 179
Confucius Classroom 57
Confucius Institute (CI) 57
consequence of assessment 4, 62; high-stakes 4, 62; moderately high-stakes 4, 62
consequential stakes: low-stakes 62
construct for language assessment 3–10; co-constructed 22–4; discrete-point 10–11, 17, 155, 156; global 18; specific constructs 18; syllabus-based 19; theory-based 19
construct-irrelevant variance 142
constructs for assessing L2 Chinese 46–51; grammatical (GC) 121; listening (LCC) 143; orthographic (OC) 170; Pinyin (PC) 134; reading comprehension 178; speaking (SCC)152; vocabulary (VC) 112; writing 190
contextually rich tasks 21
converted writing (CW) 34, 134, 166, 187
corrective feedback (CF) 99–100; strategies 100
correlation coefficient 72
Coulthard, R. M. 94
criteria for assessment of OC 167
criterion-referenced assessment 39, 78
cycle and process for developing summative CBA 64–5; stages 65–71

Damböck, B. 56, 61–2, 74, 84
Davies, A. A. 7–8, 60–1, 73, 81, 153, 157
default listening construct 141
DeFrancis, J. 8, 33, 179
dictation exercise 10, 13–14, 18, 23, 99, 135, 145, 170, 172
direct item/task 152–3, 156
discourse completion test (DCT) 127
discriminability of assessment 67

Douglas, D. 21
dynamic assessment (DA) 23, 85

Elicited Imitation Test (EIT) 155
error analysis 188
European Benchmarks for the Chinese Language (EBCL) 2, 29–34, 43–6, 49–52; Can-do Statements 30; graded lists of characters and lexical items for A1 and A2 33, 113; graphemic/orthographic control (GOC) 30, 34, 49; Pinyin reading and writing competence (PRWC) 30–4, 46, 49; sinographemic competence (SC) 30–2
Everson, M. E. 39, 113, 166
examiner/rater training 81, 149, 156
experiential/world knowledge 13
explicit and implicit mode of assessment 56, 81

facility in L2 155
follow-up move (Fo) 94
formative assessment strategies (FAS) 84–7, 89–91, 106; FAS1 89, 95; FAS2A 91–3; FAS2B 94–6; FAS3 90–8; FAS4 98–100; FAS5 100–2
Fox, J. 66, 71, 77, 99
Fulcher, G. 25, 64, 66, 147, 162

gap filling question 12, 18, 23, 79, 182
Genesee, F. 61, 73, 78, 97
grammar translation method 133
grammaticalised lexis 50–1, 111, 120
grapheme-phoneme relation 24, 28
graphemic and orthographic control/competence 14, 21, 23–30
Green, A. 10–11, 19, 28, 60, 64–5, 74, 76, 119, 148, 156, 159, 161–2, 195
Guan, C. Q. 48–9, 166, 169, 173, 185, 186
Guder, A. 8, 30

Halleck, G. B. 22
Hanban (Office of Chinese Language Council International) 3, 18–19, 29, 37, 45
handwriting Chinese characters 2, 16–30
Harding, L. 102–5
He, A. W. 22–3
heritage learner 58
holistic rating 158–9, 195–6
homophones 111, 175, 187
HSK (Hanyu Shuipin Kaoshi, Chinese Proficiency Test) 11, 28, 60, 80, 182; Level 3 and 4 41, 76; Level 5 191;

listening papers 142; New HSK 28, 152; writing papers 15
HSKK (Hanyu Shuiping Kouyu Kaoshi, Chinese Spoken Test) 37, 155–6
Hughes, A. 13, 60–1, 64, 71, 74–6, 79–80, 127–8, 174, 176, 182–3, 191–2, 195
Hulstijn, J. H. 47, 85, 149
Hymes, D.H. 10, 18

implicit constructs 60
indigenous assessment 22, 81
indirect test 152–3, 155–6, 163
information transfer 144, 182
interactional competence (IC) 23, 148–51, 153, 155, 157–9, 161–3
interactionist approach to construct definition 21, 39, 86, 177
intercultural competence 42
interlocutor effect 22, 147–50, 157
interlocutor script 148, 157
interlocutor variability 81, 155, 157–8
International Curriculum for Chinese Language Education (ICCLE) 39–45; learning objectives/CDSs for Stage 3 41–3; stages of learning 41; structure of Chinese language competence 4
I-R-F structure 94
item difficulty 72, 143, 162

Ji, Y. 188
Jiang, W. Y. 188
Jiang, X. 115, 166

Ke, C. 48, 109, 132, 174, 176
knowledge and competence for assessment (KCA) 57–9, 102–6; components 103; levels 105
Kremmel, B. 102–5

Lado, R. 9–10, 24
Lantolf, J. 82, 85–6, 100
Lazaraton, A. 158
Li, C. N. 50, 119, 122
Li, P. H. 8, 159, 166
Li, R. 48, 115
Ling, V. 8, 16, 48
Little, D. 28
logogram 8, 165
logographic script 5, 8, 186
Long, M. H. 19
Lu, Y. 8, 15, 22, 32–3, 34, 75, 86, 157

McNamara, T. 20, 22, 76, 153, 156, 162, 193
mediated interaction 179, 181
mediated learning 7, 162, 181, 194

metacognitive strategies 22, 47, 51, 142; *see also* strategic competencies
Min, G. 187–8
modes of assessment 56; explicit 56, 81, 84; implicit 56, 65, 81, 85
monosyllabic characters 33, 110
morphological characteristics/features 50, 109–10, 117
motor activity 166
multiple choice 11–12, 16–20, 80, 114, 118, 144, 181–2, 191

Nation, P. 112, 114
non-alphabetic writing systems 13, 35, 133
non-character 169
non-character background learner 58, 78, 176
norm-referenced test 19, 39, 60
Norris, J. M. 19

Oller, J. W. 10, 13, 18
Online Dynamic Assessment System 6, 179–80, 194
opening, maintaining and closing conversations, initiating and developing topics and interacting with 50
oral proficiency interview (OPI) 149
orthographic awareness 166–7, 170
orthographic control/competence 16, 43–4, 48–50, 165–74
O'Sullivan, B. 22, 77, 147

Palmer, A. 18–19, 45–51, 65–6, 74, 102–3, 153
Pearson product-moment correlation 46–47
peer assessment 97–8
peer learners 162–3, 165–72
Perfetti, C. 166
periphery metacognitive components 47
phonetic components of Chinese characters 23–4
Pinyin /Hanyu Pinyin 8, 49; aspirated and unaspirated consonants 48, 133; double or triple vowels tones 48, 132; finals 132; initials 132; sandhi/changes of tones 132; tone pairs/order of tones 132
Pinyin reading and writing competence (PRWC) 30–5
planned and unplanned formative assessment 87–9
Poehner, M. 82, 85–6
post-test validation 65, 69–72
practicality of assessment 20, 76, 203
Pressley, M. 88
primary trait scoring (PTS) 201–2
proficiency test 19, 37, 80, 100, 164

Index 225

prosodic features 48, 133
Purpura, J. 17, 20, 22, 50, 81, 118, 122–3, 129
Putonghua 24; Standard Chinese 2, 131
pseudo-character 169

question-word questions 121, 129

rater leniency and severity 80, 162
rater reliability 80–1, 153; inter-rater 80, 156, 195; intra-rater 80–1, 153, 156
rater variability 80
reduplication 50, 110, 112, 117
reliability 11, 73, 77; administration 78; student-related 77–8; test 78–80; *see also* rater reliability
Romagnoli 48, 109, 111–12
Romanised phonetic system 8, 14, 31, 43, 131–5, 138; *see also* Pinyin
rules for writing characters (正字法) 167

self-assessment 62, 81, 96, 198
semantic-phonetic compound 31, 116
semi-scripted texts 146
Shen, H. H. 16–17, 48, 174, 176, 224
Shi, Z. Y. 167, 169
short-answer question 79–80, 145–6, 182
Sinclair, J. 94
Sino-Tibetan language 2, 9
socio-interactional approach to construct definition 21–3, 50–1, 81
socio-linguistic competence 74
Song, L. Y. 32–3
spatial literacy 49
specific-purpose language-ability construct 21
standard deviation 41, 49
Sun, C. F. 109–10, 119, 169
Swain, M. 10, 18

task-centred approach to construct definition 19–21, 23, 26, 148, 189
Taylor, L. 102–5
techniques for assessing L2 Chinese competence, grammatical (GC) 122–9; listening (LCC) 142–7; orthographic (OC) 170–81; Pinyin (PC) 134–8; reading comprehension 178–83; speaking (SCC) 152–6; vocabulary (VC) 113–18; writing 191–4
Teng, Y. J. 11, 15, 28
test authenticity 18–20; continuum of authenticity 20, 51, 192–4; interactional authenticity 53; real-world authenticity 153; strong version 20, 76; weak version 20, 24, 76, 153

test fairness 1, 55, 63, 70–1
test usefulness 1, 18
Thompson, S. A. 50, 119, 122
TOCFL (Test of Chinese as a Foreign Language) 11, 13–14, 28, 57, 80, 113, 118, 154
top-down processing/processes 6, 45, 139, 175–8, 182–203
topic-prominence 147
trait-based approaches to construct definition 17–19; communicative competence 18–19; discrete-point 17–18; unitary 18
trends for defining construct for assessment 10–14; communicative competence 11; formative 11; master learning 11; pre-scientific/traditional 10; psycholinguistic sociolinguistic 10; psychometric structuralist 10
true or false question 11, 70, 183
Tsui, A. 94
types of listening tasks 144; extensive 145; intensive 144; interpretive 145; responsive 144; selective 144–5

underlying ability 20, 76
unique sentence construction 119–21, 125
Upshur, J. 61, 73, 78, 97

validity 1, 73; concurrent 73, 75; construct 74–6; content 73; criterion-related 73; predictive 74–5
variant forms of strokes 168
Vygotsky, L. S. 84–5

washback 55–7, 62, 76–7, 105, 183
Weir, C. J. 19, 28, 52, 76, 191, 194
William, D. 84–7, 89
word order 50, 119–20, 140, 176
word segmentation 5, 175
World-Readiness Standards 37–8

Xiang, C. H. 188
Xing, J. Z. 50, 118–19, 122, 132, 140

Ye, B. B. 48, 115
Young, R. 22–3

zero-subject sentence 9, 146
Zhang, H. 48, 133
Zhang, Q. 187–8
zone of proximal development (ZPD) 84, 86, 97, 99–100

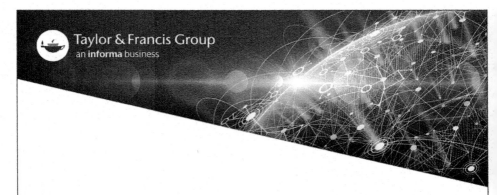